29 MAIN STREET

Living with Partition

BY

DERMOT MCMONAGLE

PUBLISHED BY

Dermot McMonagle
dermot@gnp.ie

First Edition 2013
29 Main Street - Living with Partition

ISBN 978-0-9574771-0-0

Editor: Brian Maye

Cover Design: Ray Fadden
Cover Images from Historical Files

Printed and Bound by Blacks of Cavan
Typesetting in Times
Layout Design: James Brady
Photography: Lorraine Teevan
Cover Map: Dermot Walsh

*Dedicated to those who have gone before and
to my grandchildren who are the future.*

*He who knows not the story of the past cannot judge
the present or wisely plan for the future.*

Arthur Griffith

TABLE OF CONTENTS

Foreword

Acknowledgements

Introduction

Abbreviations - Explanations

Chapter 1	....	Ballyconnell.	P. 14
Chapter 2.	....	Awaiting the Third Home Rule Bill	P. 25
Chapter 3	....	The Home Rule Bill and Ulster Day	P. 41
Chapter 4	....	The Volunteers and the Great War.	P. 56
Chapter 5	....	Arthur Griffith and the Growth of Sinn Féin	P. 67
Chapter 6	....	The War of Independence in West Cavan	P. 85
Chapter 7	....	Self-Determination or Partition	P. 102
Chapter 8	....	Local Elections and the Dáil Courts.	P. 122
Chapter 9	....	Conciliatory Unionism	P. 137
Chapter 10	....	The War Continues	P. 150
Chapter 11	....	The King Speaks	P. 169
		Lloyd George's Dream	P. 182
Chapter 12	....	The Great Divide	P. 184
Chapter 13	....	20 Years On; Sean Milroy Reflects	P. 199
Chapter 14	....	Living With Partition	P. 209
Appendix 1	....	Lloyd George's Speech at Caernarvon	P. 229
Appendix 2	....	Sinn Féin Court Case re. 1919 Local Elections	P. 237
Index	....		P. 254

FOREWORD

"We anxiously wish to see the day when every Irishman shall be a citizen, when Catholics and Protestants, equally interested in their country's welfare, possessing equal freedom and equal privileges, shall learn to look upon each other as brothers, the children of the same God and the natives of the same land, and when the only strife among them shall be who shall serve their country best." Thus wrote Arthur Griffith in his newspaper *Sinn Féin* on 5 May 1906.

Arthur Griffith had an Ulster Protestant ancestry. The Griffith family was originally from Co. Cavan – so he said opening his by-election campaign at Bailieboro in that county on 28 April 1918. He told his election workers that the family had originally been farmers at Redhills, Co. Cavan. There are 18th century records of lands leased at Redhills by Griffiths, who were Protestants and who lived at Cornapaste, Co. Monaghan. There is a belief that his grandfather converted to Catholicism. His oldest brother, who was born in 1865, was given the very Protestant name William George, as was his sister, Marcella, born the following year.

Pilib Ó Mordha has shown that Griffith's ancestors most likely came from Laurelhill, Cornapaste and Fastry in Co. Monaghan. Although he found no clear documentary proof of it, Ó Mordha speculated that it was his great-grandfather who converted from Protestantism.

A favourite point that Griffith used to make was that the Protestant Unionist was as national as the Catholic nationalist and the British made use of religious differences in Ireland for their own ends. A respect for Protestant political thinkers was an aspect of the Sinn Féin movement that he founded. He esteemed Jonathan Swift, Henry Grattan and above all Thomas Davis, whom he claimed as his political mentor and about whom he wrote: "He softened our asperities and dispelled much of the bigotry and misconception that kept Irishmen apart, and he opened the way to national reunion - When the Irish read and reflect with Davis, their day of redemption will be at hand."

Griffith saw his dual-monarchy policy as a means of attracting the widest possible support in Ireland as a whole. He explained to the political activist and historian, P. S. O'Hegarty, that he was willing to forgo his separatism in the interests of unity.

His early Sinn Féin movement attracted a number of Protestant supporters, among them the Rev. J. O. Hannay, better known as the novelist, George A. Bermingham and the Presbyterian essayist, Robert Lynd.

When Unionist opposition to Home Rule intensified after 1912, Griffith's Sinn Féin went much further than the Irish Parliamentary Party to try to assuage Unionist fears about Dublin rule. In my book *Arthur Griffith* I deal at length with Sinn Féin's initiatives at this time.

The importance of the north east for the rest of Ireland, in Griffith's thinking, cannot be over-emphasised. That part of the country represented what he wished to see achieved all over Ireland. The ideal to which he hoped his policies would lead was an industrial revolution in the rest of Ireland based on the model of the north east.

Dermot McMonagle has researched extensively the history of the Arbitration Courts (sometimes called Sinn Féin or Dáil Courts) in his native county of Cavan, where indeed this significant form of civic disobedience (the cornerstone of Griffith's policy) began. Now he extends his study to look at how partition developed and the reality of living with it in his native area of west Cavan and south Fermanagh. He draws particular attention to the role of constructive Protestantism/Unionism. As he says in his introduction:
"There were many from all religions who wished for, in time, an independent Irish nation but a substantial minority were forced to indicate differently. It is regretful that the substantial minority of Protestants or liberal Unionists, who supported Ireland and Home Rule, were not listened to. Wolfe Tone and Henry Joy McCracken were let down."

As Dermot points out, the reality on the ground for most people may be summed up in the phrase, "live and let live". If only such a sensible-minded attitude had prevailed among a majority of those in power, the history of Ireland and indeed of these islands might have been so different.

Brian Maye

ACKNOWLEDGMENTS

This publication is only possible because of the many early conversation on the War of Independence in west Cavan with my mother and her sisters who were born and reared in 29 Main Street, Ballyconnell. The extended family also contributed.

The people from the area – Frankie Dolphin, Tony Connolly, Monica O'Reilly, Jack Maguire, Monica Finn, Julia McGovern, Frankie O'Reilly, Annet Kavanagh and Seamus McCaffrey, - all volunteered their recorded documents and memories, which helped verify many events.

Savina Donohoe and her staff at County Cavan Museum were always at hand to assist, as was Eugene Markey who could always be approached for clarifications.

Columba O'Hare, Newry, contributed 'The Kaiser's Dream' and the missing lines from 'Lloyd George's Dream.

Paddy Dolphin and Capt. Seán Sheridan who were active in the War of Independence, contributed much to understanding the political and military issues of that time.

Willie O'Hanlon's comments on the East Cavan by-election of 1918 coupled with Maura McNally's MA thesis on that historical event have been crucial to my research.

As I was living with a bank of comments and memories, it was my wife Phyllis and daughter Sarah who encouraged me to start researching, if only for personal satisfaction. Starting at the reference section of Cavan County Library, this task was made easier by the assistance and enthusiasm of Brian Connolly and Tom Sullivan. They guided and directed a mere amateur through the library's archives of newspapers and historical documents. The assistance of the staff at Cavan County Library in getting this book to publication cannot be overlooked – a service always at hand to help and direct.

Mary Sullivan at the Genealogical Research Centre, Cavan did much in researching my maternal ancestors, which forms the basis for this publication.

The staff at the Fermanagh Co. Library, Enniskillen were most welcoming and efficient while always interested in how my research and book were progressing.

The Church of Ireland Archives at Braemor Park, Dublin hold much valuable information on The Home Rule question - records of great historical, religious and social value.

The National Archives Dublin is a national treasure where important elements were discovered to help adapt the local to the national question in Ireland's turbulent years.

"Journalism is the first rough draft of history." (Philip L Graham).

The volume of vital political information and editorial comments published in the local newspapers the Anglo-Celt Cavan and the Impartial Reporter Enniskillen from the early decades of the twentieth century are a library in their own right. They were the Sky news of their time, where selected important information was pursued and published in the interest of their readers, at a time when they were the only media available to many. Journalists had a great vision for truth and those newspaper archives are now of great historical benefit.

As a reader of history I am fortunate to live in an age when so many Irish writers and historians have published stimulating books and journals on Anglo Irish events and how they shaped us. It is gratifying that many prominent historians, especially Jonathan Mattison and Gordon Lucy could be approached for their clarifications. They were most supportive with their comments and material for this publication.

Brendan McCann and Phyllis, my proof readers provided much advice and support.

To Brian Maye my editor, a special word of thanks, for his ongoing encouragement. He was always available to discuss, clarify, suggest and correct.

The good wishes and encouragement received from many associates and friends towards 29 Main Street cannot be overlooked and hopefully this publication, on our shared history, will not disappoint.

Thank you all.

A very special acknowledgement for the assistance of Cavan-Monaghan LEADER, Breffni Integrated Limited, Monaghan Integrated Development Limited, the Minister and Department of the Environment, Community and Local Government, the EU and EAFRD in part-funding this project. (National Development Plan 2007-13)

Is fiontar comhpháirteach é LEADER Cabhán-Muineacháin idir Breifne Aontaithe Teoranta agus Forbairt Aontaithe Teoranta Muineacháin chun an Clár Forbairt Tuaithe Éireann 2007-2013 a thoirbhirt i gcontaetha Cabhán agus Muineacháin.

Cavan-Monaghan LEADER is a joint venture between Breffni Integrated Ltd. and Monaghan Integrated Development Ltd. for the delivery of the Rural Development Programme 2007-2013 in counties Cavan and Monaghan.

INTRODUCTION

Modern Irish political history and the religious, social and economic complexities around partition are the elements on which this book is based. Looking at the local history of west Cavan and south Fermanagh (that part of south Ulster which was divided), much had to be relearned about the political thinking and strategies on both sides, which influenced the area. Irish history has conspired against itself for decades by "airbrushing" important people, some events and parliamentary debates for reasons unknown. This book tries to reopen that which has been pushed aside while looking at local events of national importance. The beauty of history is that it is a social science and always open to reinterpretation.

Reflecting on the history of one's native place, family, its people saying or doing the unforgettable are all interwoven and now recorded simply to be enjoyed. Ballyconnel could have ended up on either side of the Irish political divide. With its own social and political history, it cannot be divorced from the broader national question, i.e., the political and military turmoil imposed on the Irish people within the union and afterwards and how these events affected the people of south Ulster.

Growing up in the Irish border area, one very soon caught and accepted difference as a normal everyday thing and seldom questioned why the country was partitioned. The economic benefits were, more importantly, there to be grasped.

This book is based on related and observed events, newspaper reports, researched facts, political and parliamentary debates on Home Rule leading to partition. Parliamentary debates at Westminster and related newspaper comments in England and Ireland have been examined to bring a broader understanding of the political "shenanigans" within the mother of parliaments from 1909.

The time frame dips into the last years of the 19th century and the determination of the Irish people to own land and to remove the landlord from Ireland. The introduction of the third Home Rule Bill and the counter anti-Home Rule campaign in Ulster were the beginning of partition and the question has to be "for whom". "The Great War" had a greater immediate impact on Ireland than the Easter Rising of 1916 — only for Dublin Castle to waste the opportunity. The political rise of Arthur Griffith and Sinn Féin from 1917, particularly in Co. Cavan where the Sinn Féin Parish Courts were formed, saw the beginning of the people's campaign of civil disobedience to weaken the British hold on Ireland. The 1918 general election victory for Sinn Féin and the formation of the first Dáil leading to the War of Independence and the Partition Act of 1920 are interlinked. The historical intervention by King George V, which led to the truce and the Anglo-Irish Treaty of 1921, was critical in bringing to an end the political, bloody and religious battles between the union and the Irish where "poor God" was used for political gain. The Irish Civil War speaks for itself.

So much military and political activity in a small country within a few years.

The historical and accepted county and parish boundaries within Ireland never made much sense as they seldom showed natural lines of demarcation. Geographically based self-contained communities were in turn divided by partition. Prior to the introduction of the third Home Rule Bill, religious and social beliefs were mutually accepted and were part of the development and growth of Ireland within the union. There were many from all religions who wished for, in time, an independent Irish nation but a substantial minority were forced to indicate differently. It is regretful that this minority of Protestants or liberal Unionists, who supported Ireland and Home Rule, were not listened to. Wolfe Tone and McCracken were let down.

Emigration was always a safety valve to relieve many situations for a plethora of reasons.

Yet a divided country still survives.

ABBREVIATIONS AND EXPLANATIONS

Catholic Nationalists within Co. Fermanagh were classified as either **"Hibs"** or **"Fenians"**. Those who were members of the **Ancient Order of Hibernians (AOH)** were referred to as Hibs. The AOH was founded by Irish exiles in the USA in 1836 and grew in strength in Ulster in opposition to the Orange Order (see below). It was very close to the Irish Parliamentary Party (see below). Ulster nationalists who retained the ethos of Wolfe Tone's United Irishmen, the Young Irelanders etc. were commonly referred to as Fenians.

The **Orange Order** is an exclusively Protestant organisation founded in 1796 based mainly in Ulster. It became closely identified with Unionism (see below), taking a very active part in opposition to Irish Home Rule. There are different strands of Orange Societies/Lodges.

The **United Irish League** (**UIL**) was a follow-on organisation to Michael Davitt's Land League from the later 19th to the early 20th centuries. It continued the fight for land reform and ownership in Ireland. It was absorbed into the IPP.

The **Irish Republican Brotherhood** (**IRB**), formed in 1858, was classified as a secret society, whose members influenced most voluntary Irish organisations. Its motto was "success through silence" and it led the Easter Rising 1916.

The **Irish Parliamentary Party** (**IPP**) comprised Irish nationalist MPs elected to Westminster representing Irish aspirations for Home Rule. The representatives were from all religions but its supporters were in the main Catholic nationalists.

Sinn Féin (Ourselves) was founded in 1904/5 by Arthur Griffith and became the prominent political party after the 1916 Rising. It re-established parliamentary democracy in Ireland.

Irish Unionists or members of the **Ulster Unionist Council/Party** aligned themselves with the Conservatives or Tories at Westminister and supported the Act of Union. Many adherents to Unionism were members of the various strands of Orangeism.

Liberal Unionists were a substantial minority of Irish Protestants who supported Irish aspirations for self-government and some form of Home Rule. They were, in the main, business or professional people who opposed mainstream Orangeism. Some were members of Independent Orange Lodges.

The **Ulster Volunteer Force (UVF)** was formed in early 1913 as a Protestant militant force to oppose the third Home Rule Bill and to protect the Act of Union. Many wanted a separatist state from southern Ireland.

The **Irish Volunteers** were founded in late 1913 as a reactionary force in support of Home Rule and a mirror image of the Ulster Volunteer Force. When the Third Home Rule Bill was on the statute book at Westminster and the Great War broke out in 1914, many Irish Volunteers enlisted to fight in the war under Redmond's National Volunteers on the understanding that Home Rule would be granted to all of Ireland.

The **Royal Irish Constabulary (RIC)** was the police force for all of Ireland until 1922.

The **Royal Ulster Constabulary (RUC)** was the police force of the six counties of Northern Ireland from April 1922. It was founded as an extension of the Royal Irish Constabulary (RIC). The RUC was supported by the **Ulster Special Constabulary** who were commonly referred to as the **B Specials** and sometimes in Fermanagh as the **B Men**. This reserve force was disbanded in the early 1970s

The **Irish Republican Army (IRA)** was originally the Irish Volunteers until 1919 and fought Ireland's War of Independence. After 1922 the IRA split on pro- or anti-Treaty lines. Most pro-Treaty men formed the Free State army while the anti-Treaty IRA members were commonly known as "republicans".

The **Sinn Féin Parish Arbitration Courts** were established in Co. Cavan in 1917. They were also called the **Sinn Féin Courts.** From June 1920 they came under the control of Dáil Éireann and became the **Dáil Courts.**

Irish Republican Police (IRP) were senior IRA men appointed to act as local policemen from 1920 by the Army Council or by the Dáil Courts.

From 1922 the Irish Free State remained within British Sterling or in the old £. s. d. system. The Saorstát Pound was created from 1928 and was aligned to Sterling. This was retained until Sterling went decimal in February 1971. The Pound had twenty (20/s) shillings. Each shilling had 12d. or pence and there were 240 pence in the pound. The full coinage then was: a half-penny, penny, three pence 'bit', six pence, shilling, a florin or two shilling piece, half a crown, a crown or five shillings. Banknotes were ten shilling (10/s), £1, £5, £10, £20 and £50. With the introduction of decimal currency the pound equalled 100 new pence and the old coins were replaced in decimal units.

John Drum and Annie Malanaphy are the maternal grandparents of the author.

CHAPTER 1

BALLYCONNELL

(i) Annie Malanaphy

On New Year's Eve 1869, Annie Malanaphy came into this world, the third child and first daughter of Frank Malanaphy and Catherine Dolan in the townland of Drumbar, Swanlinbar. Lying in the panhandle of County Cavan, this must have been a cold and wet place. It is high up on that line of hills south east of the Cuilcaghs, which straddle the Cavan and Fermanagh boundary and run from Swanlinbar to Slieve Rushen, above Ballyconnell, and around to Molly Mountain and Doon, from where they slope gently towards Knockninny Rock and the shores of Upper Lough Erne.

Francis Malanaphy and Catherine Dolan were children of the Great Famine, born in the early 1840s and surviving the greatest human and social catastrophe in Irish history. We have never been allowed to forget those who died in the Irish Famine or those who had to emigrate. However, we must be thankful to the numbers who lived through it, which had to be a sign of inner and physical strength and a will to live through one of the toughest tests of physical and mental character in human history.

All that we know about Annie Malanaphy growing up in Drumbar comes from something she often said to her own children about the place: "where the land was so bad, that the crows wouldn't light on it". This was said to let them know that they did not come from the peerage and to keep their feet firmly planted on the ground. Drumbar was said to be a townland on the hills with some of the better land in that area or at least the best of a bad lot and it is now producing evergreen trees for the paper and furniture industries.

The people living on this hilly area formed a community in their own right. The many families who lived there had been banished from better lands by the planters or by landlords in penal times – banished to survive on what was left of their dignity. While their lives and living were very basic at best, they were a people who developed a unique sense of survival and direction, guided by the elements by day and the moon and stars at night. They could find their way across bog and bracken to visit friends, go to wakes or to sell their produce at local fairs and markets. This inbuilt sense of direction and understanding of nature would stand them well in later life, be it in the new world or when smuggling became part of border living in Ireland.

Annie Malanaphy emigrated to America shortly after leaving national school, sometime in the mid-1880s. Annie spoke little about her time in America. It is not known where she went, be it New York or Boston, or what she worked at, but more than likely she worked "in service". Getting work with the right people or in the right place was obviously problematic for an immigrant girl of her age at that time, but fortunately for her, like many others from the area, she had a good contact or sponsor.

There was a senior police officer in America whose family hailed from Fermanagh. There was very high regard for him as a contact in the USA as he used his uniform and power to source sustainable employment there for people from the area. He was known to be a grand uncle of Terry Curry "of the Ford", who lived in Fermanagh, about two miles from Ballyconnell. A lineage of blood relations could be traced without much difficulty in rural Fermanagh or Cavan and one could be readily told, whether you wanted to hear it or not, where a third or fourth cousin could still be called "a friend".

In late 1896 Arthur Griffith, a young Dublin printer and journalist emigrated through economic necessity and on medical advice to the drier climes of South Africa to seek a cure for his chest problems. He undertook some administrative work in the mining industry and while there he also did some reporting on the Boer War. At around this time, the 26-year-old Annie Malanaphy returned home to Ireland and west Cavan with dollars in her purse to buy a property or business. She was positive about settling back in her native county and obviously made serious enquiries as she was brought to Ballyconnell in a pony and trap by "Coffey" the auctioneer from Bawnboy. Ballyconnell was then a small town with railway connections to Leitrim and to the Great Northern Railway and national rail networks at Belturbet. Annie Malanaphy and Arthur Griffith would meet some two decades later in Ballyconnell, in the political cause of Sinn Féin.

(ii) Ballyconnell

Medieval historians accept that Ballyconnell or Béal Átha Conaill (the Mouth of Conall's Ford) had its origins as far back as the time of the Red Branch Knights of Ulster. It was a place where there was a shallow crossing point on the River Gráinne. The settlement got its name from Conall Cearnach of the Red Branch Knights who, it is believed, was slain by Queen Maeve's husband in a fit of jealously. As Conall was returning to Ulster after trying to resolve Queen Maeve's quest to get ownership of the Donn Cúailnge or

Brown Bull of Cooley, he was killed. Tradition is that he is buried where the Cearnach Stones are at Ballyheady near Ballyconnell. However, a study of the contents of this Iron Age tomb was conducted in the 1930s and the remains found are said to predate the time of the Red Branch Knights by 1,000 years. It is thought that Conall was buried elsewhere along the banks of the River Gráinne. The legend lives on. Later the river became part of the boundary between the territories of Breffni O'Raghallaigh and Breffni O'Rourke.

Under an Act of 1842, it was proposed to transform the River Gráinne into a navigable canal to improve the arterial drainage of the adjacent lands with the potential of the controlled waters to produce water power. Work commenced in June 1846 with an estimated cost of £131,858, but the canal did not open until 1860 at a cost of £228,651. Very few commercial boats used the Ballyconnell-Ballinamore Canal, as the railways were now developing. *

The old territories of Breffni are now, in essence, the Catholic Dioceses of Kilmore, which covers most of counties Cavan and Leitrim, and small parts of Meath, Sligo and Fermanagh.

According to *Slater's Directory of Ireland 1824*, Ballyconnell had a population of 450 people and very few traders. Seventy years later, things had changed very much according to the same source as the population was reduced to 291 and now there were many traders – obviously influenced by the railway network. The reduction in the population had to be the result of the Great Famine 1845-49 and emigration. However, Ballyconnell was showing some prosperity as the leading market town in west Cavan, with a monthly fair and a pork market every fortnight.

According to the Market Deeds:

The rights to hold fairs and markets in the town of Ballyconnell, was granted by Letters Patent of the tenth day of November in the third year of the reign of King James II of England (1688) to Meredith Gwylyn Esquire and all the rights and privileges incident thereto conferred by the Letters Patent constituting the Manor of Gwylynbrook.

These rights were transferred to the Vesey-Knox family and later to the O'Kane family. Annie Malanaphy's son-in-law, Dan McMonagle, purchased these rights in 1951, which also included ownership of the town's fairgreen. The market rights to Ballyconnell are still in his name and are now of historical value.

In *Slater's Directory* 1894, the following were named as principal people in

*[Inland Waterways Association of Ireland]

the locality of Ballyconnell: Dr Alan T. Peachy, Medical Practitioner; Patrick O'Kane, Cranemaster; Ralph Montgomery, Postmaster; Rev. Hugh Newman, Parish Priest; Rev. Orange Sterling Kellet, Rector at Cranaghan House (now Slieve Russell Hotel); M. Netherfield, Courthouse Clerk and Caretaker; David Wells, Station Master; Michael Curry (Corry), National Teacher; Thomas Griffin, assistant NT and Thomas H. Griffith, Clerk of the Parish.

Annie Malanaphy was shown a closed-down thatched public house on Main Street, Ballyconnell and a small parcel of land at Laghernahone for sale at £200. She purchased all for £150. She must have seen some potential as it was adjacent to the Market House. A further advantage was that it had a square perch of bog bank in the chapel bog, the need for energy sources and supply was paramount and the bog was beside the town. Her anxiety to purchase or to invest her hard-earned dollars proved somehow controversial and to her personal and family disgust, the property which she had just purchased had been sold to her by "the Bank". She was not aware of this until the money was paid and the deal was done. The empty property had been on the market for some years and it was told to her afterwards that the Jones family, who lived next door, then one of the leading merchant families in the area, had offered £100 for the premises. It was not the done thing to bid for, let alone purchase, a property that "the Bank" was selling and so Annie Malanaphy knew that she would not be very welcome in business in the town. She returned to America.

The premises she had just bought at 29 Main Street was called The Gaelic Bar. This had been the home of Tom O'Reilly, the man who along with John Alex Clancy established the first Gaelic football team in Co. Cavan and Ulster in late 1885. The club was originally called the Ballyconnell Joe Biggars, named after the serving Irish Parliamentary Party MP for West Cavan and was later known as The First Ulsters. This was confirmed in conversation with the late Brian O'Grady, a native of the town and former County Development Officer for Cavan. His grandfather and granduncle played in the first recorded Gaelic football game at Ballyconnell on 25 April 1886. An article in *United Ireland* of 13 March 1886 reported: "Ballyconnell members played their first regular match under GAA Rules on 7 March and the local constabulary tried to stop it under The Sunday Observances Act". Brian O'Grady also confirmed that it was in this same house which Annie Melanaphy had purchased, that the first Gaelic club in Ulster was formed. This was why the premises was known as The Gaelic Bar — printed on its invoices for over a century.

Tom O'Reilly was politically very active and a member of the Irish Republican Brotherhood (IRB) and a prominent supporter of Parnell and Home Rule. Later he was a founding member of the Volunteer movement and the local Sinn Féin Club. He became chairman of Bawnboy Workhouse Board of Guardians, a member of Bawnboy District Council and a member of Cavan Co. Council. He was an active local politician and acted as a legal advocate and sometimes a reporter for the *Anglo-Celt*, Co. Cavan's local newspaper.

According to the *Anglo-Celt* (1891) and as reported in "The Stag Hall Story", the following incident occurred in Ballyconnell:

> This was a time when people had strong convictions on the land question, Home Rule and even Parnell: parades and demonstrations offered a legal outlet for these feelings. One Saturday in 1891 as Thomas O'Reilly was working in his bar, he heard music and marching feet. On going to the door, he saw a large number of people turning off the Bawnboy Road and down Main Street. They carried banners and placards on which there were the following slogans: "Down with Landlords", "Kinawley to the Front" and "Home Rule for Ireland". Six bands followed the banner-wielding crowd and each played music in turn. After the demonstrations, many retired to O'Reilly's bar. Later in the evening, as they were leaving, a fight developed amongst them and a vicious confrontation took place, with stools, forms and musical instruments freely used. When the police established peace, most of the musical instruments, drums and O'Reilly's stools and forms were destroyed.

This incident was a reflection of what was happening nationally, which saw deep divisions develop within the nationalist or Catholic community following the political fall of Parnell through the O'Shea affair. These divisions were created and led by the Catholic bishops who controlled the anti-Parnellite movement. They openly preached against the pro-Parnell people, who were in the main members of the nearly defunct IRB and the old Fenian movement. It is noted in *Oscailt Oifigiúil* for the opening of Páirc na gCéad Ultach (First Ulster Park) at Ballyconnell in 1983: "In 1890, Ballyconnell [football] was on the decline. Games were impossible to control; politics and drink motivated much of the fighting."

In July 1890 the *Anglo-Celt* was regretfully recording that "football under Gaelic Rules was a thing of the past in parts of Cavan. The Parnell split in 1891 completed the decline and the GAA in Cavan was moribund until 1903.

The Ballyconnell club broke up in 1891." In fact, the GAA itself almost imploded in that year, were it not for the sporting-focused people at the helm of the then fledgling association. They ousted those with solely political motivations. Were it not for these actions the GAA might not have become the great national movement it is today. Tom O'Reilly, like many before him and since, was forced to emigrate to America. Why he had to go was often questioned and it is probably correct that, after the riot in the pub, he could not afford to refurbish it and more than likely he owed the bank a few pounds and so he had little option but to leave. The bank, as part of the "establishment" and O'Reilly being a noted political activist, was probably disposed to "squeeze him", which resulted in his premises being put up for sale. Emigration for Tom O'Reilly had another consideration. Those who sided with Parnell after the O'Shea affair were often ostracised in their community by the preaching of the Catholic bishops. O'Reilly's premises was not recorded as trading in *Slater's Directory1894*.

Annie Malanaphy returned to America and some time afterwards her father came to Ballyconnell and started to restore the premises and applied to the local courts to have the licence renewed. There were objections. Annie returned to Ireland in 1900 and started to trade from the premises. There was still local agitation and she often told her family that at first her turnover was as little as one shilling and two pence a day. In the census taken on 31 March 1901, Annie Malanaphy was recorded as living at 29 Main St, Ballyconnell. She was single and aged 27. Her mother was also residing there and was recorded as being married and aged 57. In fact, they were 31 and 61 years old respectively. As the recording census enumerator was a member of the local Royal Irish Constabulary (RIC), the old saying came into play: "Whatever you tell them, don't tell them the full truth." Meanwhile, Francis Malanaphy and three daughters were recorded as residing at Gortacashel, Swanlinbar, and their ages were also incorrectly recorded.

(iii) **John Drum**

On the eastern slopes of Slieve Rushen lies the townland of Gortahurk in Fermanagh, about three miles from Ballyconnell. The same census showed that the Drum household consisted of Mary Anne Drum, a widow, who had three eligible sons, Francis, John and Patrick, all in their thirties, their younger sister and a grandson. It was said within the family, however true it may be, that there was a match made between two of the Drum men and two of the Malanaphy girls. It was nearing formal agreement, with John Drum to marry a sister of Annie Malanaphy. However, that was not to be, as love struck between John and Annie, two strong personalities. They were married in Ballyconnell in June 1901. Perhaps it was a love story about which Percy French could have penned a ballad.

John Drum was a local self-taught veterinary practitioner in the south-Fermanagh/west Cavan area and he owned a small farm. He was very much involved in his community and he was a founding member and first drum major of the Mountain Road Fife-and-Drum Band in 1895/96, which is still going strong. The formation of the Mountain Road Band was a political statement and formed as a breakaway "Fenian" group from the Knockninny Fife-and-Drum Band, which was in existence in his parish for many years. The Mountain Road Band was formed as a reaction to Joseph Devlin re-establishing constitutional nationalism in Ulster with the support of the Ancient Order of Hibernians (AOH) and their pro-Catholic stance. The AOH at that time in Ulster was looked upon as sectarian where members had to be Catholic and green, an ethos that was very much a reaction to the growth of the re-forming Orange Order and a mirror image in many ways. This was far removed from the AOH and its radical political and social influence in America. There its members were leaders in the formation of the trade-union movement and its identity with the "Molly Maguires". The AOH also established the tradition of holding St Patrick's Day parades throughout North America.

The Drum family and most of the people of "the Mountain Road" were known Fenians in an area where the nationalist community was classified as being either Fenians or Hibs. Those who were called Fenians were nationalists who believed in the traditions of Wolfe Tone, the Young Irelanders and the original Fenians. Fenianism was growing under the influence of Bulmer Hobson who was reforming the IRB in Ulster. The IRB wanted an independent republic for all of Ireland, where Catholic, Protestant and Dissenter would live in harmony.

When John Drum married Annie Malanaphy he moved to Ballyconnell. The licensed house was small and would still have been in a poor state of repair and so plans were drawn up to build a larger premises on the site. This newly built pub and boarding house was to become a popular place for Fermanagh people. It retained The Gaelic Bar name for another 90 years and attracted patronage from all sides of the community. The new building was completed in 1904. It was constructed by local builder Willie Bennett from Gortmullan. Bennett was a member of the Church of Ireland and employed men irrespective of their creed. This was how the people of west Cavan and south Fermanagh then lived and worked. It is sad to say that within a decade that same community would see division on the Home Rule question, as political and religious differences were used to prop up the political establishment at Westminster. As division was becoming politically obvious in north-east Ulster, thankfully the majority of people in west Cavan and south Fermanagh still respected and lived among each other irrespective of the church they went to on Sundays.

The new premises as constructed by Bennett at 29 Main Street, Ballyconnell, has walls up to a meter in thick and still stands today — regretfully empty and unloved.

In south Fermanagh and west Cavan many families were known by their nickname, as names like Reilly, O'Reilly, Maguire and Curry were common. Why they were given a nickname is a little amusing. The Curry family who worked for Willie Bennett was better known as the "Stan Ups", so called as they had a very giddy "jennet and cart" for drawing building materials and rubble. The only command that the jennet knew from his masters was "Stand Up" and so the constant use of these words sealed the nickname. One of the Drum girls married into the "Fat" Maguires. In west Cavan where the names McGovern, McGoldrick and Dolan were common, most could be identified by the Irish tradition of Christian name, father's name and grandfather's name – in other words, generational name identity. Around Ballyconnell there were people known by their nicknames only, like "The Dockens", "The Braddas", "Charlie the Salmon","Mary from Heaven", "Buttons and Bows" and many more. Nobody referred to their proper surnames.

In 1904 John Drum was offered a place at Queen's University Belfast to study for one year to become a fully qualified veterinary surgeon, which he declined. (Veterinary practitioners were recognised professionally by the Royal College of Veterinary Medicine until 1952.) He was obviously very busy attending to his family and business. In the census of 1901, there were only two people residing at 29 Main Street, Ballyconnell, but in the census taken 10 years later, there were 22 people recorded in the premises. John and Annie now had seven children, from nine years old to an infant, three servants and 10 boarders. It must have been mighty crowded house.

Seven of the boarders in Drums were plasterers and joiners and all were Presbyterians and Episcopalians from Belfast and Co. Antrim. They were probably employed in the construction of the new Masonic Hall at Church St., Ballyconnell. Obviously these tradesmen had no problem boarding in a well-known Fenian establishment. When the Masonic Hall was opened in June 1912, it was completely free of debt. The Ballyconnell Masonic Lodge (405) had 23 members and the master was Richard Kells, Glendoon House, who donated the site.

With the introduction of the old-age pension, rural Ireland was socially uplifted and the Irish and global economies were improving. The population of Ballyconnell had grown to exceed 500, some 25 per cent of whom were non-Catholic. The political changes at Westminster from 1910 were pointing towards the introduction of a third Home Rule Bill for Ireland, which was generally accepted by the majority of the people in the area, including a sizable number of the Protestant community.

With a growing population Ballyconnell had a new Catholic school opened in May 1910. The site for the school was donated by Surgeon-General Roe, CB, of Ballyconnell House who was later killed in action in the early days of the Great War. The construction cost of the school exceeded £1,000 and was borne by a levy imposed on business people and farmers. Others contributed according to their means. Later that year two new young teachers came to Ballyconnell, Master J.B. Mulligan from Virginia and Miss Molly McCabe from Derrada, Ballinamore. Master Corry, the principal teacher in the boys' school, was fond of a "drop" and on his way to school in the mornings would call to Drums for his usual "hair of the dog" to start the day. On one such morning John Drum in making conversation, referred to the fine young man he got to assist him, to which Corry retorted: "Yes Drum, fine indeed; he's so fine he could tramp meal in the barrel of a gun" – referring to the young Master Mulligan who was and remained a very thin man.

During this time, the business people of the town were in negotiations with the legal representatives of Lady Annesley for the purchase of the their tenanted properties in the town.

(iv) Politics

In the early days of the 20th century political activity in most parts of Ireland was at a minimum as many of the representatives at Westminster continued to be appointed and anointed to their uncontested seats. From the general election of 1892, the majority of Irish seats at Westminster were not contested and so a democratic choice was seldom available to the people.

The British Empire was engaged in the Boer War in South Africa, in the last years of the 19th century. Arthur Griffith, who had emigrated to South Africa reported on the events of this War. The treatment of the Irish regiments by their British commanders in South Africa influenced his political attitude and thinking.

Being politically and culturally motivated, Griffith returned to Ireland to co-establish the *United Irishman* paper in 1899 and with many others he became active in Cumann na nGaedheal to revive the Irish language and culture. In 1904/5, he published his 27 essays entitled "The Resurrection of Hungary", which formed the principles on which Sinn Féin was founded. These principles were based on the 1849 rising by the Magyars of Hungary against the Austrian Empire in pursuit of Hungarian autonomy. This rising was militarily crushed. The Hungarian people undertook a silent campaign of passive resistance and civil disobedience against the Austrian Empire. This 17-year long "bloodless war" impressed Griffith as an alternative to the many "botched" revolts by the Irish against English rule. Griffith's Sinn Féin policies of civil disobedience and moral resistance were very much respected and were in turn followed by Mahatma Ghandi in India's pursuit of political independence from the British Empire.

With the introduction of the progressive scheme for land acquisition through the Wyndham Act of 1903, political and social agitation for land ownership by tenant farmers was now being addressed and in the main accepted by the Irish people. Charles Stewart Parnell, former leader of the Irish Parliamentary Party, had always advocated and believed that the land question had to be addressed first and Home Rule would follow. With a growing economy, the agitation for land reform and the end of landlordism was transferred to a campaign for self-government for Ireland by the introduction of a third Home Rule Bill. This campaign was now politically led by the Irish Parliamentary Party (IPP). It had the support of the AOH and the United Irish League, an Organization active throughout Co. Cavan which had its roots in Michael Davitt's Land League. Political and land reform was not confined to the Catholic or nationalist community.

The *Anglo-Celt* reported that some small Protestant tenant farmers suffered evictions from their holdings carried out on behalf of Lord Farnham at Portlongfield, Killeshandra and at Kilmore. A Protestant family, now in Fermanagh, who was evicted from its holding beside the Benison Estate at Ballyconnell in the 19th century always held the view that Lord Benison was pro-Catholic. John Joseph Benison was a land agent and landlord and was always referred to locally as Lord Benison, while not having the formal title. The census of 1911 shows that all his employees in residence as well as his older sister were Catholic. Benison was lauded in the west Cavan song 'Swanlinbar Chapel' for his role in saving the chapel at Swanlinbar from being burned down by another land agent over unpaid tithes in the early 19th century. The following is a verse from the song:

> You sons of old, round the hills of Macken,
> Would lose their lives or their Chapel save.
> I'll lay down my pen as the case is settled,
> Fill up your glasses with rum and gin,
> And drink a health to your friend Montgomery,
> To noble Maguire and brave Benison.

On 15 August 1912, a mass Home Rule meeting was held in O'Kane's field, Daisy Hill, Ballyconnell and it is said that on the same place many years earlier one of the first Home Rule meetings in Ireland was held. At Westminster, the third Home Rule Bill for Ireland was to become part of a programme of government, but it was to become a political football within parliament. The Tories and the Irish Unionists, with the support of the House of Lords, were to try every means possible, using the Irish situation, to try to kill Home Rule and oust the Liberals from power.

Life in Ballyconnell would appear to be somewhat very tranquil and at peace with itself in 1912, when a meeting was called and a local string band or light orchestra was formed. The area was fortunate to have the much praised music teacher Miss Veitch, Carramore House, a member of the small Methodist community. Under her direction this local orchestra gave its first concert in May and performed again in November that year in the Town Hall or Market House. There were 14 members in the orchestra and among them were names which are still known in Ballyconnell, like the brothers Bryan, Frank and Leo O'Grady, all flautists, Tom Gormley on clarinet, Frank Dolphin and Joe Clancy on violin and others now long forgotten.

CHAPTER 2

AWAITING THE THIRD HOME RULE BILL

(i) William E. Gladstone

When Liberal Premier William E. Gladstone introduced the Home Rule Bills for Ireland to the British Parliament in 1886 and 1893, they were both welcomed by nationalist Ireland. They were designed to introduce political reforms for self-government in Ireland within the British Empire. On both occasions the bills were not politically popular as they were going to break the 1801 Act of Union. The Irish Unionists, Tories and the House of Lords used this Act to ensure their defeat. Eighty-six members of the House of Lords had extensive landed estates in Ireland.

From the Act of Union of 1801, after the Irish Lords and Commons had voted themselves out of existence, with the encouragement of Lord Castlereagh, the Dublin Castle administration did not have an elected Dublin assembly to oversee it. Being geographically remote from Westminster the result was an uncontrollable growth in the cost of Irish administration. This coupled with the continued abuses in Ireland by the Lords and their landlords were a concern to Gladstone. In simple terms, Ireland was costing the British Exchequer, while the Irish Lords with distant governance continued with their corrupt ways on a greater scale (charging rack-rents). Therefore Gladstone wanted an effective Irish assembly which would govern Ireland and be self-sufficient. Gladstone, being a religious man, must have been aware that the absence of self-governance in Ireland had contributed much to the helplessness and hopelessness endured by the Irish people during the Great Famine. As the potato crop failed in Ireland the landed gentry continued to send foodstuffs to Britain and nobody with a conscience or political clout within Ireland was in a position to cry stop on behalf of the destitute.

On becoming Prime Minister in 1868 Gladstone wanted to right the many wrongs of Ireland. He disestablished the Anglican Church in Ireland by the Irish Church act 1869. It then became the Church of Ireland from 1871. The act meant that non-Anglican property owners and farmers were no longer obliged to pay tithes to that church. Gladstone's first Land Act gave tenant farmers some legal rights — an evicted farmer had to be compensated by his landlord for any improvements made to the holding during his tenancy. Gladstone's second Land Act introduced the Three Fs — fixity of tenure, fair rents and free sale. The Home Rule proposals for Ireland would mean severe administrative and expenditure cuts within the country. Gladstone's Home Rule Bills of 1886 and 1893 were defeated, as orchestrated by those who wanted to maintain the Act of Union and to save ownership and income from their landed estates in Ireland. The insecurity created among the ascendancy and the Anglican Church in Ireland by the Irish Church Act must have left a residual underbelly of hatred and mistrust towards Gladstone within the British establishment. His Home Rule Bills had little chance of success. Queen Victoria and Gladstone did not have a comfortable relationship.

In 1909, the Liberal Government at Westminster through its then chancellor David Lloyd George, presented the People's Budget to parliament, a revolutionary political move based on social-democratic principles. Its objectives were the introduction of much needed social reform in Britain and to finance the modernisation of the British navy. This budget proposed to increase taxation on liquor and tobacco as well as a super income tax on the rich and the introduction of death duties. This was targeted at the wealthy unelected and land rich members of the Lords. The House of Lords voted down the people's budget — an act that was totally against parliamentary convention to veto budgetary proposals as passed by the House of Commons. This precipitated a political crisis in Britain and it was Ireland that was to suffer the consequences.

There were two general elections in 1910 when the Liberals and Herbert Asquith were returned to form a stable government with the support of the 82 Irish nationalists after the second general election in December. For the IPP support, a new Home Rule Bill for Ireland was part of the bargain, as was the abolition of the Parliament Act, to remove absolute power from the House of Lords. The Liberals' agenda, which had the King's support, had the intent of political revenge on the Tories and the Lords.

Dublin Castle and the Irish civil service had anticipated that a Home Rule Bill for Ireland was on the cards. They started to plan for their own self-protection and for the handover of administrative duties to a new Irish assembly, which they assumed would be led by John Redmond. Ireland's financial deficit in 1910 was £1 million and growing. In 1912 Irish expenditure exceeded revenues by over £2 million. The problem facing Westminster was how to overcome this great financial quagmire and grant financial autonomy to a country that was basically bankrupt. The third Home Rule Bill for Ireland would not be acceptable to the Unionists and Tories. The Protestant Churches were targeted to sell the campaign to their congregations under their great new fear — Home Rule would be Rome Rule.

It has to be noted that at this time the 'Ne Temere decree' of 1908 (under which with a Catholic marrying a non-Catholic, both parties had to promise to have all their offspring baptised in a Catholic church and brought up as Catholics) and other such decrees from the Vatican were contentious issues between the churches. This added much fire to the divisive debate on the Home Rule question to come. Religious differences would now be used by the political ascendancy and some industrialists to polarise political and religious allegiances, which would eventually lead to new divisions within Ireland. The passing of the Parliament Act, which took absolute power from the House of Lords, would also be used to bring down the third Home Rule Bill. Ireland was to be the battlefield for another British political war.

(ii) Protestant opponents of Home Rule

The debate on the Home Rule question commenced in Fermanagh on New Year's Eve 1911, when Fr Bernard Maguire gave a fund-raising lecture in aid of St Michael's Church Enniskillen, "Would Home Rule be Rome Rule?" where he said:

> There was not a shred of decent argument in support of the contention. The Catholics of Ireland had ploughed, harrowed and steam-rolled for centuries in the name of religion, and now when they were lifting their heads they were asked to give assurances for good behaviour. And the answer they might give was - "Have we not a right to our place in the world as well as you; and do we owe you an apology for accepting it? If the truth must be told, we were here before you, and when you came it was uninvited and as intruders. Do you in defiance of the law hold us guilty until we prove ourselves innocent..?"

On the following day a nationalist rally in support of Home Rule and the King was held at Derrylin where the nationalist MPs, Patrick Crumley, South Fermanagh and F.E. Meehan, North Leitrim spoke. The speakers were aware of their audience as they verbally attacked the Unionists for their anti-Home Rule stance. The most appeasing words at Derrylin came from a Mr John Crozier, a Methodist from Blacklion, who said: "Politics of the present day was not a question of religion. He was sure that under Home Rule everyone –

– both Catholic and Protestant — would get fair play. If he was under the impression for a moment that this would not be the case — he was sure everyone would be contented — he would not stand on a Nationalist platform."

Both these meetings were recorded in the *Impartial Reporter*, which also reported on the annual reunion meeting of the McKinley Loyal Orange Lodge, held in the Protestant Hall, Enniskillen on 2 January, where C. F. Falls, District Master, said:

> There was one subject which transcended in interest every other one that night. That was the far reaching and tremendously important decree promulgated by His Holiness the Pope. The past year had been a very dark and serious one for them in Ireland... He thought that the Irish Unionists should return to the Pope their sincere thanks for what he has done for them in this fight against Home Rule by the decrees he had issued.

Many Protestant leaders gave the impression that they were against the Ne Temere decree. In fact they were delighted as they saw it as a Protestant defence against any further mixed marriages and their own flocks would be further removed from Rome's influence.
Instead the Ne Temere decree was used as a political weapon.

W. Copeland Trimble and K. Fetherstonhaugh MP speaking, attacked John Redmond and Westminster, the very political establishment they wanted to adhere to, while rejecting Home Rule. They spoke of past Protestant repressions and their fears if the Act of Union was broken. From what was being said there was going to be no appeasement. The as-yet-unpublished Home Rule Bill was going to have a fight on its hands and the *Impartial Reporter* under Trimble's editorship was leading the Unionist campaign in Fermanagh.

The *Church of Ireland Gazette*, a weekly publication by the Church for its fraternity, was an obvious organ to be used to get the anti-Home Rule campaign under way among the ordinary Protestant people. It commented in January 1912:-

> In former years on the eve of Home Rule Bills, the Church of Ireland expressed her voice with unmistakable unanimity. We are not primarily concerned as a Church with politics, but as long as Irish Churchmen continue to believe that under a Home Rule Bill the highest interests of their Church and of their country would be gravely imperilled, they

will do wisely to impress the fact upon the electorate. A few observations occurring in a speech delivered at a Belfast Church Conference which seemed, however wrongly, to indicate that the opposition to Home Rule was slackening in its intensity, were greedily snatched at, and had a liberal circulation at the hands of those who were glad to find any support for views to which Churchmen are, as a body, strongly opposed. Any silence on our part at the present juncture would be similarly misinterpreted, and we are glad that a special meeting of the General Synod is to be summoned, by which date it is expected that the details of the forthcoming Home Rule Bill will be before the public. We have little doubt that Churchmen will be as keenly alive to the vital importance of the issues involved, and will express their convictions no less forcibly than of yore. Any failure to do so would be quickly interpreted by our political and ecclesiastical enemies as a token that we were not so earnest or convinced in our opposition to Home Rule as the many great men who have spoken on the subject in special Synods in 1886 and 1893.

This article shows that the Church of Ireland leaders and the majority of its people were against impending Home Rule while preparing themselves to protect their own interests be they land, property or perceived freedom. The church was saying to its flock, as it had in the past, to do what they considered best for themselves and Ireland. It also recognised that there were some members who supported Home Rule and who wanted the subject debated. It showed a willingness to debate or share their fears of the contents of the impending Home Rule Bill with other Irishmen issued later that month...
"Mr. J.J. Horgan republishes his series of articles from *The Leader*, and places them before us as a critical consideration of Home Rule. He wants to awaken intelligent discussion concerning the details of Home Rule, but neither we nor him are in possession of them."

So far the anticipated Home Rule Bill was raising old fears and suspicions in north-east Ulster, as a February issue showed with extracts from a speech by Bishop Darcy of Down, who spoke on Home Rule at a Young Mens' Christian Association in Belfast and was quoted:

* The Leader, edited by D P Morgan was a strongly pro-Catholic weekly

I trust that one effect of this meeting may be that there may go forth an influence which will make for peace and self-restraint amongst our people throughout this whole week. The Bishop asked, how could Home Rule make for prosperity, when it consisted of putting the progressive elements under the control of the unprogressive and demonstrate the very grave peril to their liberties which Roman supremacy would mean. Where the Popes found it impossible to enforce their decrees, they winked at or overlooked the breaking of their decrees by persons who owed them allegiance, on the score of necessity; when the necessity disappeared, the law at once assumed its validity. The bearing of these facts on the present situation is evident. A Government in Ireland under papal patronage would make short work of our liberties.

Bishop Darcy did not mince his words and was uncompromising in what he said — that Protestants were a different class, the Church of Rome would rule, other Irishmen were unfit to rule and non-Catholics would lose their freedom.

The *Gazette* reported on the gathering of Presbyterians in Belfast in February, which had much written about it in the British press:

It was a remarkable occasion. Never before in Ireland did so many Presbyterians assemble. There was no mistaking the stern reality, the grim determination of these men... represented the class that does not sympathise with Orangemen. In ordinary circumstances great numbers of them would be found thoroughgoing Radicals. It remains to be seen whether their appeal to their co-religionists across the water will be listened to. A developing feature of this demonstration was the number of businessmen who took part. The heads of many of Belfast's commercial firms made speeches, men not previously seen or heard on political platforms. The purpose of the Ulster Presbyterian was plainly summed up by Sir William Crawford, Chairman of the York St. Spinning Co. - "A Dublin Parliament, the Presbyterians of Ireland would not have; its laws they would not obey; its demands for money they would throw into the fire. Let an Irish Government be formed, let it send its officers to Ulster to take taxes by force. They would not pay. Their decision was final and unchanging, their duty was clear". It is difficult to see how a Dublin Parliament could enforce its authority...

It was now apparent that the majority within the Church of Ireland and Presbyterian communities had begun a very focused campaign with new-founded objections based on taxation, against the as yet, unpublished Home Rule Bill. The campaign was initially confined to the greater Belfast area. The *Impartial Reporter* reported on this Presbyterian assembly and on a Methodist assembly later in February and both on predictable grounds.

In March The *Gazette* notified the faithful that, "The Archbishop of Armagh is calling a special meeting of the General Synod, to take councel as to the duty of the Church in the present crisis..." What crisis? They were making a crisis out of an unknown issue based on past fears.

The *Gazette* said:

> Many of our readers will remember that after the fate of Mr. Gladstone's Home Rule Bill in 1893 people said: "Home Rule is dead". Then indeed our island entered upon a period of prosperity, unparalleled in its history, wise and beneficial legislation settled the long vexed question of land tenure, and established the small farmers as peasant proprietors; trade and commerce flourished, poverty fast decreased, the savings of the people accumulated enormously. Then came the disastrous election of 1906 when the Unionists were flung out of office. Had the English and Scottish Liberals been returned in sufficient strength, matters would not have been so bad. As it was, it required the strength of the Nationalist party of Ireland to enable them to take office, and, accordingly an alliance ensued, and under its leadership our unhappy country is being rushed along a road, which threatens an invasion of our liberties as Churchmen and citizens...

The Irish writer George Bernard Shaw, took a swipe at the religious Home Rule debate when in February his letter to the *Christian Globe*, London, was published:

> What is wanted on both sides of the Channel is a little real Protestantism. This craven terror of poor old Rome - of a Pope who is less free personally than any Atheist and less powerful than the nearest surgeon - is not Protestantism; it is the cowardice that is the invariable symptom and penalty of want of faith. There is one force, and only one, that Rome cannot face, and that force is democracy. In democratic America, Irish Roman Catholics desert their Church by tens of thousands. In oligarchic Castle ruled Ireland, the bitterest enemies of the priests

would die rather than desert in face of the enemy. In France the Roman Church cannot get even common justice. In Italy the Pope is a prisoner in his own palace. In Spain priests and nuns depend on police and military protection for their personal safety. In Ireland alone the priest is powerful, thanks to the hatred, terror, faithlessness and folly of the Protestants, who stand between him and his natural enemy, democracy. There is only one chance for priestly tyranny under Home Rule, and that is the chance of the Protestants insisting that the Irish Parliament shall be denied the power to set the Roman house in order.

The most pressing need in Ireland today is the establishment of the Roman Catholic Church. At present the priests levy taxation without audit or responsibility, and their charges for their official services - for marriages, funerals etc would make an English farmer gasp. This taxation should be levied by the Irish Parliament, which should pay the priests and regulate the charges, besides controlling ecclesiastical patronage. Factory Acts should be applied resolutely to convent workshops and the like, and the inspector of education should exact as high a standard from convent schools as from lay ones.

Enough then, of these drunken Ulsterics and maudlin singing of 'Rule Britannia'. The north used to sing 'The Protestant Boys will Carry the Drum'. It was manlier than clinging to Britannia's skirts for protection against the bogey-men with the triple tiara.

I suppose it is useless to remind the Orange North that honour and humanity are to be found in Roman Catholic Ireland at least as conspicuously as in Belfast, and that as, though Calvin burnt Servetus, and priests have been quite as horribly persecuted as parsons, the Roman Catholics have managed to survive Protestant domination, perhaps there may be some hope for Protestants under Home Rule.

At all events, pure materialistic cowardice will not save the situation.

Weekly attacks were made on the proposed Home Rule Bill and interestingly all comments were becoming stronger with the fear of what Dominion Home Rule might bring. There was no evidence in the *Impartial Reporter* that Protestant people or societies undertook any form of communication with nationalists, and if they did, in all probability their good intentions would have been suppressed. However, the paper did report on nationalist and Sinn Féin meetings and comments. The editor W. Copeland Trimble was forging a focused campaign against Home Rule during 1912, where week after week, he put the message across to his readers, the Unionist people of Fermanagh and adjoining counties.

Historically it was the Protestant people of Ulster who were the free thinkers and leaders in Ireland. Why now, was this line of enlightenment being trampled upon in the interests of the English ascendancy and against the progressive majority in Ireland? From the many press reports from the Protestant churches and Orange societies, there was a common thread with constant references to the Pope and papal decrees. The Protestant population at that time would appear to have been made more aware of Rome's teaching than the ordinary Catholic population, who were always probably poorly informed of such and cared less. The Ne Temere decree from the Vatican was now subject to legal challenges in some British Dominions and was contributing much global divisions between the Catholic and Protestant churches. All churches appeared to be using their positions to control through fear contrary to what Christianity was and is all about.

The special meeting of the General Synod of the Church of Ireland to debate the impending Home Rule Bill was held in Dublin in late March 1912. It was presided over by the Primate of Armagh, Dr Crozier, who said: "The sense of responsibility cast upon him in calling the meeting and the question before them concerned the very existence of their church and the welfare and prosperity of the country. The vast majority of Protestants were absolutely united in this matter, more than a million of the cream of Irish life..."

In moving the first resolution at the Synod, Rev. Dr. Peacock said: "Home Rule would not bring peace and harmony and material good will to Ireland. For these reasons he deprecated its establishment, and he cordially endorsed the resolutions of the Presbyterian and Methodist brethren protesting against it." The Bishop of Kilmore (Cavan) supporting the resolution, asserted that:

> The attitude of the Synod, was not one of political bias. To Irish Unionists, Home Rule was a moral and social cataclysm, and if it became a fact it must, to say the least, deprive them of their natural heritage as freeborn citizens of the British Empire. Should they, then, be asked to keep silence with a heterogeneous coterie conspired to rob them of that birthright? They objected to having their aspirations confined to Ireland, or to a Parish Rectory, or to a Donnybrook Fair...

If the synod, as asserted by the Bishop of Kilmore, "was not one of political bias", certainly his utterances and tone had to be of a religious or class bias, or both. The bishop's own words denying it as a political matter questioned his own understanding and position on the issue of Home Rule and Ireland and the relationship of his own flock with their Catholic neighbours throughout his dioceses.

(iii) Protestant supporters of Home Rule

At the Synod Rev. J. O. Hannay, the distinguished rector of Westport, said:
> He opposed the resolution, and said he believed in the policy of Home
> Rule for Ireland ... and in dissenting from the resolution he thought he
> spoke for a minority in the Church of Ireland, a minority not
> insignificant in the matter of numbers, and certainly not insignificant
> in intelligence and capacity. You will forgive me perhaps if I quote you
> the same words spoken by no less a person than Oliver Cromwell to an
> assembly something like this — ' I beseech you gentlemen, to believe
> it possible that you may be mistaken'...

Mr. McMurrough Kavanagh said:
> He disagreed with the resolution. He emphatically protested against
> raising a political question in the Synod Hall or turning the Synod Hall
> into a political debating ground. They as Unionists were against Home
> Rule, they condemned it and would have none of it, and they had a
> perfect right to oppose it as politicians, but not as Churchmen and
> certainly not in the Synod Hall. It had been stated by the Bishop of
> Ossary that if Home Rule were passed, their Cathedrals would be
> taken from them. Well if those statements had been made outside on a
> platform, they would not have been taken seriously, but they were
> different when uttered in all solemnity by a Bishop of the Church. Did
> they really believe it (Cries of 'Yes'). Did they really believe an Irish
> Parliament would rob their Church ('Yes' and 'Why not'?). Well, after
> all it was only a matter of opinion. (Laughter) These statements were
> made on no facts, either past or present. If they believed any of these
> things, he would not believe them. (Cries of 'We Do'.) He believed the
> Church and Property would have the same protection as of old.

The speaker was proceeding when the President ruled him out of order, as
he was not speaking on the motion.

Mr Pierce O'Mahony, speaking to a United Irish League meeting on the
anticipated Home Rule Bill in Dublin at that time, said:
> That week at the Synod, the Lord Primate and head of the Church to
> which he belonged — the Church that claimed to be the Church of
> Ireland — said 'God save Ireland from ignorance and superstition,
> from bigotry, intolerance and strife, and make that Church herself the
> saviour of the warm-hearted, kindly and impulsive people who formed
> the great mass of our fellow countrymen, and with whom we might

live for ever in peace but for the unscrupulous politicians'. That was to say, he accused him and every member of the Church who held nationalist opinions of the desire to overthrow the Church to which they belonged. That was a base and wicked accusation to bring against them, and it was a disgrace to the man who made it. In using such language at the Synod, his Grace had degraded it to the level of a political meeting. 'Ireland', his Grace went on to say 'was never a nation and never could be a nation' and that to be a nation she must have an army and navy of her own and control her own Customs and Excise. Apparently it was hard to please his Grace. The present Home Rule Bill was bad in his opinion because it did not go far enough.

Mr O'Mahony set out to prove the Primate of the Church of Ireland wrong in his assertion that Ireland never was and never could be a nation:

Was Ireland not a nation long before the Normans set foot upon her shores, when she evangelised Europe, when Saxon kings and nobles sent their sons to her schools of learning to get education they could not get at home? Was she not a nation in 1772 when she won her independence, and when the English Parliament passed an Act renouncing for ever its right to legislate for her, and declaring that the Irish Parliament alone was competent to make laws to govern the people of Ireland? Ireland had always been a nation, she was a nation now, and would continue to be a nation, and when the Home Rule Bill became Law she would be able to develop her national life on true national lines. He would like to know if the Primate meant when he complained about Ireland not being given the control of customs and excise that because she would not be able to fix the price of whiskey sufficiently low, therefore she would not be a nation.

There was a resolution moved at the Synod by the Provost of Trinity College — a resolution, which he, as a Protestant, was heartily ashamed of.

Had it come to this — that all the Protestants of Ireland could now put forward as a reason against the granting of Home Rule was that they could not trust themselves to a Parliament in which they would be outnumbered by their Nationalist fellow countrymen. What a falling away from the spirit and character of the Protestant patriots of the eighteenth century. What a difference between the men in the Synod the other day and Henry Grattan and his compatriots in College Green. The Protestants were just as small a body then as the Protestants of today are, and they were not afraid to trust to their fellow countrymen.

So it has come to this — that the benefits of over a hundred years of the Act of Union have been the making of the Irish Protestant so cowardly, base, and suspicious that they are now afraid to trust their fellow countrymen. He was almost ashamed to belong to them except for one thing, that quietly, but slowly and surely, there was a large mass of Protestant opinion coming round to support the claim for full self-government for Ireland. It was not equality that the Protestants, for whom the Primate of Ireland and the Provost of Trinity spoke at the Synod on Tuesday, wanted, but ascendancy, and that is what they will never get again in Ireland. He was a communicant and a synodsman of the Church of which the Lord Primate was the head, and he resented deeply and indignantly his accusation that he and other Protestant Nationalists were seeking to destroy the Church to which they belonged. The statement was absolutely and wickedly false...

A monster meeting in support of Home Rule was held in Sackville St, (O'Connell St.), Dublin on 31 March 1912 where the main speaker was John Redmond, the leader of the IPP. The other speakers were Eoin MacNeill and Padraig Pearse, both of whom addressed the mass gathering. Pearse said:

We have no wish to destroy the British. We only want our freedom. We differ among ourselves on small points, but we agree that we want freedom, in some shape or other...

But I should think myself a traitor to my country if I did not answer the summons to this gathering, for it is clear to me that the Bill we support today will be for the good of Ireland, and that we will be stronger with it than without it. Let us unite and win a good Act from the British; I think it can be done.

If we are tricked this time, there is a party in Ireland, and I am one of them, that will advise the Gael to have no counsel with the Gall but to answer henceforward with the strong arm and the sword's edge... If we are cheated once more there will be red war in Ireland.*

Pearse was now speaking from his soon to be adopted IRB position of historical mistrust of the British parliament (he joined the IRB in 1913) and the growing opposition by the Ulster Unionists to the impending Home Rule Bill.

* Joseph E.A. Connell Jr., History Ireland, 2012, Vol.20 No2.

(iv) Militarised opposition and Tories fan the flames

The *Church of Ireland Gazette* reported on "A Unionist Demonstration" in Belfast on Easter Tuesday 1912 which was a new development, saying:

> The Unionist Demonstration has largely occupied attention in Ulster lately. For weeks and months men have been preparing for it. Drilling has been going on in all parts. Large bodies of men might be seen constantly in the evenings practising marching in military formation through the streets of Belfast and along country roads, some contingents carrying 'dummy' rifles, and some are said to be armed with real rifles. One disquieting feature is the enormous number of revolvers that have been sold. It is no exaggeration to say that thousands of working men are in possession of these dangerous weapons. The enthusiasm of the crowds is quite spontaneous and the spirit and determination to resist Home Rule is intense...

The Church of Ireland through the *Gazette* was starting to look at its role in the anti-Home Rule campaign, as there was now evidence of public militarism which was being shown in the Belfast area. The wording used in the report of the events in Belfast over that Easter week were somehow muted, when Bonar Law, the leader of the Tory and Unionist Party, paid a visit to the city and was greeted by a reported crowd of 100,000 anti-Home Rulers in the Balmoral Showgrounds. Bonar Law arrived by train from Larne, where he was welcomed by a civilian guard of honour drawn up in double lines, the full length of the station platform, with Sir Edward Carson and the Lord Mayor of Belfast present. It was reported that on that day there were some 8,600 members of this citizen army, mostly armed, of whom an estimated 4,000 were from the Belfast shipyards. This was a major show of Unionist feeling against impending Home Rule and a demonstration of their determination to have it defeated by "whatever means".

The *Impartial Reporter* writing on the military aspects of this Belfast gathering said: "The permanent agricultural showground at Balmoral lies at the point where country and city join. The city soldiers and country soldiers met at the gates at the end of a march of many miles, and side by side, each army, eight deep swung into the main fairway. As they came onto the paved way the rhythm of the marching feet rang out clear above the drums and fifes, above the cheers and brought as clear a sense of the pomp and circumstances of war as if every man had been in red uniform."

The following Resolution was put before the Balmoral gathering:

We, the Ulster Unionists gathered in this vast assembly from all parts of the province, hereby accord a most hearty and enthusiastic welcome to the Rt. Hon. Andrew Bonar Law MP, on the occasion of his first visit to Ulster as leader of the Unionist Party in the House of Commons.

We most emphatically ensure him — and we ask him to take the message to the people of Great Britain — that the opposition of the Irish Unionists to a separate Parliament for Ireland, in any form, is unaltered and unalterable. We are convinced that the government of Ireland by a Home Rule Parliament would infallibly lead to bitter racial and sectarian strife, to lasting injury to our commerce and industries, would involve ruin to our civil and religious liberties and the degradation of our citizenship in the United Kingdom, and would be the first step in the disintegration of the great Empire, to the up-building of which Irishmen and in no small degree the descendants of the Ulster plantation have contributed their full share.

We most earnestly reaffirm, and once more pledge ourselves to, the historic resolve of the great Ulster Convention of 1892, and under no circumstances will we submit to be torn from the protection of the Imperial Parliament and to be forced under the control of a separate Irish Legislature. Our resolve is confirmed by the consideration of the dishonourable tactics by which it is proposed to rush a Home Rule Bill through Parliament without any mandate from the electorate of Great Britain — from whom, indeed, its provisions have been studiously concealed — and thus to secure its enactment as a result of the unprincipled bargain with the Nationalist Parliamentary group, and under cover of a constitution mutilated by the Parliament Act.

We solemnly assert that the disastrous consequences of such legislation will lie at the door, not only of the reckless who seek to enact it, but also at that of every elector who, by his vote or influence supports them.

The *Impartial Reporter* continued: "The inclement weather made the atmosphere dour and determined rather than gay and triumphal in the Balmoral Showgrounds on that day as the crowd waited and sang 'Rule Britannia' and 'God Save the King' before the Church of Ireland Primate gave the opening prayer. Sir Edward Carson, waving a Union Jack tied to a blackthorn stick, said: 'Raise your hands and repeat after me'. With that, 30,000 heads, hands and arms stretched to take the oath – 'Never under any circumstances will we have Home Rule' – which was also taken by the massed crowd. On the platform, packed with prominent Unionists, Members of the House of Lords and Parliament, Bonar Law joined Sir Edward Carson who said: 'I only ask in the presence of this our nation that he and I should shake hands over this question'."

Bonar Law then spoke:

I come to you as the leader of the Unionist Party in the House of Commons with two objects. I come to give you the assurance, and I give it now, that we who represent the party regard your cause, not as Ulster's alone, nor as England's alone, but the cause of the Empire. We will do all that men can do to defeat a conspiracy as treacherous as has ever been formed against the life of a great nation. As in 1886 and 1893, Ulster holds the key of the position. I come with the expectation that we will send to the people across the Channel the message that your hostility to Home Rule, which twice before has killed it, has not diminished with time – but has grown stronger with every passing year and is burning with a flame that shines brighter and steadier than ever. I expected that this would be a great gathering, but the result has far exceeded my expectations... With you, there is neither doubt nor hesitation. You are men, to quote words once used by Cromwell to describe his Ironsides, 'who know what you are fighting for and love what you know'... The two previous Home Rule Bills, if carried, would have Ireland bankrupt and would have destroyed the unity of purpose upon which the safety of the nation depended.

Continuing, he pointed to the example of Austria and Hungary, of Sweden and Norway and how Austria and Hungary were still united but by a tenure so frail. The whole history of the modern world is a history of movement towards a closer union and great nations are centralising their resources. Italy, Germany, the United States, our own Colonies all teach us the same lesson. Everywhere the centralising of power is being increased, everywhere the authority of new states is being diminished. And we, we alone, who have been the Empire builders of the world, are asked to reverse that movement, to begin a process of disintegration, to set up a separate parliament in Dublin which, at best, means friction if that parliament were always friendly...

The Tory leader was telling the Belfast people what he wanted to say about centralising powers, but failed to tell them that Norway had won its political independence from the Swedish Empire in 1904 and Bulgaria got its political independence in 1908, leading to the break up of the Ottoman Empire.

He continued: What good can Home Rule do Ireland? I have no ill feeling – and I am sure I speak for this vast assemblage as well as for myself – towards our Nationalist fellow-subjects. We claim for ourselves no privilege, which we are not willing to extend to them. They can point to no grievance, no single grievance, which the British people and the British Parliament has not been ready to redress. They are in the main a Roman Catholic population in a Protestant country, but enjoying, and they will always enjoy, freedom for the exercise of their religion to an extent as great, probably greater than in any Catholic country in the world. Not the least of the evils of this great conspiracy is that it rouses again the whole hostilities of race and religion which all of us would like to see buried…

The government has erected by their Parliament Act, a boom against you to shut you off from the help of the British people. You will burst that boom. That help will come and when the crises is over, men will say to you, in words not unlike those used by Pitt: "You have saved yourselves by your exertions, and you have saved the Empire by your example."

There were four speaking platforms that day from which every noted Unionist spoke to the assembled Unionists from Belfast, Co. Antrim, Co. Down and Co. Derry. Special trains brought some 1,400 Unionists from the far south as well as Wexford and Wicklow. A special steamer brought supporters and acquaintances of Bonar Law from Glasgow, while the Orange lodges from Northumberland were represented among the Ulster volunteer militia.

The *Impartial Reporter* stated that one of the speakers was a Mr J. C. Coffey BL, Dublin, who said: "There were thousands of his co-religionists, Catholics, who were against Home Rule, and he was certain his church was. He regretted that there were numbers of his co-religionists who were afraid to come out and express their opinions. They had Catholic England with them, and Catholic England would see that they did not get Home Rule."

What J. C. Coffey had said could also be said for many liberal Unionists who were afraid to speak out and had little option but to be seen to go along with the anti-Home Rule campaign. Fear is a strong but terrible political weapon.

CHAPTER 3

THE HOME RULE BILL
AND ULSTER DAY

(i) Third Home Rule Bill

As The White Star Line was launching the Harland and Wolff-built Titanic liner on its maiden voyage from Southampton to New York, the Westminster government was introducing the Third Home Rule Bill, on 11 April 1912. The bill proposed the granting of self-government to Ireland with dominion status within the British Empire. Everything was looking well for Ireland politically and for its future among the nations of the world. The bill as presented by the Prime Minister Herbert Asquith to parliament was hailed as being superior in every way to the two previously defeated Home Rule Bills of 1886 and 1893. It was widely welcomed with many good wishes received by John Redmond, the leader of the IPP, from the dominions, such as Canada and Australia.

The principal details of the Home Rule Bill were that the Irish parliament would consist of the King, an Irish Senate of 40 members and an Irish House of Commons with 164 members. The parliament would make laws for the peace, order and good government of Ireland only. For the Senate, 40 members were to be nominated for the first time by the Imperial Executive and to hold office for six years, retiring in rotation. As members retired, the Irish Executive would nominate their successors. The 164 members of the lower House of Parliament were to be elected by the existing Irish constituencies. No constituency was to have a population of fewer than 27,000 people. This would give representative seats as follows: Ulster 59, Leinster 41, Munster 37, Connaught 25 and the Universities 2. In case of disagreement the two houses would sit and vote together.

The Home Rule Bill stated that the Dublin parliament would be forbidden to pass laws affecting the Crown or the making of peace or war. It would have no responsibility for the army or navy, treaties, treason, the amendment of the Home Rule Act, the Irish Land Purchase Act and the 1893 Act. There was a right to appeal to the Privy Council on all acts of the Irish parliament. It was forbidden to make any law directly or indirectly to establish or endow any religion or to prohibit the free exercise of it or to give a preference, privilege, or disadvantage on account of religious belief or religious or ecclesiastical status or to make any religious belief or any religious ceremony a condition of the validity of marriage. (This was probably included to allay Protestant fears, to prevent a Dublin parliament enacting any legislation on marriage in line with the Vatican's Ne Temere decree.)

Westminster temporarily reserved control of old-age pensions, national insurance, the police, Post Office Savings Bank, loans made to Ireland before 1912 and the collection of taxes, which were to be collected in Ireland as per the practice of the time. The Irish parliament would have power to impose new taxes under certain limitations. It could also reduce taxes and have a free hand in excise. It could increase customs to the amount of 10 per cent and all taxes were to be paid directly into the Imperial Exchequer.

In finance, Ireland's projected deficit for 1912 was put at £2 million to reduce to £1.5 million in 1913. Every year there would be transferred from the Imperial to the Irish Exchequer an amount for Irish services, estimated at £200,000; a further sum of £500,000 would be transferred in the first year and £50,000 less in every following year, reducing to £200,000 for the expenses of the Irish legislature. If that sum was not sufficient, Ireland would have to find the rest herself. There would be a separate Irish Exchequer and consolidated fund.

Ireland would have 42 members in the Imperial Parliament. Universities would not be represented. There would be eight boroughs and 34 counties with representatives – eight Unionists and 34 nationalists.

Prime Minister Asquith made the following points on why Ulster could not be excluded when introducing the Government of Ireland Act:

> They could not admit the right of a relatively small minority in Ulster to veto the verdict of the vast body of people in Ireland. At that time, Ulster (9 counties) was represented by 17 Unionists and 16 Home Rulers, this disproving the pretence that Ulster would die rather than accept Home Rule … Home Rule could no longer be represented as a concession to violence. He had always presented the case for Home Rule for Ireland as the first step in a larger scheme of devolution. The claims of Ireland came first and must be separately dealt with. Local interests must be dedicated to local management. The cardinal principle of the Bill was that the Imperial Parliament would not surrender its supreme authority and the Bill would confer on Ireland in regard to Irish things a real autonomy and it would have power to make laws exclusively relating to Ireland.

During the debate on the Bill's second reading on 29 March, the MP for East Cavan, Samuel Young, said:

He had lived 91 years amongst these people in Ireland, and he asserted that there would be no despotism, no tyranny, no attempt at putting down the minority of the country who were Protestants. On the contrary, they would give perfect fair play to all the Protestants with whom they came into contact. He represented a Catholic constituency for 20 years and he could speak with perfect freedom. It was surely time to settle this national question, which had disturbed the peace of Ireland and retarded the progress of business in that House for so many years. It had often been a puzzle to him why the British people did not get rid of this diseased limb, which had been a source of much weakness of the body politic, that the patent remedy known as self-government had not been applied earlier, when it was known to be so effectual in allaying discontent in Canada, South Africa and other colonies. The Bill before the House was ardently desired by three-fourths of the people of Ireland, by the people of Scotland and Wales and by all the colonial parliaments. The opposition came from about half the constituencies of England and the north-eastern corner of Ireland, where the people were actuated by religious and irreligious feelings. A few here and there of the ascendancy class feared to lose place and power. It was not true that the majority of the people of Ulster were opposed to Home Rule. There were 45 per cent in Ulster who were Catholic and desired Home Rule and 12 to 15 per cent Protestants in the northern province in harmony with the Bill. It was quite a mistake to say that there were only a few Protestants who were in favour of it.

In their largest hall they could get 2,500 to attend a lecture. The fact was that the majority of Protestants in Belfast were Tories, and the Liberals feared to lose their trade unless they kept quiet. Now there were a large number who were beginning to come out and take courage. When Mr Churchill came to Belfast, there were about 15,000 people to listen to him. It was not true to talk of Ulster as Unionist; it was Belfast that was Unionist. There was a little gang of six Unionist leaders who met the Liberal Unionist Association in Belfast and issued manifestos in panoramic succession through the widely circulated Tory journals. This little band in Belfast acted like a refracting atmosphere and distorted the true shape of the Irish demand for the Bill before the House. They were incapable of emancipating themselves from the tyranny of their sectarian prejudices. The great world of thought was for devolution, but it was difficult for those who practised the chief role of bluster and noise to subside into stoicism. The Unionists of Belfast must have felt the weakness of their case when they imported Sir Edward Carson to assist with threat and bluster. It was the ascendancy class that was making so much noise because they feared to lose place and power. They offered no real argument against Home Rule. They simply said: "We will not have it."

From the professional politicians in the House, now and again, they might be told that the people were unfit for self-government, as if the Irish people were inferior to the people of South Africa or any civilised people in the world. They were told also that they would quarrel among themselves, just as if this state of things did not exist under British rule, and encouraged too, so that ascendancy and the present state of things might be maintained by keeping the people asunder. They were told it was disintegration Irishmen wanted. That was absurd. It was a greater union with England they wanted and the Bill was sure to accomplish this real union. Then they were told that Ireland could not support herself, that she would go into bankruptcy, as if they had been living on the benevolence of Great Britain these hundred years. He asked those who did not reason to turn their thoughts to Denmark, Holland and Belgium, much smaller countries than Ireland, whose inhabitants live and prosper by their own industries. Why not Ireland? It appeared to him that an Irish parliament would possess all the elements of harmonious action, so many burning questions having been already disposed of. Unlike Wales and Scotland, in Ireland and England there was no longer an established church, no university question, not even the land question to be settled, nor need there be a franchise or redistribution question, nor any alteration in local government. And, as for legislative schemes, as it was sometimes asserted, for persecuting the Catholic or Protestant, no sensible person believed in such childish bogies.

It was difficult to know what to do with that impossible class in the north of Ireland, which knew not the history of their country and would not reason. Imagine the fourth wanting to dominate three-fourths. When the affairs of Ireland were stagnant and the people were in a state of reasonable unrest, the cry was "No Home Rule". Prosperous or not prosperous, no Home Rule for Ireland. What was the opposition to this Bill? From the north-east corner of Ulster, it meant bigoted hatred from the opposition in this party spirit. If the Unionists came into power tomorrow, they would have to give Home Rule in order to make it possible to govern Ireland. All sorts of reforms were now promised by those opposed to the Bill, but it was too late. No system of government could succeed in opposition to the wishes of the people. In all sincerity, he declared that if that House wanted a panacea for all the ills of Ireland, if it wanted to end sectarian strife, if it wanted Ireland to take her progressive place with other nations, if it wanted her inhabitants loved and contented, if it wanted to make her a strength to the British Empire, it would give her people the right to manage their own affairs, and thus concentrate the energies of her sons on the physical and moral elevation of their country.

The Home Rule Bill as presented gave some recognition to the people of the north-east corner of Ireland as being different. An amendment to the bill by the Liberal member for Cornwall, Agar-Robartes, that the counties of Antrim, Armagh, Down and Londonderry should be partitioned from the rest of Ireland was defeated by 69 votes. However, Carson and the Unionists grabbed the opportunity to support the amendment, not for what it intended, but as an opportunity to use it to defeat the Home Rule Bill. According to a report in The *Irish Times, (the then voice of Unionism)* the IPP members were hopeful that the Unionists would vote against this amendment and by doing so would support Home Rule and not abandon their southern Unionists. The paper went on to say that this amendment was a trap, set by the cabinet, which they hoped the Unionists would blindly walk into.

Although the amendment was defeated, the partitioning of the north-east from the rest of Ireland had Tory and Unionist support within parliament and was now on the record of the House. It is important to note that this motion proposing the partitioning of Ireland was supported by Sir Edward Carson and his fellow Unionists at Westminster. This was only a short time after the monster anti-Home Rule rally at Belfast on Easter Tuesday when the Tory leader Bonar Law said: " The whole history of the modern world is a history of movement towards a closer union and great nations are centralising their resources." He spoke these words to stress the Tory and Unionist's campaign to maintain the Union and to remain under the Imperial Parliament. It would appear that the anti Home Rule campaign did not have a coherent policy in 1912.

Four Ulster counties were too small to administer and a nine county Ulster would not guarantee a consistent "Protestant parliament for a Protestant people". A six county province would be born later.

On 21 June, the *Church of Ireland Gazette* praised a report of the Belfast Chamber of Commerce against Home Rule "calling it" to be "an important document in the fight against Home Rule." It states many facts that are deserving of being remembered. For instance, it points out that since the rejection of the Home Rule Bill in 1893, the population of Belfast had increased by over 50 per cent and its economy has grown by over 100 per cent. The income derived by the Imperial Revenue from Belfast was more than double for the rest of Ireland and was only surpassed by three cities in the United Kingdom. The registered tonnage of vessels sailing from Belfast was 74 per cent of the total of the ports of Ireland. This is the more remarkable when it is remembered that practically all of the raw materials such as iron, flax and tobacco have been imported and that the chief markets for finished products are outside of Ireland.

The Belfast Chamber of Commerce was working on its commercial strengths by claiming to be the fourth port city of the United Kingdom after London, Liverpool and Bristol. It also claimed that Belfast was responsible for 74 per cent of all Irish commercial activity, while contributing a similar percentage of Ireland's total taxation into Imperial coffers. These figures could well be disputed, as the combined ports of Dublin, Cork and Waterford would have handled a substantial percentage of Ireland's trade. On the basis of population alone, that claim by the Belfast Chamber of Commerce can be questioned. From the census of 1911, Dublin had a population of 304,802 while Belfast had 386,947 people.

(ii) "Enniskillen Horse" and Sir Edward Carson

In defiance of the Home Rule Bill and the passing of the Parliament Act earlier, the Unionists of Enniskillen and Co. Fermanagh were eagerly preparing for the visit of Sir Edward Carson to the town on 18 September 1912. It was the first meeting in his 10-day crusade to promote "Ulster Day" and the signing of the Ulster Covenant. According to the *Impartial Reporter*:

> Enniskillen put on its gay aspect, like the great occasion in 1904 when the two Inniskilling regiments met in the town. The event was of vast significance and of thrilling interest...
>
> Sir Edward Carson travelled by car from Crom with Lord Erne and Lord Hugh Cecil, and the party embarked on a special carriage to Enniskillen, where it was met by two squadrons of yeomanry on horseback, said to be 235 strong, carrying lances bearing the pennon of the Inniskilling Dragoons and who proceeded to escort them through the town, in military fashion, to Portora Hill, where the mass meeting of an estimated 40,000 [probably more like 25,000] people were there to greet him.

This open display by the squadron, (known as the 'Enniskillen Horse') was the beginning of militancy against Home Rule in Fermanagh under the leadership and command of William Copeland Trimble. He had freely distributed literature, from late August, throughout north and central Fermanagh and as far south as Lisnaskea, seeking men with good well-groomed horses for the occasion. "Such a show of Unionist militancy would grow and prevail within Fermanagh and was noted and reported at that time by military people present. The protocol of the Enniskillen Horse, was later questioned by the Member from Montrose at Westminster, on the legality of men on horseback bearing the pennon of the 'Inniskillen Dragoons' through Enniskillen – a form of welcome reserved only for the Monarch".*

Following the 235 men on horseback, a battalion of some 200 men marched on foot followed by Unionist and Orange representatives from throughout Co. Fermanagh. This was said to be the first show of Ulster Volunteer forces in Fermanagh, where on that day, according to reports they were extremely well disciplined and did not appear to be armed. Next in order in the parade came the Co. Cavan representatives with Unionist Clubs from Cavan town, Kilmore, Ballyhaise, Drumalure and Blacklion, each accompanied by a band and Women's Unionist Association members. The officers of the County Grand Lodge Bro. R.H. Johnstone DL and Lord Farnham, took their place as leaders. There were also Unionist and Orange representatives from counties Donegal, Leitrim, Monaghan, Tyrone and Sligo. It was reported that some 10,000 people (very doubtful as Enniskillen Railway Station could not cope with such numbers) were conveyed by special trains to Enniskillen for the occasion. This was a new step in organised militant Unionism's fight against the Home Rule Bill in Ulster, "day one" leading to the partitioning of Ireland.

After lampooning Winston Churchill, Sir Edward Carson in his Enniskillen address, stated:
We are here on serious business; more serious perhaps than some realise, and I hope that you and everyone of you realise it. We are not to be trifled with any longer …
Speaking at length on the on-going campaign against the Home Rule Bill he said: The government only cared about the English non-conformists who for their own purpose, and to their shame, were prepared to desert their co-religionists in Ireland … In all that the government had been trifling with them and in the words of Bonar Law

* Turning Points of The Irish Revolution – Benjamin Grob-Fitzgibbon 2007.

"the government had made it perfectly plain that if they had any policy, it was to force this million of people in Ulster to accept an allegiance which they looked upon with horror and refuse to accept". To ask a man to live under a constitution which he never got an opportunity of expressing his views on amounts to a tyranny, which is unparalleled in the history of civilisation. We are driven now to do what we think right and we will not shrink ...

They propose with the most solemn deliberation – if the Unionists of Ulster approved – to advance on Ulster Day. They would lay the foundations for their defence, and they would enter into a solemn covenant in all humility and in no sense of defiance: a solemn covenant, one with the other, to resist this scheme if it becomes law. They would advance as one man.

Referring to the Battle of Newtownbutler and the cry of Colonel Wolseley in 1689, Sir Edward said with great passion: Do you want your leaders to advance? Were they ready to have two and a half centuries of their history blotted out by this terrible Bill?

In concluding he said: I shall deem it an honour to be the first to sign the Covenant ... He declined to give up any inheritance through love of liberty of those gone before them, and based his whole action on the love of his own country and his reliance on the justice of the people of England. No inducement of any kind and no fear of any penalty would ever deter him from doing what he believed to be right.

At the end, when the carriage containing Sir Edward Carson was ready to depart, the mounted escort was in waiting. Before departing he said to their commanding officer: "I beg to thank you cordially for this great honour you have done me, and this great compliment represents the great county of Fermanagh..."

(iii) Solemn League and Covenant

In 1912, the political and religious division of Ireland and its people had commenced. The leaders of the Protestant churches were supportive of their Unionist representatives and the ascendancy in promoting the anti-Home Rule message. However, as the anti-Home Rule campaign was now being strongly influenced by militant Unionism, this forced the five northern Church of Ireland bishops to pause and promote a reflection in prayer in the interests of all Irishmen in a pastoral letter. The Church of Ireland was now looking at its own position and was being squeezed between militancy and moderation.

The signing of the Ulster Covenant on 28 September 1912 by Unionists was for them a very solemn occasion on which they believed their future depended. While the Unionist leaders signed the covenant in the Ulster Hall Belfast, arrangements were made at local level throughout Ulster and elsewhere to ensure as many signatories as possible. In Enniskillen there was a united prayer service in the Church of Ireland, where clergymen from the three Protestant churches led the service. The Bishop of Clogher and the Earl of Erne led the congregation to the Town Hall to commence the formalities for signing and 1,365 people with Enniskillen postal addresses signed the Ulster Covenant and Women's Declaration on Ulster Day in Enniskillen. A total of 14,885 men and women signed throughout Co. Fermanagh.

The text of the Ulster Covenant was as follows:
> Being convinced in our conscience that Home Rule would be disastrous to the material well being of Ulster, as well as to the whole of Ireland, subversive to our civil and religious freedom, destructive to our citizenship, and perilous to the unity of the Empire, we whose names are underwritten, men of Ulster, loyal subjects to his gracious Majesty King George the Fifth, humbly relying on God, Whom our fathers in days of stress and trial confidently trusted, hereby pledge ourselves in solemn covenant throughout this our time of threatened calamity to stand by one another in defending for ourselves and our children our cherished position of equal citizenship in the United Kingdom, and in using all the means which may be found necessary to defeat the present conspiracy to set up Home Rule in Ireland. In the event of such a parliament being forced upon us, we solemnly and mutually pledge ourselves to refuse to recognise its authority, in sure confidence that God will defend that right. Hereto we subscribe our names and, further, we individually declare that we have not already signed the covenant.

The women's pledge of support or declaration ran as follows:
> We whose names are underwritten, women of Ulster and loyal subjects of His Gracious Majesty, being firmly persuaded that Home Rule would be disastrous to our country, desire to associate ourselves with the men of Ulster in the uncompromising opposition to the Home Rule Bill now before parliament, whereby it is proposed to drive Ulster out of her

cherished place in the constitution of the United Kingdom and to place her under the domination and control of a parliament in Ireland. Praying that from this calamity God will save Ireland, we hereunto subscribe our names.

471,414 men and women signed the covenant and declaration on that day in total. Of that number an estimated 25,000 men and women of Ulster birth and descent signed the covenant in Dublin, Britain and in other parts of the world.

Arrangements were made throughout Co. Cavan for the observance of Ulster Day. According to the *Impartial Reporter*:

> There seemed to be unanimity of opinion everywhere. In Cavan town, service was held in the Protestant Hall at 7.00 p.m. and the spacious hall was crowded. The solemn service began with the singing of the hymn 'O God, Our Help in Ages Past'. A portion of Holy Scripture was read by Rev. Gabriel J. Spence, Methodist Minister. Special prayers were said by Rev. E.D. Crowe, Rector of Cavan parish. After the religious ceremony, Lord Farnham was moved to the chair and addressed those present with a few well-chosen words appropriate to the occasion, after which the Solemn Covenant was signed by all the men and women present. A service was held in Ballintemple Parish Church at 7.00 p.m. The Rev. E.H. Weir, rector of the parish, conducted the service. The Covenant was afterwards signed in the Orange Hall. There was an exceedingly large attendance at Kilmore Cathedral where a service was held at 7.00 p.m. Special hymns and prayers were used and an appropriate address delivered by Rev. W.J. Askins, rector of the parish. The Covenant was signed in the old church by the hundreds who had attended.
>
> Similar services were held in Killeshandra Memorial Hall, Ballyhaise Parish Church, Cootehill Parish Church, Killoughter (Redhills) Parish Church, Derrylane Parish Church, Cloverhill Parish Church, Belturbet Parish Church, Drumlane Parish Church, Bailieborough Parish Church, Ballyconnell Parish Church and in Templeport Parish Church. After the service in each, the Covenant was signed. The churches were well filled with devout congregations and the solemnity of Ulster Day was befittingly observed by the Unionists throughout Co. Cavan, who are as determined in their opposition to Home Rule as their brethren in other parts of Ulster.

From figures obtained, in excess of 8,000 men and women in Co. Cavan signed the Covenant and Declaration.

L.S. Kirkpatrick claimed in a recent article (Sept. 2012) in the Belfast *News Letter* that of the 1,225 Protestant clergy (Church of Ireland, Presbyterian and Methodist) in Ulster, only 798 signed the covenant on Ulster Day. Among those who did not sign was J.F. McNiece, the Rector of St Nicholas in Carrickfergus and father of the poet Louis McNiece. These clergymen did not support the covenant for many personal reasons, the principal ones being on religious grounds and the growing militancy and militarism visible within Unionism.

Based on the above figures it appears that at best two-thirds of Ulster's Protestant adults signed the covenant and the remaining third were liberal minded Protestant people who were indifferent or supported Home Rule. So it seems that the majority within Ulster were not against Home Rule.

Rev. J. B. Armour, Trinity Presbyterian Church, Ballymoney, Co. Antrim, a liberal Unionist living in the radical tradition of the United Irishmen in his area, was so incensed with the "ballyhoo" associated with Sir Edward Carson and the signing of the Ulster Covenant, that he set up a pro-Home Rule Covenant in north Antrim, which was endorsed with 3,000 signatures on Ulster Day. Armour was a well-known Home Ruler in his area and within his church from 1893. In that year with his friend J.B. Dougherty he forwarded a Presbyterian memorial with 3,535 signatures to Prime Minister Gladstone expressing their heartfelt gratitude for his past services and their sympathy with him in his present efforts to secure better government for Ireland.

The Ulster counties which showed the highest percentage response to the covenant were Armagh, Tyrone and Monaghan and surprisingly Belfast had the least response. In many areas women's signatures were in the majority.

It is highly improbable that any Catholics signed the Covenant as the leading Catholic Unionist Denis Henry chose not to sign.

Against this political backdrop, normal life in Ballyconnell continued. In December 1912, a community meeting was called to see if the town could have its own electrical supply and this was followed through. Mrs Josephine Arnold (Lord Benison's sister) turned on the first electric lights in Ballyconnell in December 1914. The town generator was housed at the rear of the town creamery, along the banks of the canal. The project cost the people of Ballyconnell £1,100. There certainly appears to have been a strong community and creative spirit prevailing, which was not too bothered by political developments in Ulster.

(iv) Moderate Unionist voices

Moderate Unionism was reflected in the views of many of Ulster's writers, intellectuals and the business elite. These liberal views were expressed by the Fermanagh writer Shan F. Bullock. He adopted the pen-name, Shan Fadh, in recognition of his Irishness. Bullock wrote part time while working as a civil servant at Somerset House in London. He was sympathetic to the Irish cause through his experience of seeing at first hand subsistence living on all sides in rural Fermanagh, a subject on which many of his books were based. His first novel, *The Awkward Squad*, was published in 1893, and *By Trasna River* followed in 1895. His final autobiographical memoir, *After Sixty Years*, was published in 1931. Shan Bullock's writings were mostly about his native Fermanagh and are recognised as being exceptional for their interpretation of the Fermanagh dialect of that time and are important sources of social history.

Shan F. Bullock was born at Crom Castle in 1865, where his father Thomas was land steward to the Earl of Erne. In his position, Thomas Bullock was aware of political agitation for land reform and the ultimate demise of the landlords and so opted instead for life as a tenant farmer at Killynick, near Aghalane in Fermanagh, which had a Belturbet postal address. Politically he was a moderate or liberal Unionist who abhorred Orangeism. Interestingly, Bullock's employer, the Earl of Erne, was Irish Grand Master for a number of years and an avid anti-Home Ruler.*

The novels of Shan F. Bullock are now a rarity, but thankfully the reference section of the County Library in Cavan houses his writings. His novels were read by children in national schools throughout the area in the early part of the 20th century and were often heard quoted many decades afterwards.

Sir Horace Plunkett, agricultural reformer and founder of the Irish cooperative movement, wrote some of the introductions to Bullock's earlier books and it was through their friendship that they both accepted the inevitability of Home Rule and opposed partition. When Lloyd George established the Irish Convention 1917-18 under the chairmanship of Sir Horace Plunkett, Shan Bullock was seconded from his duties at Somerset House to work as secretary to Plunkett.

Bullock was totally opposed to any form of partition and he did not like the idea of an Ulstershire being tagged onto Britain. He felt that the Unionists should make the best terms they could from their unrepeatable position of strength to control.*

*Patrick Maume, Bullock Paper, Belturbet 1997.

The Rt. Hon. T. Lough, ex-MP, His Majesty's Lieutenant for Co. Cavan, was a liberal Unionist who maintained a political interest in Ireland's affairs. He expressed his views in many letters to *The Times*, always advocating Home Rule with a dominion parliament as a solution to the Irish question. He encouraged Asquith on the Irish question in 1913-14. On economic grounds, Lough believed a Home Rule parliament in Dublin could run the country politically and economically as opposed to a partitioned country.

(v) Opposition continues

Michael McCaffrey recalled as a boy seeing the local Ulster Volunteers drilling with wooden rifles on the Chapel Square in Swanlinbar in 1912. There was also a corps of the same force in the Bawnboy/Templeport area – a reactionary force against the Home Rule Bill. County Cavan being part of the province of Ulster, this would appear to be a natural progression as militant Unionism had its origins and strengths within the Orange Lodges, which were prevalent throughout Co. Cavan. R.H. Johnston of Bawnboy House was Co. Cavan Grand Master during these turbulent years and it was his sister who re-established the Association of Loyal Orange Women of Ireland in 1911. It was reported that "the Covenanters" at Corglass, Bailieboro, Co. Cavan were openly drilling with arms in 1913.

Orange societies in Ulster were becoming militarised by the procurement of arms from the mid 1880s. Militant Unionists continued to import small quantities of arms prior to the formation of the Ulster Volunteer Force. In 1913 small quantities of arms destined for Ulster addresses were seized by the authorities. At the port of Drogheda four boxes containing 60 "Fabri Turini 1888" Italian rifles, including some bayonets, were seized. These were destined for addresses in counties Down and Fermanagh. The seized shipment came on board the SS Coleen Bawn from Glasgow and was consigned by an agent in Newcastle-upon-Tyne. In the port of Derry a consignment of 26 Italian rifles and 16 bayonets was seized on its way to an address in Strabane. In another instance, an off-shore customs' patrol intercepted a fishing boat carrying arms and ammunition for the Ulster Unionist Council, seizing it near the small fishing port at Carrigart, Co. Donegal. These seizures were only part of many consignments of arms brought into the north east. In 1914 the Larne gun-running by the Ulster Volunteer Force took place, an operation carried out openly with military precision, which was noted and reported by the police but also went unchecked. This importation consisted of 35,000 rifles and five million rounds of ammunition, all ironically illegally imported from Imperial

Germany. In the same year, the Irish Volunteers imported a consignment of 1,500 rifles with ammunition through the north Dublin harbour at Howth, also brought in from Germany.

In 1912 the Third Home Rule Bill was passed by the House of Commons and defeated in the House of Lords. The bill was passed by the House of Commons on two more occasions only to be rejected by the Lords in 1913 and 1914. However, the government using the provisions of the Parliament Act, sent the bill for royal assent and it came into law in September 1914, to be enacted in 1916. Due to the Great War the Home Rule Act was left on the statute book, and as understood, would be implemented within two years or when the Great War was over.

Carson's campaign against Home Rule continued with many public demonstrations held in England and Scotland, only to be followed within days with pro-Home Rule rallies by Irish nationalists in the same cities. Carson held a demonstration in Glasgow before a reported 5,000 people only to be followed by a nationalist pro-Home Rule rally.

The following is a report from the *Anglo-Celt* of that pro-Home Rule rally in Glasgow, April 1913:

Not since Gladstone's great campaign in Midlothian has such a reception been given a political leader as that accorded Mr. John Redmond and Mr. Joseph Devlin in Glasgow on Monday, when 40,000 enthusiastic Scotchmen headed by 1,500 torchbearers marched through the city cheering for Home Rule and justice for Ireland. The demonstration was of such a character as to fairly amaze the Irish leader who, although he knew Scotland was solid, had no idea of the intensity of feeling.

At the great meeting in St Andrew's Hall, 'Annie Laurie' and 'God Save Ireland' were played and the speakers referred to the dismal failure of Sir Edward Carson's trip against the Irish problem being solved. The chair was occupied by Prof. Latta, Professor of Logic, University of Glasgow, and the attendance included all the leading Liberal MPs and many Presbyterian ministers of the city. The chairman said:

The Ulster Covenant was nothing but a clever and rather unscrupulous advertising trick, there being no analogy between the Covenant of Scotland and that identified with Sir Edward Carson – who had endeavoured to trade in the name of the other. The chairman believed in Scottish Home Rule, but they in Scotland had their own criminal laws, marriage laws, property laws, educational system and so forth. These things Ireland had not got and should they not sympathise with Ireland? They wanted Scottish Home Rule in order that they might more easily be able to reform their institutions. On the other hand, they had in the Home Rule movement, a movement which it was not necessary to commend to Scotsmen. It was a spirit, which was showing itself more throughout the world. If it were a mere narrow spirit of nationality, it might be evil. It was the great glory of their great country that it should be possible to unite in one great freely governed empire any number of diverse nationalities, being governed according to their own ideas, yet loyal members of one great country. Ireland wanted to join this band of nationalities. Should they be asked to refuse it to her? (No).

John Redmond addressed the meeting:

During the Land War – which ended with the principle for which the Irish nationalists had fought being inscribed on the statute book of England – Sir Edward Carson was instrumental in sending thousands of men (Mr. Redmond amongst) to jail for acts and for words which in light of the gospel according to north-east Ulster today seemed innocent and harmless. The same Sir Edward Carson had only promised a 'minimum of support' to Mr. Wyndham's great Land Purchase Act of 1903, and when the Local Government Act was introduced, he denounced it as a betrayal of the Unionist Party in Ireland, of which he was a member.

Carson's tactics were often reported and questioned in the British and Irish newspapers at this time. *The Globe* reported:

... In reference to the Irish Unionist campaign, either Sir Edward is sincere in this attitude or he is not, and if Ulster is just a political 'brief', well and good. We know where we are, and also how far we shall be led by him along the gory path. This is what we have been telling the Orangemen all along, that Sir Edward Carson, the lawyer, was dealing with them from a lawyer's point of view, using all the skill of an advocate to frighten the more timid into returning the verdict, he sought.

CHAPTER 4

THE VOLUNTEERS AND
THE GREAT WAR

(i) The Irish Volunteers

In June 1914 the first corps of the Irish Volunteer movement in Co. Cavan
was formed in Ballyconnell. This was a logical reaction to the growth of the
Ulster Volunteer Force throughout the province and the formation locally of
units in Swanlinbar and in the Bawnboy/Templeport area. The main objective
in forming the Volunteers was to underline Irish nationalist support for the
third Home Rule Bill. Some men joined the ranks, however, thinking that
they were getting ready to fight the English. The call to join the Volunteers in
Ballyconnell was made by J.F. O'Kane, and Tom O'Reilly. It was reported
that over 100 men enrolled and this increased to nearly 200 within a week.
Tom O'Reilly was appointed captain and J.F. O'Kane and J. McCaffrey were
appointed lieutenants. J. O'Kelly was appointed drill sergeant, as he had
British military experience and T.A. Hussey was secretary. The men drilled
on the Fair Green twice weekly but had only one mock rifle among them.
The co-founder of the Volunteers, The O'Rahilly came to the town in July
1914 to review the local corps and afterwards he met with the local command
in Dolphin's Hotel, where he was lobbied to send some rifles. They
eventually got five Italian rifles but no ammunition. The Volunteers' rifle drill
was carried out in McGovern's field at Derryginney.

From recorded comments by some Volunteers who participated in the
Easter Rising of 1916, these Italian rifles were as good as useless as they
heated up rapidly and could not be held in the bare hands after three shots.
Maybe it was just as well that they had no ammunition in Ballyconnell.

In September 1914 with the Home Rule Act now on the statute book at
Westminster, the Volunteers had a celebratory parade through Ballyconnell
with bands and a bonfire on the Fair Green. Within a short time the corps of
Volunteers collapsed as many members joined John Redmond's National
Volunteers while others had gone to England or Scotland to work (replacing
British men who had enlisted). Later many of these men enlisted in various
regiments to fight on the Allied side in Europe. Others emigrated to America
to avoid possible conscription. Many Irishmen joined the American forces
after a German U-boat sank the Lusitania in 1917 off the south coast of
Ireland. America entered the war, siding with the allies in Europe.

The Great War was sold as "the war to end all wars in defence of small nations" and would be all over by Christmas. Initially there was much support for the war effort within the general west Cavan community from local women led by Mrs Arnold, Slieve Russell House. They organised craft events and entertainment to collect clothing and home produce to be sent to local men at the front. The Irish Catholic bishops supported the war effort to liberate Catholic Belgium, while in the north-east counties of Ulster, posters were displayed urging men to enlist to defeat Catholic Austria.

Irish men from the National Volunteers and civilians enlisted to fight for many reasons, from the right thing to do, it being adventurous, and also simply as a means of earning a living and even to get free clothing. Many men believed sincerely that Home Rule would come when the war was over while others were advised by the local Volunteer command to enlist to get military training and experience, in readiness to fight the British later. There was still a sizable minority of IRB people who for historical reasons never believed or trusted the British establishment or parliament and this attitude applied to the Home Rule Act.

The first letter received in Ballyconnell from the front in Belgium was from a Private Fitzmartin. Though believed to be a native of Wexford he had been an apprentice shoemaker to James McCabe, Main St. He wrote in early 1915 of observing better farm equipment in Europe and said "the farmers are more 'Up' than in Ireland", adding, "when more young men come out to Belgium they will see for themselves and learn". In a second letter to Ballyconnell he told of the mass of dead bodies around and said he would find it hard to stick it. A third letter in June of that year was sent from his hospital bed.

Another volunteer, James Brady, recalled himself and a Private Cassidy from Belturbet in their trench one evening having tea with mud all around them, when a German shell landed beside them and "ruined their supper". Some other local men who fought and survived the Great War were Felix O'Hara, Ned Farmer and two McDermott brothers. Johnny Creamer, who lived in the Clinty area, was a known veteran of the Great War and was an employee of Ennis' Mill, formerly Laing's Mill. Johnny had a reputation for making "the best poitín" in the area, which he made for himself and not for sale. Johnny got a grain recipe from Galway men he met while at the front and instead of using the traditional potato of the area, he used grain to make "a drop". There was an elderly man called "Crigs" Drum who lived on Main St, who it is believed survived the Boer War and the Great War. There were others who came to town occasionally and who carried external and internal scars of war – a subject seldom mentioned.

There is "a story told" – and probably told in many parts of Ireland – about a married man who volunteered to fight in the war. As there was no conscription, the British army would send a lorry to an area on a given day to collect those who had enlisted. When the man got up on the back of the military lorry in Ballyconnell he looked at his wife and asked her would she miss him, to which she replied: "I won't and I hope the Kaiser doesn't." When he was almost two years out at the front he got word that his wife had just had a baby and he went to his commanding officer looking for compassionate leave. The obvious question put was: "How long are you out here without leave?" to which he replied "nearly two years sir." "And you mean to say that you are out here nearly two years and you want to go home to see a baby that's...?" To which the reply came: "That's no problem, sir, 'shure' there's nearly two years between me and me brother."

Away from the horror of the trenches normal life continued in Ballyconnell. On 18 September 1915 the local light orchestra gave a concert to a quayside audience from a number of boats on the Woodford Canal. It was hard to think that a World War had been raging for a year and that an Irish revolution was pending.

(ii) Easter 1916

As the Easter Rising of 1916 was taking place in Dublin, and Ireland declared a Republic, very few people outside of the capital had any idea of what was going on. The IRB-led rising was planned mainly for Dublin and other urban areas of Leinster, Munster and Connaught but not Ulster. In the original plan, the Volunteers in Ulster mainly from Belfast and Tyrone were small in number and poorly organised. They were ordered to assemble in Coalisland and to proceed west of the Shannon to fight. The confusion surrounding the countermanding order in the newspapers on Easter Sunday resulted in the rising being deferred for a day in Dublin and there was little or no activity taking place in other parts of the country. The news of the rising trickled outwards from Dublin and it was a number of days before the people of west Cavan were made aware of what was happening.

The Easter Rising of 1916 is the landmark event in modern Irish history and was not fully accepted by the majority of the Irish people as they were not aware of it until well after the event. People probably thought of it as unnecessary because Home Rule was on the statute book at Westminster and John Redmond was assured that it would be fully enacted within two years or when the Great War was over. Dublin was ready for revolution in 1916 because of social and economic issues along with the armed uprising as planned by the IRB.

At the time of the Act of Union, which ended Grattan's Parliament in Dublin, the city was always referred to as the second city of the empire. This status was now well diminished due to lack of investment by the ruling classes and the very obvious neglect on the part of the British establishment by not extending the industrial revolution of the 19th century to Ireland. It is accepted that the British did their best to destroy the textile industry in the south and west of Ireland, while supporting the linen industry in the north east.

Dublin's revolutionary zeal was triggered by "the great lockout" of 1913/14 as the trade union leadership of Jim Larkin and James Connolly fought for better wages and working conditions for workers. As employment was inconsistent at best, working-class Dublin was poverty stricken and living conditions in tenement buildings were dire with large families living in one-room accommodation in buildings that were suited only for demolition. Disease was rife and Dublin had the highest infant mortality rate in the empire. Two tenement houses collapsed in 1914, with the death of many children. This, in addition to the shooting of four civilians on Bachelor's Walk by soldiers of a Scottish regiment, added further flames to the fire for revolution.

Dublin was a very divided city, with sides supportive of and opposed to Irish involvement in the Great War for both personal and political reasons. The Great War resulted in an increased demand for food and so Dubliners saw the cost of living rise substantially – another spark for revolution. This was not seen so much in other parts of Ireland as farming and food production were doing well due to higher prices because of the war.

During this time on all the major spring fair days in Ballyconnell, upwards of 100 carriages of cattle were transported from Ballyconnell Station to the rich pastures of Meath for fattening and then onwards to the British market. The fortnightly pork market in Ballyconnell was an essential outlet for pork meat produced in west Cavan for the Irish and British markets. Live pigs were brought to town where pork agents or dealers would offer a live or dead weight price according to quality. Pigs purchased dead weight were slaughtered in Baxter's slaughter-house and then brought to the Market House to be officially weighed. Refrigeration was not available and so the fresh pork was packed in straw-filled crates and a little salt to maintain freshness during transportation. Willie Hunt was one of the pork butchers who looked after the slaughtering of pigs in Baxters and when his day's work was over, he would head to one of the local pubs where his first drink was not a pint, but a quart. The monthly fair was an important part of rural Ireland for economic and social reasons. Livestock and farm produce were traded and travelling suppliers would come and set up their stalls to sell their wares to those who had money to spend after selling their livestock. It was an occasion for people to meet and enjoy a day out. Perhaps the most important fair days in the year were the hiring fairs held half yearly on May Day and on All Saints' Day, when farm hands who were out of work would seek farm employment for six months on large farms. This employment offered poor wages and meagre boarding but there were few alternatives for gaining employment. For many, getting hired on All Saints' Day meant a roof over their heads for the winter months. The principal hiring fairs in west Cavan were held in Arva.

Given the little Volunteer and political activity in Co. Cavan it is not surprising that there were only three Cavan people involved in the Easter Rising. One was Peter Paul Galligan. He was born in Carrigallen, Co. Leitrim but his home was in Drumkilly, Ballinagh where he was arrested and charged in 1916 as the officer in charge of rebel troops at Enniscorthy, Co. Wexford. From 1915, Galligan was employed in Bolger's Drapery Store in Enniscorthy after serving his time in Dublin, where he had joined the IRB and the Volunteers. Galligan travelled to Dublin on Easter Saturday for orders. The following day after meeting with Padraig Pearse, James Connolly and Joseph Plunkett he was sent back to Enniscorthy with orders to be ready to block British troops coming into Ireland via Wexford. Galligan mobilised his battalion of some 100 men in Enniscorthy who were armed with 20 service rifles and 2,000 rounds of .303 ammunition. The balance of arms was made up of pikes, all recently made in the same style as used in 1798.*

Hugh Farrelly, born in Mullagh, was an active member of the IRB in Dublin, as was Castlerahan native Noel Caldwell, both having fought in the GPO during Easter Week. Hugh Maguire, a Volunteer from Crosserlough was in Dublin but returned to Co. Cavan because of the countermand order where he became a leading figure in the War of Independence. In 1916 there was little volunteer activity in Co. Cavan. The most active unit was in the Ballinagh/Drumkilly area, which was an original base for some members of the famous North Longford Brigade under Gen. Seán MacEoin.

*Easter Commemoration Digest, Vol. 10 1968.

(iii) Peace Convention 1917-18.

In May 1917, Lloyd George initiated an attempt at an Irish settlement, by proposing to John Redmond Home Rule with six counties excluded, subject to reconsideration by parliament after five years. There would be a Council of Ireland with equal north/south membership, with powers to extend, or to initiate the ending of the area of exclusion.

This proposal failed to evoke a positive response from Redmond, and so Lloyd George set about establishing an Irish Convention which opened at Trinity College Dublin, in late July 1917 under Sir Horace Plunkett.

From day one, this convention had little chance of success as Sinn Féin was hostile to it. Sinn Féin had already defeated the IPP in three by-elections and was well on its way to becoming the party representing the vast majority of Irish nationalists. The Ulster Unionists attended the convention but were determined to wreck it by demanding the permanent exclusion of all nine Ulster counties. Had the southern Unionists known the position of the northern Unionists, they would not have taken part in the convention. The outcome as eventually reported by Plunkett in April 1918 was, that agreement had been reached between the IPP and the southern Unionists on all-Ireland Home Rule with disagreement on the control of customs. But this was accompanied by a flat rejection from the northern Unionists and, of course, by the equally flat opposition of Sinn Féin from outside the convention. The calling of this convention was a foreign policy issue for Lloyd George and Britain. The failure of the convention did not worry Lloyd George too much, as in calling it, it showed that he was doing something about Ireland and helping to calm opinion in the United States and in the Dominions.

(iv) The Great War

More than eleven hundred men with Co. Cavan addresses volunteered to fight in the Great War. From west Cavan (Present Belturbet Electoral Area), it is known that 165 men gave their lives while serving in the King's regiments, Canadian, New Zealand, Indian and American forces as officers, sergeants, lance corporals, privates and in the merchant navy. It is known that 654 Co. Cavan natives or those with Co. Cavan postal addresses died in the Great War. The Church of Ireland Parish of Tomregan (Ballyconnell) has a roll of honour of 25 of its members who fought in various regiments, five of whom died in the war. This had a huge impact on this minority community.

From the lists as reported on 4 May 1918 *(Anglo-Celt)*, among the casualties in the recent fighting on the Western Front were the following from the Ballyconnell district:
Pte. Smith, Crossmakellegher, gun shot wounds;
2nd. Lt. McElroy, Daisyhill, wounded, and his brother Cpl. McElroy, missing; Edward Farmer, Labour Battalion, killed (there was a Ned Farmer from the area who survived the war, so this may be an error); Trooper W. Bennett, Gortmullen, died of wounds;
Lt. Hamilton, son-in-law of Mr Donohoe, "The Ford", prisoner of war.

The "Roll of Honour" of men from the immediate Ballyconnell area who lost their lives in the Great War, was:

Pte. James Bannan, Templeport, Royal Irish Fusiliers, killed in action 27.03.18

Lt. Robert Burton Benison, Connaught Rangers, died 20.09.14

William Bennett, Gortmullen, died of his wounds 28.04.18

Pte. Patrick Boles, Altnadarragh, Corlough, Royal Irish Fusiliers, killed in action 8.7.16

Sgt. William Colston (Coulston?), Royal Inniskillen Fusiliers, died 09.09.17

Pte. J. Connor, Aughrim, Ballyconnell, Irish Guards, died 08.05.1918

Pte. Thomas Connor, Aughrim, Ballyconnell, Irish Guards, died 12.09.16

Pte. John Cunningham, Bocade, Ardlougher, Royal Irish Fusiliers, died 17.07.18

Lance Cpl. Thomas Curnan, Cortonn, Corlough, Irish Guards, died 24.02.17

John D'Arcy, Corlough, died 15.08.15, Gallipoli, Turkey

John E. Daly, Tomregan, died in France 25.09.16

Pte. J. Farmer, Ballyconnell, Gordon Highlanders, killed in action, 25.02 16

Pte. Patrick Farrell, Ardlougher, Royal Irish Fusiliers died in Egypt 04.11.18

Pte. Patrick Healy, Templeport, Leinster Regiment 22.07.17

Pte. Terence Keating, Bocade, Ardlougher, Australian Infantry, died 10.09.16

Thomas Kiernan, Stranadara, Bawnboy, died 31.03.18

John Kinsella, Templeport, died 03.04.17

Pte. Alex Maguire, Corlough, Bawnboy, Royal Irish Fusiliers, killed in action 24.06.16

Pte. Alfred McElroy, Ballyconnell, Royal Irish Rifles, missing 05/18

Capt. Fred McElroy, Ballyconnell, Machine-Gun Corps, died from wounds 1918

Lance Cpl. William Morton, Greenville, Ardlougher, Canadian Infantry, died 09.04.17

Pte. Peter Patterson, Ballyconnell, Royal Irish Fusiliers, died 07.10.18

Gunner John Prior, Tullytrasna, Corlough, Royal Garrison Artillery, died 22.02.16

Pte. J. Reynolds, Bawnboy, Canadian Infantry (Alberta Reg.), died 14.03.18

Capt. S. G. Roe, Ballyconnell, Royal Inniskillen Fusiliers, killed in action

Pte. John Francis Shannon, Bawnboy, Irish Guards, killed in action 15.09.17.*

In early 1921, Mr Philip Connors, Aughrim, Ballyconnell received from the King, through the Records Office, the 1911 and 1915 Stars awarded posthumously to his sons. John and Thomas Connors left lucrative employment in Scotland and volunteered for service when the war broke out.

The Ballyconnell and Belturbet postal areas served a generous part of south Fermanagh prior to partition — a fact that was soon forgotten afterwards. This was confirmed in a postcard sent by Lieutenant or Regimental Sergeant Major Harry Hamilton, Royal Irish Fusiliers. He had been captured by the Germans and taken a prisoner of war (POW no. 60003) in April 1918. Military officers and men of rank who were POWs were photographed and images were put on postcards to send home to their families to show that they were alive. While still in a German POW camp, Hamilton sent a postcard, postmarked 2 December 1918 (the war was over at this stage) to his brother-in-law Pat Donohoe, Drumderg, Ballyconnell, Co. Cavan. Drumderg is in Fermanagh and this showed that the Ballyconnell postal area serviced a good part of the Teemore area prior to partition. This was logical as it was a natural administrative region. From the list of World War I dead from the Ballyconnell area, William Bennett, Gortmullen, Peter Patterson, Ummera and William Colston, Cloncoohy in Co. Fermanagh, had Co. Cavan postal addresses. Capt. Thomas William Bullock, Dorset Regiment, Pte. Fredrick McMullen, Inniskilling Fusiliers, and his brother William Arthur, Irish Guards, were from Aghalane in Fermanagh, which had a Belturbet postal address.

Irrespective of cultural or religious beliefs there had to be a great sense of brotherhood among the many Irish men who fought in the Great War. Whether they were regular members of the forces or volunteers, whether they met in the trenches or behind the lines in France or Belgium a spirit of comradeship grew. Of the 25 men from the greater Ballyconnell area who lost their lives, it now appears that six were from the Church of Ireland

---

* From Co. Cavan World War Dead, 2012

community and the rest were Catholics. Reflecting on the fear-filled agitation in Ulster for and against Home Rule before the Great War, there had to be many instances where those from the opposite Irish traditions helped each other out, fought and died together while not waiting to question their political or religious allegiance.

One major instance from the Great War was at the Battle of Wijtschate — Messines Ridge in June 1917. Irishmen from the 36th Ulster Division and the 16th Irish Division re-took the Belgian village and gained control of Messines Ridge. Earlier these two divisions lost heavily during the Somme campaign. In late 1916 they moved north to Flanders and became part of the Second Army which was to hold the line against the well-defended German machine-gun positions. In the spring of 1917, they underwent intense training in readiness for the attack on Wijtschate. The symbolism of this historic coming together and battle was believed among some Irish politicians to be an opportunity to build a new Ireland among Unionists and Nationalists to uphold the Third Home Rule Bill. If they could fight and die together there was no reason why they could not live together.

In December 1916, Willie Redmond MP wrote to Sir Arthur Conan Doyle: "There are a great many Irishmen today who feel that out of this war we should try and build up a new Ireland. The trouble is, men are so timid about meeting each other half way. It would be a fine memorial to the men who have died so splendidly, if we could, over their graves, build a bridge between north and south."*

During this time the different divisions played many soccer matches. The Ulster teams won them all while the bands from each regiment entertained each other and the native Belgians. There were some instances of bad relations but they were minimal in the greater scheme of things. There were UVF men in the 36th Division and National Volunteers in the 16th Division, men of opposing views, who, were it not for the common enemy, would have been arch-enemies. There were many positive comments on the relationships which developed between these army divisions. The words of Rev. J. Redmond, Church of Ireland Chaplin to the 9th Inniskilling Fuisiliers were apt:

*Tom Burke, 'Brotherhood Among Irishmen; History Ireland, Vol. 15, No. 5, 2007

It was impressive to see what a feeling of security before the battle the Ulster Division had in having the 16th. Irish on our left flank and that the 16th. Division had in having the Ulster Division on their right flank. This feeling of goodwill and confidence between the two divisions had been growing for some time. I wish the entire north and south that they represent could participate in the same spirit.

One area of the Great War which probably influenced Ireland's future and the non-enactment of the third Home Rule Act, with partition to follow, was the Dardanelles or the Gallipoli campaign. From early 1915 Britain and France, led by a poor naval fleet and inept planning, tried to take the straits for access to Istanbul and the Black Sea.. The Allied campaign did not produce any decisive results, only major casualties due to poor tactics, a shortage of ammunition and inexperienced troops. A year later the Allies abandoned this campaign. This led to the formation of a national coalition government at Westminster from December 1916. David Lloyd George succeeded Asquith as Prime Minister and he appointed Sir Edward Carson as Minister without Portfolio to the War Cabinet. James Craig was appointed to junior Ministries in the Treasury until he succeeded Carson as leader of the Unionist party in 1921. The influence of these two men in their positions at Westminster cannot be overlooked in the ultimate demise of the third Home Rule Bill, as passed by parliament in 1914. John Redmond the leader of the IPP refused a cabinet post.

Propaganda is always a noted feature of any war and used as a psychological mechanism to keep the forces and the public focused on the positive news at hand, while entertaining them by lampooning the enemy. One such example of words in poetry or song employed by the British public-relations machine against the Kaiser and the Germans is The Kaiser's Dream. This would later be transcribed, mocking the British Premier, David Lloyd George (See page 182 - 183).

The Kaiser's Dream.

There's a story now current, though strange it might seem,
Of the great Kaiser Bill and a wonderful dream.
Being tired of the Allies, he lay down in bed,
And amongst other things, he dreamt he was dead.

On leaving the Earth to Heaven, he went straight.
Arriving up there, he knocked at the gate.
But St Peter looked out, and in a voice loud and clear,
Said: "Be gone Kaiser Bill, we don't want you here."
"Well," says the Kaiser, "that's very uncivil,
I suppose after that I must go to the Devil."
So he turned on his heel, and off he did go,
At the top of his speed to the regions below.
And when he got there he was filled with dismay,
For, while waiting outside, he heard Old Nick say
To his imps: "Now look here, boys, I give you all a warning,
I'm expecting the Kaiser down here in the morning.
"But don't let him in, for to me it's quite clear,
He's a very bad man and we don't want him here.
If he ever gets in we'll have no end of quarrels,
In fact, I'm afraid he'll corrupt our good morals".

"O Satan, my dear friend," the Kaiser then cried,
"Excuse me for listening while waiting outside.
If you don't admit me, then where can I go?
Oh do let me in, for I'm feeling quite cold.
"And if you want money, I've got plenty of gold.
Let me sit in a corner, no matter how hot."
"No, no," said Old Nickie, "most certainly not;
We do not admit folks for riches or wealth.
Here are sulphur and matches, make a Hell for yourself."

Then he kicked William out, and vanished in the smoke.
And just at that moment the Kaiser awoke.
He jumped out of bed in a shivering sweat
And said: "Well that dream I shall never forget;
That I won't go to Heaven I know very well,
But it's really too bad to be kicked out of Hell."

CHAPTER 5

ARTHUR GRIFFITH AND THE GROWTH OF SINN FÉIN

(i) The aftermath of the Rising

The 1916 Proclamation of the Irish Republic was read in the names of the IRB, the Irish Volunteers and the Citizen Army. There was no involvement by Sinn Féin, contrary to what many Unionists and British media believed and often quoted as "the Sinn Féin Rebellion". This IRB-inspired rising, under the adage "England's difficulty is Ireland's opportunity", was done in the belief that Ireland's time for open revolt had come. The Volunteers, who were for the most part Dublin based, were small in number, poorly armed but reasonably organised. They fought for their cause and surrendered after six days.

The debate around the Easter Rising continues. However, we must always uphold the aspirations of those who fought and died, especially the signatories of the Proclamation of the Republic who were executed. This was a turning point from perceived fools at first to Irish heroes. The Irish diaspora and world opinion condemned the actions of the British military in Dublin and support for Ireland's struggle for political freedom as an international right grew. The executions of the rebel leaders ceased on the orders of Prime Minister Asquith when he visited Dublin in May 1916. Those who survived and surrendered were sentenced and detained in English jails and Ireland's declaration of a Republic was, in the eyes of Dublin Castle, quashed – but not for long.

The Irish armed rebellion was now dormant and it was replaced by new political activities in 1917 under the banner of Sinn Féin, as founded and led by Arthur Griffith. The year 1917 saw the rapid growth of political Sinn Féin when the real democratic foundations of the Irish State were established. Under the direction of Arthur Griffith and with support and encouragement from the trade-union movement, Sinn Féin brought Ireland's fight for political autonomy to the people.

The fledgling Sinn Féin party had fought and lost its first by-election in Leitrim in 1908. Apart from Griffith's many writings and publications; the party lay politically dormant for the next nine years. The constitutional nationalist IPP at Westminster was becoming older, many members had died and so by-elections to fill these parliamentary seats were to become very common in Ireland in 1917. The IPP still believed that the Home Rule Act of 1914 would come into force when the Great War was over. However, with a national government in power in Westminster from December 1916, the IPP were to be outwitted by the new British Premier, David Lloyd George.

Sinn Féin under its abstentionist policy fought and won by-elections for Westminster seats, in February 1917 with Count Plunkett in Roscommon, and in the summer months with Joe McGuinness in Longford, Eamon de Valera in Clare and W.T. Cosgrave in Kilkenny. These political victories led to the rapid growth of Sinn Féin Clubs throughout the non-Unionist parts of Ireland. Sinn Féin also contested and lost by-elections in East Tyrone and South Armagh. The Catholic or nationalist vote in Ulster was controlled by the Ancient Order of Hibernians and the United Irish League, based on anti-Parnellite nationalism. Sinn Féin wanted to capture this electorate in the province to establish its mandate for an Irish parliament and Irish independence. Sinn Féin had to counteract the Unionist campaign to have Ulster and the north east treated differently to the rest of Ireland. To establish its political status in Ulster, Sinn Féin had to target a seat in the province and the one seat that was most likely to be contested first was the constituency of East Cavan.

(ii) Winning East Cavan for Sinn Féin

The then MP for East Cavan was 95-year-old Samuel Young who had been elected to represent the constituency in 1892, as an anti-Parnellite Protestant nationalist, when he defeated the Unionist candidate Beresford-Clements. He was returned unopposed for five general elections and had not attended parliament for some three years. He was chairman of Bernard Hughes Ltd, Bakers and Millers, Belfast and head of the firm Young, King & Co., Distillers in Belfast and Limavady. He appeared to have little in common with the people of East Cavan. However, as a 91 year old, he delivered a most notable speech at Westminster at the second reading of the Home Rule Bill in 1912 (as detailed in chapter 3). As the electors of East Cavan had not had an opportunity to cast a vote since 1892, Sinn Féin, with its campaign of building the party and growing national popularity, got to work in Co. Cavan and gave the electorate an appetite for a democratic contest.

Notices covering events and meetings of the Ancient Order of Hibernians (AOH) and the United Irish League (UIL) throughout Cavan and adjoining counties were common in the *Anglo-Celt* newspaper in the early years of the

20th century. The AOH had a strong presence but there were splits in the UIL in Cavan, which had started from 1912 when the then county secretary, John "The Leaguer" O'Reilly from Templeport, resigned on grounds of indiscipline within the organisation. From 1916 in East Cavan there was open revolt developing within the nationalist community, principally between the UIL in Cootehill and the AOH in Bailieboro, which allowed Sinn Féin to step into the impending breach. One former UIL supporter and prominent man in Cootehill, the Rev. P. O'Connell PP, changed his allegiances to Sinn Féin and became its champion and accepted leader in East Cavan.

The first Sinn Féin notice appeared in the *Anglo-Celt* in May 1917: "A Sinn Féin testimonial function was held in Ballinagh for released prisoners. Mr Philip Baxter, County Council Chairman, West Cavan Sinn Féin, was removed as a Justice of the Peace by the Lord Chancellor." The first recorded activity of Sinn Féin in East Cavan was of Seán Milroy speaking publicly at after-Mass meetings on Ascension Thursday at Middle Chapel and Maudabawn, and on the following Sunday after Masses at Cootehill and Drung.
In a June edition of the *Anglo-Celt* there appeared this report "Sinn Féin in East Cavan" — Rev Fr P. O'Connell PP Cootehill, spoke to a large gathering at Middle Chapel 'to whip up the district'. Mr Fidgeon agreed to work the Shercock area, Mr McCabe will look after Mullagh, Mr J.P. O'Brien is to look after Kingscourt and J.J. Lynch is to attend to Ballyjamesduff." Key people were now in place to build the organisation, to canvass the electorate and to sell the Sinn Féin policy in order to win the East Cavan seat.
At this time a Sinn Féin conference took place in Kilkenny, where the provisional executive was formed under the continued presidency of Arthur Griffith until a full national convention was held in October. The *Anglo-Celt* continued to report Sinn Féin activities nationally and locally through announcements from Sinn Féin offices in Dublin. The organisation under Seán Milroy had a very focused political campaign under way throughout Co. Cavan to win the East Cavan seat when it came up for election. The hearts and minds of the people of Co. Cavan were to be won over by Sinn Féin's policies, as were the people in adjoining counties and constituencies.

In July 1917 Eamon de Valera won the by-election in East Clare. Many new Sinn Féin Clubs were formed in Counties Cavan, Monaghan, Leitrim, Meath and Fermanagh. In a July issue of the *Anglo-Celt* there appeared a report of a Sinn Féin meeting in the Town Hall, Cavan, under the heading: "Cavan Sinn Féiners – All Council and Other Seats to be Captured."

In the same edition, notices from 24 Sinn Féin Clubs in Co. Cavan were published – a sign of its growing popularity.

There had been an attempt to establish a Sinn Féin Club in Ballyconnell in early 1917 but it failed to win support. It was on the evening of the announcement of de Valera's victory that a Sinn Féin Club was eventually established. It was founded in James Baxter's sitting room to accommodate the 20 or so people attending. The first tricolours were put up in the town on that evening but were removed by the RIC on the following morning, only for them to be replaced. Local youths were arrested for this. The Sinn Féin Club officers elected in Ballyconnell were:

President: John Drum
Chairman: Tom O'Reilly
Vice-Chairman: T.W. Murphy
Secretary: Barney Rudden
Joint-Treasurers: James Baxter and Ed Shannon

From this inaugural meeting, it was claimed that membership grew to over a hundred within a week. There were only four Sinn Féin Clubs in Co. Cavan in early 1917 and this grew to 53 clubs by year end with in excess of 2,600 members. This could not have happened without the presence and ability of Seán Milroy, who paved the way for Arthur Griffith's first visit to Co. Cavan. This was planned for Belturbet but with Tom O'Reilly's influence, Griffith's visit to his adopted political county was transferred to Ballyconnell. Here on 15 August 1917 Griffith was met by thousands of people and accompanied by recent converts to Sinn Féin, Cllr Larry Ginnell and Ald. Tom Kelly, Dublin.

The *Anglo-Celt* reported:

> At a largely attended Sinn Féin demonstration in Ballyconnell on Wednesday, arches of green white and orange spanned the streets of Ballyconnell. At four o'clock there was a parade headed by the Ballinagh Brass and Reed Band and The O'Rahilly Sinn Féin Club with cyclist corps in the charge of Capt. Paul Galligan Irish Volunteers. Thirty Sinn Féin Clubs and fourteen bands represented Cavan, Leitrim and Fermanagh.

This was a very formal well-choreographed political occasion, where a platform was erected at Mount Pleasant (now Woodford Park) to accommodate the gathering. This date was strategically chosen as it was a traditional day for the AOH to hold their parades and public meetings in non-

Unionist parts of Ulster. The platform had all the Sinn Féin District and Urban Councillors (they would not have been elected under Sinn Féin but had recently pledged their allegiance, having been members of the IPP or Independent councillors) of the region. Philip Baxter chairman of the West Cavan Executive of Sinn Féin acted as chairman. John Drum, Thomas O'Reilly and Barney Rudden were on the platform representing Ballyconnell Sinn Féin Club. Barney Rudden, secretary Ballyconnell Sinn Féin Club, in his address of welcome said:

> The sons of Breffni are in thorough sympathy with the ideals and principles on which Sinn Féin is fighting: the right for Ireland to have a place among the nations of the earth as a free and independent nation. Too long we have trusted our leaders; too long have we been deceived but the blood that has flown in streams from Ireland's bravest sons has not been shed in vain. The men of Breffni appreciate their motives and their sacrifice and shall never yield until our people and our country take their place among the nations of the Earth. We have seen our fields laid bare and our countryside made orphan of our bravest and best because there was denied to Irishmen the right to live in their own country. Under the folds of our flag, the green, the white and the orange, we take our stand and with it we will conquer or die.

A letter from Rev. M. McLoughlin CC, Belturbet, was read: "It is only future generations that will fully realise what our country owes to Mr Griffith. He is the father of Sinn Féin and in Irish history he will yet be known as the Father of his Country."

The address of welcome was far removed from Griffith's original concept for Sinn Féin, which was dual monarchy as a basis for settlement of the Irish question. This was now overtaken and influenced by the events of Easter 1916, the rise of militant Unionism and the faltering Home Rule Bill. Griffith was a writer and propagandist with an international reputation, producing papers, journals and speeches, putting forward the Sinn Féin message by lambasting the IPP and British rule in Ireland. He was a commentator and philosopher who moulded the ideals of Sinn Féin – policies of moral resistance through non-violent civil disobedience, passive resistance and non-cooperation.

Arthur Griffith speaking on that day in Ballyconnell, said:

The sending of Irish representatives to the British parliament is a recognition of the British right to rule Ireland and is a basic error of Irish politics because it turned the minds of the people from their own strengths. The Sinn Féin policy is clear and distinct, that the Irish people are by national right and by international right a free people; that anything that obstructs that freedom is tyranny and must be removed and the way Sinn Féin proposes to remove that tyranny is by non-recognition of English authority in Ireland...

He quoted Parnell, "Keep a firm grip on your homesteads", and continued: English government in Ireland will be broken, not by playing the game of politics in the enemy's stronghold and according to the enemy's rules but by acting on the Sinn Féin policy. Ten years ago in neighbouring Leitrim the first Sinn Féin election was fought by Charles Dolan, when the Irish Party told the people, "Keep Sinn Féin out and you'll have Home Rule within three years". What has happened since? Ireland's taxation had risen from £12 million in 1914 to £30 million while the population had decreased by six hundred thousand.

Sinn Féin tells the Irish people to turn their backs on England, to deny that country's right to rule them, to elect supporters of that policy for the parliamentary constituencies and representatives to councils and having done that, they will set up a constituent assembly, an acting government of Ireland endowed with the moral authority of the Irish people.

With the passing away of Parnell, Biggar and Davitt, the Irish Party became the tail of the English Party and the first step was to get rid of them. While the Irish Party were saying that they have accomplished great reforms in Ireland, two things were happening – Irish taxation was growing and the population was going down: that is the road to national extinction. They are not the representatives of Ireland in England but England's representatives in Ireland.

As farming was the principal commercial activity at that time, Griffith continued:

When an embargo was placed on the Irish cattle trade in English markets four years ago, the Irish Party held the balance of power in the British Parliament, and when asked why it did not throw out the government responsible for the embargo, Mr John Dillon said: "If we throw out the Liberals, we let in the Tories". That was an absolute confession of the impotence of parliamentarianism. At that time, a few men in Dublin who believed in the Sinn Féin policy were arranging alternative markets for Irish cattle in Germany or Italy. The Irish farmer sending cattle to Hamburg or Genoa would realise 15 shillings to £1 more per hundredweight than prices pertaining in British markets. One of the things a National Council sitting in Dublin and attending to the interests of the Irish people will see to is the opening of world markets for Irish cattle.

Was Arthur Griffith our first politician with a vision of the benefits of European free trade? What he said in Ballyconnell in 1917 was in essence similar to what politicians and farm leaders had to say of real benefits of Ireland's application for entry into the European Economic Community in the early 1970s. This prompts a valid question: What happened economically in Ireland in the next 50 plus years? Emigrants were the country's biggest export.

This political speech by Griffith was simple in its content. He laid out his plan for Sinn Féin national and local assemblies, while lambasting British rule and the IPP. He told the people how the British system was hurting their pockets while advocating better markets for Irish farm produce in Europe rather than Britain.
He concluded by saying:
> That day was one which would gladden the heart of any Irishman as he had not expected to see on his first visit to Cavan such a magnificent display of national feeling. He claimed the Sinn Féiners were the real successors of Parnell, Biggar and Davitt, whose policy was to make English government impossible.
> He added that there were many things said of him and other leaders of the movement that they had agreed to treat with contempt. It had been said of himself that he was a Welshman or a Scotsman but his father told him that the family came from Fastry near Redhills, Co. Cavan, for which reason he was very proud to be speaking that day in which he felt was the county of his ancestors.

Griffith connected with the people by saying that Co. Cavan was the home of his ancestors. Fastry is actually in the parish of Currin, Co. Monaghan and a mere stone's throw from Co. Cavan.
Arthur Griffith stayed overnight in Clancy's Hotel, Ballyconnell. He met

many Sinn Féin activists from the area in 29 Main Street on the following day. Annie Malanaphy welcomed him to her home. Griffith held many private meetings in the upstairs drawing room. Ellie Drum had memories of that day when Griffith met many Sinn Féin people from the area, including Protestants like Robert Crawford, footman to Lord Benison. This is contrary to some contemporary republican perceptions. Prominent Protestants in west Cavan were sympathetic to and supportive of Sinn Féin. At this time Arthur Griffith appointed John Drum and John 'The Leaguer' O'Reilly as judges to the Sinn Féin Arbitration courts.

Molly Drum, Ellie's eldest sister, recalled this occasion in Ballyconnell and said that Arthur Griffith paid two further visits to their home, one she remembered well when Griffith implored her father to stand as a Sinn Féin candidate in an election. She could not recall the year or the election or the purpose of Griffith's third visit.

The RIC were keeping a close eye on proceedings in Ballyconnell as was their wont. They somehow brought a charge, which resulted in a subsequent hearing at Ballyconnell Petty Sessions in September before J.D. Gerrard RM and seven Justices of the Peace on the Bench. District Inspector McEntee, Cavan, prosecuted James S. Mullery, Cavan, for an alleged infringement of the petrol regulations by driving passengers to Ballyconnell on the occasion of a Sinn Féin demonstration on 15 August. D.I. McEntee read three orders made by the military authorities authorising the use of petrol in the case of ambulances, hearses, medical officers, army officers, munitions workers, government officials, veterinary surgeons and farmers on business and not exceeding a radius of 10 miles. Constable McGoldrick, Cavan, said that he saw the defendant leaving Ballyconnell and named the passengers, one of whom was waving a Sinn Féin flag and singing 'A Soldier's Song', to which Mr Fay JP retorted: "The singing of a song has nothing to do with this case".

Cross-examined by Mr W.J. Fegan, Mr McEntee said: "Mr Walsh [one of the passengers] was reporting at the meeting. There was another car with another reporter at the meeting. There was nothing against the defendant's character and the police often employed his cars... Mr Fegan said his client knew nothing of all the orders read out by the district inspector and his permit stated that the car could be 'let for public duties'. Cavan Sinn Féin Club appointed delegates to a meeting of the West Cavan executive held in Ballyconnell on 15 August and the defendant's car was engaged to take the delegates to the meeting. It would, he said, simplify matters greatly and relieve much heart-burning all over the country if 'business purposes' as referred to in the petrol regulations was properly defined. The defendant was not a Sinn Féiner but a man engaged in making a livelihood. Up to the present the government had not declared the Sinn Féin organisation illegal and he asked the Bench to hold that the car was employed for a legitimate purpose and that the defendant acted bona fide in the transaction. He quoted a recent decision in support of his argument."

Mr Gerard RM asked was it usual in such cases for a motor-car owner to apply to the police for permission to hire a car. District Inspector McEntee said it was not and he doubted if the police could sanction it without the authority of the petrol commissioners. The magistrates having consulted, the chairman announced that by a majority they had decided to dismiss the case without prejudice.

This case showed the pettiness which the nationalist population had to endure at that time from a police force who were not very sure of themselves and the law.

One of the seven JPs sitting on the bench for this case was P. E. McCorry, the first veterinary surgeon to the area. An Oxford don, he lived at Rosebank, Ballyconnell, from where he practised into the 1950s and lived out his retirement.

(iii) The origin of the Sinn Féin Courts

Arthur Griffith and Sinn Féin had a political policy that was openly active and ready to develop civil disobedience to encourage disengagement from British rule. This was advanced at a joint meeting of East and West Cavan Sinn Féin in the Town Hall, Cavan, on the last Sunday of September 1917. A resolution was adopted by the 32 clubs represented, establishing the Boards of Arbitration, or the Sinn Féin Parish Courts in Co. Cavan and nationally. The following motion was proposed by T. L. O'Brien, Lavey and seconded by J. Lynch, Carrickallen:

That the joint executives of East and West Cavan Sinn Féin Clubs hereby formulate a Board of Arbitration whose function shall be to amicably settle all disputes between members in all matters of either finance, property or person. To put the scheme on a working basis, it is proposed to appoint in each parish three reliable and trusted arbitrators (one of whom may be the parish priest or curate, the other two members or officers of the club), to whom all disputes shall be referred;
That the several executives shall appoint three members each as appeal courts to whom any aggrieved party may appeal and that the findings of

the Parish Court or Executive Appeal Court shall have the entire force of the Sinn Féin movement, financially and otherwise, to reinforce the rewards;

That the executive of each county in Ireland be furnished with a copy of this resolution in order to do likewise and therefore to deny law costs to the Crown or any traffic at all avoidable in English courts.

The many delegates at the meeting supported the motion, which was later ratified by the National Council and adopted into the Sinn Féin Constitution later that year. This meeting establishing the Sinn Féin Parish or Arbitration Courts in Co. Cavan was openly reported in the *Anglo-Celt* on the following Saturday. This was Sinn Féin political policy which lay down the foundations of a new Irish state. In so doing it was also sold to the Irish people that Sinn Féin would deal with all matters of civil dispute. This was initially accepted by the British as an internal Sinn Féin matter to settle agrarian disputes. According to intelligence reports, the authorities knew of these courts and tolerated them as they hoped that they would end up in bitter land disputes and so would bring down the Sinn Féin movement. The settling of agrarian or land disputes was nothing new to rural Ireland as there is evidence that Land League Courts were held in many parts of the south and west of Ireland in the 1880s and 1890s. In September and October 1917, there were reports that local agrarian disputes were settled in Kingscourt and Swanlinbar by Sinn Féin officers.

These Sinn Féin civil courts were used by many Protestant families to address the complexities of "entailed wills" and other impractical inheritance customs to sustain Protestant ownership of land. Historically, land was a non-tradable commodity with the Anglo-Irish who always retained ownership of the worked or tenanted lands in a family name. Entailed wills meant that the holder could not sell the property. Because of such entailed wills, the Protestant community often had to deal with complex inheritance issues of land and property. Property title was often handed on to the eldest son to ensure continuity of the name and property within the family. In cases where there was no son to inherit, this was brought to the Sinn Féin Courts for settlement. Sinn Féin made a difference at local level. Its arbitration in property matters and advice in the making of wills helped prevent expensive litigation in the future.

Arbitration or Parish Court sittings were held in the granary or loft to the back of Drums. It is recalled that on court days people were seen fighting going in and shaking hands on coming out from court sittings. This channel for resolving property and other civil matters was cost effective. These courts were a template for the costs adopted by the Dáil Courts as established by the first Dáil from June 1920.

The Sinn Féin policy was for an inclusive and united Ireland. The policy in establishing and working the Boards of Arbitration or Parish Courts, which dealt with a lot more than land disputes, sent a direct signal to the Irish people and the legal profession to commence disengagement from the British courts in Ireland. There is reported and quoted evidence that these courts started in Cavan and Clare in 1917 and they set the model for the Dáil Courts which came into being from June 1920 and continued to 1924.

The Cavan motion which set up the the Arbitration Courts was probably written and directed by Seán Milroy as part of the Sinn Féin policy. It is a pity that Ireland did not retain these courts after 1924 instead of reverting to British law and cancelling out an established and successful community forum for civil law and order. The establishing of the Parish or Arbitration Courts was a wonderful political strategy. Its consequences were the creation of a new Irish democracy and the weakening of British rule in Ireland. A stable democracy has an elected government supported by law and order, acceptable policing and an independent courts system. The Sinn Féin action in establishing these courts was a major act in dismantling British legal and political authority in Ireland, without firing a shot.

(iv) Griffith Elected for east Cavan

On the first Sunday in September 1917, on the fair green in Cootehill, Arthur Griffith addressed his first public Sinn Féin meeting in East Cavan. Eamon de Valera, Seán Milroy, W.L. Cole and Patrick Whelan spoke from the platform. This was a mass meeting in every sense with all Sinn Féin Clubs from East Cavan present and a substantial number from West Cavan, Monaghan and Fermanagh. The secretary of East Cavan Sinn Féin, Paul Smith, read the address of welcome. According to the report in the *Anglo Celt*, there were 23 named priests present, the most senior of whom was Rev. P. O'Connell PP Cootehill, now a fanatical Sinn Féin supporter, who gave the opening address. This man knew how to rouse the crowd, saying: "I have only got to say of Sinn Féin that it is a tonic in the air; it has cleared the air and it is sweeping corruption out of the land." He introduced Arthur Griffith as a Cavan man, "the Father of Sinn Féin who is engaged today by voice and pen in accomplishing the Resurrection of Ireland."

Griffith spoke explaining the Sinn Féin policy and condemning John Redmond's constitutional party saying "that by means of their "constitutionalism", Ireland was being governed by English martial law".

Quoting Reuter's Agency he said:

> Three days ago England sent to America and other countries an
> account of a diabolical plot on the part of the German government to
> divide Belgium into two areas, Flemish and Walloon, and the object
> the English said was a vile partition trick to destroy the national unity
> of Belgium. The English government that sent out this accusation
> against Germany is the same government that attempted a vile
> partition trick on Ireland 12 months ago, and believe me, we have not
> heard quite the last of that trick.

Griffith was addressing the obvious threat of the political partitioning of
Ireland.

Séan Milroy who was now well known in the region, spoke to the crowd:

> The member for East Cavan, Mr Young, was making a fairly good
> attempt at being a Sinn Féiner as he had not gone to the English
> parliament for two to three years. Referring to de Valera's victory in
> the Banner County, he wanted Cavan to be the Banner County of
> Ulster. Let Sinn Féin Clubs be formed in every centre and look after
> the register. You will have to look after the peace yourselves and see
> that the reputation for order and good conduct that has followed the
> banner of Sinn Féin since it was first flung to the skies in Roscommon
> shall be maintained. We want every Sinn Féiner to be a good Irishman
> with a high standard of civic and national patriotism.

In modern terms, what Milroy was enunciating could be called Sinn Féin's
Mission Statement and would not go astray when read and understood by
politicians today or at any time.

Five weeks later Sinn Féin held a mass rally in Bailieboro, where the main
speakers were de Valera, Griffith, Eoin McNeill and Milroy. There was the
usual large number of Sinn Féin Clubs represented, with bands and banners.
Some of the banners were former UIL banners with the letters UIL covered
over and replaced with Sinn Féin. The procession to the platform was led by
almost 100 men on horseback, probably a reaction to the Enniskillen Horse
and the local Orange Lodges as there were many in the Bailieboro area. One
noticeable factor at this gathering was that there was only one priest on the
platform and that was the parish priest from Carnaross, Co. Meath. Letters of
apology were read from Fr P. O'Connell PP Cootehill and Fr. B. Gaffney PP
Virginia. The non-presence of priests from the area was due to a ban by
Bishop Finnegan of Kilmore who forbade priests from his diocese being
present on and speaking from Sinn Féin platforms. In his memoirs, Capt.

Séan Sheridan, Ballinagh Old IRA, referred to Bishop Finnegan as a great imperialist. Both Fr. O'Connell and Fr. Gaffney had letters read out and both referred to secret societies, which they were probably told to utter by Bishop Finnegan. It is likely that they both went along with this as their reference to secret societies would be taken to mean Freemasonry or Orangism or even their church leaders and not the IRB or Sinn Féin, contrary to their bishop's intentions.

This action by Bishop Finnegan had its origins back in the 1892 general election when the Irish Catholic hierarchy split the Catholic or nationalist electorate by openly supporting the anti-Parnellite nationalists. In the nearby constituencies of North and South Meath, the supporters of the defeated pro-Parnellite candidates, Pierce Mahony and "Brian Boru" Dalton, petitioned the courts in Dublin to annul the Meath results on the grounds of undue clerical influence. The then Bishop of Meath, Thomas Nulty, on the eve of the general election, declared that, "no Parnellite voter could remain a Catholic".

This statement incensed the judges who annulled the general election results in both Meath constituencies and by-elections were held in 1893.*

From 1892, there had been very few elections in Ireland, with puppet members returned unopposed for decades. The ordinary people had lost any interest in politics, which probably played some part in the defeat of Gladstone's second Home Rule Bill in 1893. The Catholic hierarchy did not come from a democratic organisation. It was now with the presence of Sinn Féin that an open democratic opportunity was being returned to the electorate. This the Catholic hierarchy and the establishment feared – a fear which the capitalist and political establishment held against Sinn Féin's socialist or left-of-centre policies. Sinn Féin was an obvious and destabilising threat to the status quo. It was William O'Brien, the great Dublin trade unionist, who urged Sinn Féin to contest the Roscommon by-election with Count Plunkett. Later the Irish Labour Party stood aside to allow Sinn Féin a free run to contest seats at the 1918 general election. Sinn Féin and the Labour movement put forward agreed candidates in local elections to ensure socialist policies prevailed.

When de Valera spoke at that Bailieboro meeting, he lampooned the IPP and in particular its leader John Dillon for his speech on the same platform a week previously, while also speaking on the Sinn Féin policy. When Griffith spoke, he made some excellent economic and fiscal points.

* David Lawlor - 'Political Priests', History Ireland Vol. 18 No 2, 2010.

Referring mainly to an English newspaper, which questioned an independent Ireland's ability to pay its own way to fund police, army, education, pensions etc., he said:

> Last year England taxed us for £24 million, which could rise to £30 million next year. This was £2 million greater than the total revenue of Sweden, an independent country with its own army and navy and with seven million citizens. In Ireland, eleven thousand RIC members are paid £127 each per annum and eight hundred thousand children are being educated on £2.5s per capita per annum. Ireland is the only country in Europe where police are costing more than education.

The police budget probably included an allowable sum for castle hacks or informers. Children and education are always emotive and thus Griffith and Sinn Féin were gaining political points. This was a great occasion for Sinn Féin as it was just days after the Sinn Féin convention where a new constitution was adopted and de Valera was elected president on the proposal of Griffith, who after six years as president stood down. Sinn Féin was now a national political party, seeking representative suffrage at every opportunity, with 1,200 clubs nationwide and over 250,000 members.

At a Ballyconnell Sinn Féin Club meeting in December 1917, the chairman urged "the importance of dealing with the food problem at once, in view of the danger of famine next spring if foodstuffs were allowed to be exported". The years 1916 and 1917 were both inclement years for the production of food, at a time when the spade and scythe did most of the work. From January to May 1917, Ireland and the Irish people had to endure some of the severest weather conditions in over 30 years and it was little wonder that there was concern for food supplies. The export of food from Ireland to England in support of the Great War led to new concerns. The issue of food and the fear of famine was addressed at a UIL meeting in East Cavan earlier that year. The Spanish or Asian flu hit Ireland from mid-1918. This pandemic affected mostly children and young adults, whose resistance was weak due to inadequate diet. It resulted in the deaths of thousands of young people. Sinn Féin's concern for the health and well being of the Irish people at that time received little recognition.

At a food-preservation meeting in Ballyconnell in the same year, the chief steward to the Roe Estate, Ballyconnell House was asked how much seed potatoes they had in store. He said none as he had just sold all to a Belfast company for £16.10s per ton, and they were going to Scotland. He was told that the controlled price was £9-5s per ton. The RIC were patrolling the markets, checking that people selling seed or plants were charging only the fixed controlled rate. People were being arraigned in the local magistrate courts for overcharging. The Roe Estate was charged and brought to Cavan Circuit Court on the matter of overcharging and the case was deferred. There is no recorded outcome.

The arrogance shown by the Roe Estate on that occasion was to come back to haunt it later. As reported in the *Anglo-Celt* in February 1920, an auction was called to sell timber on the estate a year earlier. On the nights subsequent to the auction, 516 trees were cut down and carted away, resulting in a malicious claim against Cavan and Fermanagh Co. Councils. There were 927 trees in the wood, of which 411 were sold. Bidding at the auction was so low that the auctioneer, Mr R.H. Johnston, considered abandoning the sale. Seargent Coyle, Ballyconnell, gave evidence, stating: "At 6 o'clock on the morning of the 26 February, he saw about 200 people in the wood cutting trees and there were about 100 carts, which were going in all directions with the timber. The people told him that they had purchased the trees at auction the previous day and he believed them."

It was very probable that a small number of the trees had been purchased the previous day by those present that morning – a safeguard against any potential legal questions later. Timber merchants would not touch the sale. The estate got a decree against the councils, almost a thousand pounds less than claimed.

The Sinn Féin campaign in Co. Cavan continued when W.T. Cosgrave spoke at a mass rally in Swanlinbar in November and Arthur Griffith spoke at a New Year's Day 1918 rally in Belturbet, when he said:

> When the proposer of the resolution said that Sinn Féin was Ireland and Ireland was Sinn Féin, he stated the exact truth, for the movement was not founded as a party organisation but to achieve the same end for which Owen Roe O'Neill assembled his forces here in Belturbet 250 years ago – the independence of the whole Irish nation. We are opening a year that will be a fateful one in Irish history, a year when the map of Europe will be re-made and many nations that for centuries had lost their independence will be restored as free peoples... It was not the Irish people who deserted the IPP but the IPP that had deserted the Irish people in the interest of English ministers. Like the Slavs and Croatians, Sinn Féin claimed the same right for Ireland in justice and international law – the right to decide by the votes of its people the future of the country.

Sinn Féin activity was now focused on getting its members and electorate onto the register of electors, as was stipulated at many local Sinn Féin rallies, in readiness for the next general election. Fr O'Connell and Fr Gaffney were back speaking for Sinn Féin, not on official platforms, but on their own soap boxes. They were against impending conscription in Ireland. Home Rule as promised in 1914 was still not enacted and was faltering as the war had gone on much longer than anticipated. With members in a national government in London, Unionist political pressure for the separation of the north east of Ireland was growing as the IPP was politically fading.

In April 1918, a decision was made in Westminster to extend conscription to Ireland. Every republican and nationalist in Ireland opposed it, including the Catholic Church. This issue had a temporary unifying influence and put a lull on Sinn Féin's campaigning in East Cavan.

In the same month, the sitting MP for East Cavan Samuel Young died at the age of 96. He was described as a Protestant nationalist and as "a person who in every aspect of his character, there was never a more typical Belfast Presbyterian." Sam Young was one of O'Connell's adherents for the repeal of the union with England and always an advocate in later years of self-government in Ireland.

Seán Milroy assembled a Sinn Féin meeting within days in Cootehill and declared that Arthur Griffith would contest the vacant seat. E.J. Duffy, a solicitor from Kingscourt, was appointed constituency agent. It was a tradition within Westminster then that the party of a deceased sitting member would move the writ for a by-election to fill the seat within days of death and the subsequent by-election be held over a very short timescale, days and not weeks. The writ for the East Cavan by-election was moved by Crean, an MP for Limerick at Westminster on 4 June. In the interim, there was pressure on account of the conscription issue from nationalists and the Catholic Church for a united candidate to be nominated to fill the East Cavan seat. The reason for this was that at the time of proposed conscription for Ireland, the IPP candidate, Dooley, stood down in the by-election in Offaly, in favour of McCartan of Sinn Féin. This was because Dooley and the IPP knew they would be defeated as he had supported conscription earlier. Now, in return, the IPP wanted Sinn Féin to stand down in East Cavan in favour of their candidate. Griffith's response was not acceptable to either the Catholic bishops or the IPP. Griffith and Sinn Féin would now fight for the seat against the IPP candidate, the editor of the *Anglo-Celt*, J.F. O'Hanlon.

East Cavan had some 9,000 voters on the register, 1,000 of whom were identified as Protestant or Unionist. On one Sunday during the campaign, the IPP had 24 sitting MPs drafted into the constituency, while Sinn Féin held small and more local rallies during the campaign. Griffith suffered some name-calling from established figures when he was termed "a shirker" by John Dillon, who said, "when the rising was taking place, Griffith was at home digging cabbage". At Easter 1916, Griffith supported Eoin MacNeill's countermanding order, telling Volunteers not to turn out, and notified people to that effect. On Easter Monday when Griffith heard that the rising was taking place, he went to the GPO but he was told to go away as his journalistic and propaganda skills would be of greater importance to the Irish cause after the rising. Griffith was arrested by the British and sent to an English jail.

During the East Cavan by-election campaign the British again arrested Griffith, under what was called the German Plot. He along with many prominent Sinn Féiners were arrested and jailed in England. The German Plot reflected England's and Dublin Castle's fear that Sinn Féin was being backed by German money and arms. The plot was being mentioned by people of the establishment for some time and probably went back to the failed attempt by Roger Casement to enlist German aid and to import German arms for the Easter Rising. In the autumn of 1917, the rector at Bailieboro Church of Ireland preached to his congregation on the dangers looming from such a German Plot, — obviously the rumour and associated fears were circulating. Could the German Plot rumour be related to the old saying: "If you repeat a lie for long enough, you'll end up believing it?"

Griffith could no longer be called "a shirker" and the Sinn Féin cry for the election on 20 June was "Get the Man in Jail Out". Griffith had already spoken at many meetings and Sinn Féin rallies throughout Co. Cavan. His detention in an English prison was a political bonus. There were people who took Griffith's place on Sinn Féin platforms in East Cavan to maintain the momentum of his campaign. They were in the main G.V. Maloney, solicitor, Cavan, T.P. McKenna, Co. Council Mullagh, and Fr Gaffney PP, Virginia. G.V. Maloney's sub-office at Cootehill was the Sinn Féin election headquarters for the duration of the by-election.

When election day came, both sides had many campaigners on the ground and it was estimated that Sinn Féin had 4,000 volunteers, as they said to keep the peace (a little intimidation and personation here and there could not be denied, on either side) and the IPP had many AOH people from Belfast, Armagh and Dublin. Twenty-six years was a long time to wait for a vote and thanks to Arthur Griffith and his Sinn Féin policies, the people had their say when they elected Griffith their representative by a majority of 1,214 votes. The priests in East Cavan made their presence felt on election day as they campaigned strongly for Griffith.

John F. O'Hanlon, the defeated IPP candidate, has to be mentioned for his role, as the editor of the *Anglo-Celt* and as an election candidate. Going through the pages of the paper for that period, it has to be complimented in its objective reporting of all political meetings and events surrounding the 1918 by-election in East Cavan. Willie O'Hanlon, son of the defeated candidate recalled that, "his father was a somewhat reluctant candidate, but he always believed that the electorate had to have a choice for the sake of democracy". Willie also recalled an incident in Dublin, "when a stranger came behind his father and put what felt like a gun to his back, threatening him not to stand for election, which personally drove him to fight the East Cavan seat." The gun is not a democratic institution.

J.F. O'Hanlon was elected an Independent TD for Cavan 1927-33.

Sinn Féin went on to win 73 seats on its abstentionist policy in the general election to Westminster in November 1918. Arthur Griffith was re-elected unopposed for East Cavan and Peter Paul Galligan from Drumkilly was elected unopposed for West Cavan. This led to the first Dáil meeting in the Mansion House, Dublin on 21 January 1919. This first meeting was attended by 28 of the elected TDs as the majority of them were either on the run or in English jails. Cathal Brugha the TD for Waterford, was appointed acting-President. The international press was present to report on these historic proceedings. In his address, Brugha, declared the Volunteers to be the legitimate Army of the Irish Republic.

In the words of Griffith's biographer in the Irish language, Seán Ó Lúing: "Arthur Griffith gave the Irish nation a coherent and rational philosophy. He put forward his Sinn Féin programme as an inclusive compound of all the Irish traditions, Unionist and nationalist. Griffith, whose ancestors came from Ireland's Presbyterian province, aimed to build steel into the Irish character and mould it into the habitual acceptance of the solid material virtues of self-development, thrift, civic discipline and a full and fruitful cultivation of Ireland's native resources. Sinn Féin in its original and true meaning of self-reliance could never fail, claimed Griffith, and on this concept, through the medium of his journals, and in the language of unique persuasion, he based plan upon plan, the primary one being the withdrawal of Irish parliamentary representation from London and the setting up in Ireland of a democratically formed assembly which would command the loyalty of its people. His policy of moral resistance was respected and followed by India."

CHAPTER 6

THE WAR OF INDEPENDENCE IN WEST CAVAN

(i) Build-up to military action

When did Ireland's War of Independence start? It is generally accepted that it was on 21 January 1919 as the first Dáil was meeting in the Mansion House, Dublin, when two RIC men were shot dead as they escorted commercial explosives to quarry works in Co. Tipperary. This action was contrary to the essence and function of the fledgling new democracy being set up in Ireland. However, it can be argued that the actions of the British security forces led to Ireland's War of Independence by the arrest of leading Sinn Féin and Volunteer activists under the German Plot in May 1918. These arrests were made nationwide. Charles Dolan, Desmond Fitzgerald, J. O'Mahoney and R. Davies, all Sinn Féin organisers, were arrested in Co. Cavan. The military searched for Peter Paul Galligan at his home in Drumkilly and in the general Ballinagh area. Many English newspapers denounced the act as one of gross stupidity on the part of the government while demanding that if there was a charge against the prisoners, they should be made aware of it. Seventy-three prisoners, including Eamon de Valera and Arthur Griffith, were transported from Kingstown on board a government ship to Holyhead. The majority of detainees were lodged in Frongoch Internment Camp in Wales. The Countess Markieviez and Maude Gonne McBride were also arrested and detained in Holloway Prison London.

On 12 July of that year, Lieutenant General Fredrick Shaw, Commander in Chief of the British Forces in Ireland, declared Sinn Féin, the Volunteers, Cumann na mBan and the Gaelic League dangerous organisations. Meetings could not be held except with a licence from the police. All public addresses in the Irish language were banned. This now meant that the holding of many sporting events like horse racing, Gaelic football and hurling needed a police licence. This declaration announced on the "Twelfth" did not affect the Orange demonstrations being held on that day in Ulster and did not affect further planned Orange demonstrations in the province throughout the following week. An Orange demonstration went ahead in Ballyconnell on 19 July, where the County Grand Master, R.H. Johnstone said, "he felt a great responsibility rested on the Orange body in these times to maintain their organisation intact as there was professedly a rebel element at large in Ireland and the present government was only a weak-kneed institution". He believed, he declared, "that a man de Valera who was in an English jail was the man who gives Mr Shortt his instructions on the government of Ireland" (Edward Shortt was Irish Chief Secretary). Restrictions had been imposed on the demonstration that day – no formation or marching, no music or drum beating. The police inspector present ordered the restrictions, and that was after the licence had been issued within the required time. Eighteen lodges were represented that day in Ballyconnell from Leitrim, Cavan and Fermanagh, the majority of members having travelled by train.

However, this proclamation from a Commander in Chief was antagonistic towards the nationalist people and his motives were questionable. Ireland then and the rest of the United Kingdom were overwhelmed by news or propaganda from the war and the German offensive on the Western Front, while other global stories were either censored or totally suppressed. As Commander Shaw was banning public gatherings in Ireland, Europe was already hit with "the Spanish Flu" and it was gathering hold in Ireland. The British authorities ignored this strain of flu in spite of the high death rate among the Irish population. They could have used this mysterious illness as an excuse to suppress gatherings, but in their lack of civic wisdom, they chose to ignore its reality among the people until the spring of 1919, when it was declared a notifiable disease and the pandemic had peaked.

From 1917, Sinn Féin was becoming politically active through acts of civil disobedience. As a political and civil organisation it was totally focused on electoral contests and any question of a growth "in arms" procurement or military activities by the Volunteers was practically non-existent. They could not afford to purchase arms and what money they had was needed for the basic necessities of living. Any arms or munitions bought in Ireland would have been purchased from individual British soldiers while others were mainly stolen from policemen or the "gentry" in their large estates. There can be no other reason for Commander Shaw's announcements other than self-preservation of the ruling classes and maintenance of the British military numbers in Ireland.

The Great War in mid-1918 was reaching a climax with fierce fighting on many fronts. The officers of the British military based in Ireland in all probability wanted to avoid returning to fight in Europe. The German Plot and other unfounded allegations under the Defence of the Realm Act could be advanced to London to sustain their presence in Ireland. Here the chances of being killed in action were very much fewer than in Europe. The actions against nationalist Ireland were extreme when compared to the actions and drilling in the north east by the Ulster Volunteers on behalf of the Ulster Unionist Council from 1912.

(ii) Antagonising the people

In December 1917 at a Sinn Féin Club meeting in Ballyconnell, the issue of food shortage and impending famine was discussed. Hunger or the threat of hunger is great sauce for revolution. A motion was put to re-establish a local corps of the Volunteers, which was deferred. In February 1918, Darryl Figgis addressed a meeting of the club when the motion was re-entered to restore a corps of the Volunteers in the town. This was adopted. These Volunteers were initially under the control of Sinn Féin and the Parish Courts, for which they acted as a police force. They investigated criminality, served summonses and notified defendants and witnesses to come to court. The local Volunteers would not become militarily active in the west Cavan/south Fermanagh area for some time.

By late June it appears that the Ballyconnell community was being hassled by the police. According to the *Anglo-Celt*:

At 3 a.m. on a Saturday morning a large force of police was drafted into Ballyconnell under Head Constable Mullally, Swanlinbar. They arrested, in their beds, Edward Fitzpatrick, poultry dealer, James Baxter, butcher, Patrick Dolphin, cycle agent, William Kellegher, painter and subsequently Terence Brady and Patrick Drum, on a charge of being marched in military formation at a Feis at Wattlebridge, Co. Fermanagh on June 23. They were all taken to the police barracks and three of prisoners had not yet reached 18 years. The "towns" people were alerted and served them with breakfast and a supply of food and cigarettes for what lay ahead. At 5.00 a.m. five motors convey the men to Newtownbutler. At leaving, the men were exhorted not to give bail. About 20 members of the Sinn Féin Club set out for Newtownbutler by motor, horse car and cycle, where a special court was held in the courthouse before Mr Walker R. M. Admittance to the defendants' fathers and the public was refused. Mr Murnane DI, Lisnaskea, appeared for the prosecution and the prisoners were not represented. At the sitting of the court, the defendants were told to remove their hats but they refused to do so and they were taken off by force. Constable Collins, Ballyconnell deposed:
I was present at a meeting in Wattlebridge on Sunday 23 June last. I saw a party there from Ballyconnell and they numbered about 20. The majority wore haversacks, belts and carried hurleys at a slope; not all of them carried hurleys. They marched two deep into the field in

military formation at the head of a band. I identified the five prisoners present; they wore haversacks and belts and carried hurleys. William Kellegher wore a haversack and waist belt; I believe he was in charge. When they entered the field, Wm. Kellegher gave the following commands, halt, right turn, order arms and dismiss, and the party broke off. I don't know the hour these orders were given. I saw the same party coming out of a farmyard to the public road, two deep." Sergeant McLaughlin, Newtownbutler said that he issued the warrants and swore: "These men were a terror and a menace to the civilian population." The RM asked the prisoners if they wished to make a statement, to which Wm Kellegher replied: If you want a further contribution to this farce, I refuse to recognise this as an Irish court. Asked if they would give bail, they replied "no". The prisoners were remanded to Derry Jail to appear on Monday for trial at Enniskillen.

The *Anglo-Celt* reported in detail:

A large contingent from west Cavan travelled to Enniskillen to attend the special crimes court, Mr Gerrard RM and Mr H. Walker RM presiding. The five men were charged with taking part in an illegal assembly at Wattlebridge, Co. Fermanagh on Sunday, 23 June. DI Marks, Lisnaskea, prosecuted and the accused were not professionally represented, nor did they proffer any evidence or make any statements, merely calling out "no" when asked if they had any questions to put to the police witnesses. They appeared to treat the proceedings as a huge joke, and laughed and smiled the whole time they were in the dock.

One bit of excitement marked the proceedings when a man in the body of the court persisted in talking in a loud tone of voice. He was admonished by the bench a couple of times but refused to keep quiet. Head Constable Carland told him to hold his tongue, which he physically did. [It is believed that this man was Tom Dolphin]. The man was subsequently ordered out of the court but refused to go and ultimately was hustled out by policemen, protesting loudly. One of the accused men got very excited during this incident and attempted to jump out of the dock [this was his son, Paddy Dolphin] but was held back by the police and the other defendants. After this interlude, the proceedings were conducted quietly, only those immediately connected with the case being admitted into the court.

The report continued:

The first case heard was against William Kellegher, who was charged with being in command of 20 men on the occasion in question. After police depositions, the magistrates retired and returned to court in a few moments and the chairman asked Kellegher was he prepared to enter into sureties to keep the peace for 12 months. Kellegher replied that he was not. The two magistrates retired again and on resumption the chairman said that owing to the attitude taken up by Kellegher, who was only asked and refused to give sureties that he would act for 12 months as an ordinary citizen, he would be sentenced to two months' imprisonment, and at the termination of that period he would have to find bail himself in £50 and two sureties of £25 each, or go to jail for a further two months.

Baxter, Brady, Drum and Dolphin were similarly charged and sentenced to one month in prison and on the same terms as Kellegher. When the defendants left the court in custody, they were met outside by their supporters who immediately commenced to cheer and shout "Up the Rebels". The crowd then fell in behind the police and prisoners and an attempt was made to start 'The Soldier's Song'. The police formed a cordon across the road at the East Bridge, Enniskillen and refused to allow any of the crowd proceed until the accused and their escort had arrived at the police barracks at Belmore St.

When the Volunteers, Patrick Dolphin, James Baxter, Terence Brady and Patrick Drum, were released from Sligo Jail in early November, they received a warm welcome home at Ballyconnell Railway Station. The station platform was lined with police. The prisoners and their friends entered the Catholic Church close by and attended devotions and a novena for Ireland. The RIC proceeded alone to the town. No demonstrations of any kind took place. The prisoners had a unique experience, being arrested in Ballyconnell, tried in Newtownbutler, remanded to Derry, tried in Enniskillen, sentenced to Sligo and released there, their railway warrants carrying them only to Ballinamore, Co Leitrim, 12 miles from home.

This nonsensical administration of the law on the citizens of Ballyconnell was brought to a higher level when further antagonistic actions by the police in the town were questioned in the House of Commons in May 1919, as recorded in the *Anglo-Celt*:

At the House of Commons, Mr McVeagh for Mr Hartshorn asked the Chief Secretary whether he could state on what charge and on what evidence Messrs Thomas O'Reilly, Bernard Rudden and J. O'Brien of Ballyconnell were sentenced in Co. Cavan on 27 September to one month's imprisonment. Mr Samuels said that Thomas O'Reilly, Bernard Rudden and J. O'Brien were arrested on a charge of unlawful assembling and inciting a breach of the peace at Ballyconnell, Co. Cavan on 19 September. They were tried before the court of summary jurisdiction on 25 September and convicted. The evidence showed that the police were stoned by the crowd, booed and called "bloodsuckers" and the persons who supplied them with motor cars were also booed. They were ordered to be bound over to be of good behaviour for 12 months but they refused to give bail and were sent to jail accordingly.

Mr McVeagh then asked: "Can the Right Honourable Gentleman tell me whether it is a fact that the only evidence against these three men was that they sang The Soldier's Song?" Mr Samuels replied: "Certainly not. On the information before me, the police were booed and stoned and called bloodsuckers by the crowd." To which Mr McVeagh responded: "Not by these men. The Right Hon. Gentleman did not answer my question. I want to know, not what the crowd did, but what was the evidence against these three men. Was it not merely that they sang 'The Soldier's Song?' Mr Samuels replied: 'I said they were charged with unlawful assembling and inciting to a breach of the peace.' Mr McVeagh again asked: "On what evidence was that charge supported. So far as the three men were concerned, was not the evidence against them that they sung The Soldier's Song?" But Mr Samuels denied this and continued: "The evidence was that the police were stoned and booed by the crowd." Mr McVeagh persisted: "Will the Right Hon. Gentleman give a straight answer to my straight question? Was not the only evidence against these men that they sang 'The Soldier's Song'." Mr Samuels' response was: "I have no information on that" (laughter) to which Mr McVeagh retorted: "I have and I can give it." There the exchange ended.

Bernard Rudden's daughter, Monica O'Reilly recalled: "I remember asking my father why he was sent to jail and was it for singing 'The Soldier's Song' to which he replied: "No it wasn't. It was because I couldn't sing it".

In July 1919 it was announced in the House of Commons that Sir Edward Carson would not be prosecuted for threatening to bring out the Ulster Volunteers to repeal the Home Rule Act. Legal technicalities were put forward as the excuse. The Attorney General stated that "there was nothing in the speeches upon which it was possible to found prosecution". Attention was directed by Joe Devlin MP to the fact that the Attorney General for England was consulted and not the officers who sent Irish youths to prison for singing national songs. T.P. O'Connor MP warned the English people that "the hens would come home to roost" and that Sir Edward Carson's policy would be adopted and pressed home in industrial disputes.

During a discussion on the Peace Treaty Bill (the Treaty of Versailles), Mr Devlin asked Prime Minister Lloyd George if Ireland was to have self-determination, and was told "no". Mr Devlin responded: "There is no rule at this moment except a rule by arbitrary and irresponsible force and there is no free will and choice in the determination of the destinies of her people ... Ireland is a nation as old and with as fine deeds and as glorious a record of proud tradition as any nation in Europe. The Prime Minister, whose life has been engaged in preaching the glory of his own small nationality, has used the proud position which he occupies and the prestige which he has gathered from success in this war to level an insult at the nation to which I belong. I fling that insult back in his face. Sir Edward Carson had his triumph. The Prime Minister has been intimidated by Sir Edward Carson."

Lloyd George replied: "He had taken up no new position in saying that he could not agree to setting up a parliament in Ireland and compelling Ulster to come under it. He stood by his declaration at the general election and he was prepared to carry it out." When the Peace Treaty Bill was voted on, the four votes against its adoption were from the sole Irish nationalist members present.

On the following Friday, Bonar Law, Lord Privy Seal and Leader of the Commons, stated that Ireland was to have no referendum as to her future form of government. From statements and comments later in the English newspapers, it would seem that the government's intention was to "settle" the Irish question on federal lines, giving Ireland two parliaments, the north east of Ulster having one of them.

The partition of Ireland was now a certainty, with the north east getting first pickings.

(iii) Military action

With such actions and trumped-up charges, the local RIC officers were not endearing themselves to the people of south-west Ulster. Some forms of redress took place as reported periodically in the *Anglo-Celt* over those years:-

In July 1920, a military lorry removed the household furniture of a policeman from the town to the railway station because no locals would assist. An armed guard of police kept guard on the house while the flitting was in progress with others guarding the lorry and the wagon at the railway station. A military wagon loaded with soldiers, passed through the town at the same time. The policeman's wife, family and furniture left by the 1 o'clock train. Two weeks previously, a Belfast contractor removed the wife, family and furniture of another constable from the town."

On a fair day one of the local RIC officers was abducted into the back yard at 29 Main Street where he was stripped. He was sent on his way and his uniform and underclothing were then burned in public on the Market Square. His whistle was kept as a trophy of war.

General military and police activities took place throughout the area from 1919 onwards as the following report of a raid on 27 December 1919 shows:

Some excitement was caused in Ballyconnell at about 7.30 p.m. when extra police marched into the town and immediately the roads were blocked by police armed with rifles and revolvers, who used a rope to impede all traffic... Special attention was devoted to the bridge, Daisy Hill, Church St and the new road were patrolled in a similar manner. A large crowd assembled and passed to and fro through the barriers, through curiosity. Dr O'Rourke JP and Dr Stuart, Belturbet, on an urgent sick call, were amongst those held up. A similar military procedure happened six weeks earlier.

The night before these military actions, the people of Ballyconnell were enjoying their Christmas supper dances as was traditional in the town. One was held in the Protestant Parochial Hall and the second in the Town Hall, both concluding about 5 a.m.

The aggravation by the police forced the local Volunteers into action when in May 1920 the town's RIC barracks was destroyed. A few days later the courthouse was burned down. In July they raided a number of Protestant or suspected UVF member's houses in the townland of Killyran where rifles and a quantity of ammunition were taken. The home of J.J. Benison was also raided, but only one shotgun was found. A house belonging to a soldier returned from the war, but then living in Scotland, was also burned down. Mail vans suspected of carrying enemy mail were raided in Belturbet and Enniskillen. These acts were considered necessary to assist the Volunteers in finding "cheques in the mail", issued by the police to informers who could then be traced. As the country was now in the midst of war the acts of the Volunteers, while laudable and deemed necessary at that time, have to be questioned; not on their motivation but what immediate or direct consequences accrued for the population? Certainly they contributed to more antagonistic activities and raids by the police and military, and later backed up by the Auxiliaries and the notorious Black and Tans.

John Drum, a founding member of the Mountain Road Fife and Drum Band, donated a plot of land at Gortaree in Fermanagh for the building of a practice venue. The hall was built by the members and was called the Robert Emmet Sinn Féin Hall. It was opened on 1 August 1920. A report in the *Anglo-Celt* described the event:

There was a large assemblage for this event at Gortaree, Co. Fermanagh, on Sunday last, when bands with flags and banners with large contingents attended from the following districts: Camaleer, Carew, Swanlinbar, Kinawley, Corameen, Cornaleck and Mountain Road, where Ballyconnell provided a large turnout. At the venue, it was found that four motor lorries and a motorcar had conveyed a detachment of Cornwalls from Enniskillen, while police were drafted in from Swanlinbar and Kinawley. The soldiers carried fixed bayonets and war kit while the RIC had rifles, sergeants carried revolvers. Notification was given that if it were an aeridheacht, speeches could be made on the language movement but not otherwise. Ballyconnell United Gaels played against Derrylin O'Connells and short addresses were delivered by Rev. Fr Brady, CC Teemore, Ben Maguire and Rev. Fr McManus, Glenfarn. After the military had departed, the hall was opened and a very enjoyable dance was held.

It is remarkable that after 90 plus years this hall, the headquarters of the Mountain Road Pipe Band, is still standing and is used weekly for band practice. The band changed to a pipe band in the 1940s. While the structure is very small in today's terms, it is amusing to think back to that opening day in 1920 when so many armed military and police made their presence felt, as if this little structure and community event were a major threat to the security and good order of His Majesty's Empire and Ulster.

In September 1920 military from Enniskillen, accompanied by RIC, made an extensive raid on Ballyconnell. According to the *Anglo-Celt*:

Arriving in lorries at 2.30a.m., guards were placed at the Railway Station, Daisy Hill, New Road, Bawnboy and Enniskillen Roads, and then a general search was made, beginning at Miss Toomey's, where an assistant was inquired about but was not at home. T. McAllister's was next visited, then Ed Shannon's, James McBarron's, Frank Dolphin's, Ed Fitzpatrick's, John Drum's, Patrick Maguire's, John Maher's and Tom O'Reilly's. Several men inquired for were not on these premises. Nothing of an incriminating nature was discovered.

The report continued:

At Tom. O'Reilly's D.C. a hurley was taken and he was placed under arrest. In one or two cases, inquiries were made as to whether the Ulster Bank was boycotted in the district and if the parties had any money lodged there ... All parties entering or departing from the town were held up and searched, and a motor driver who had some Irish written in a pass book was closely examined as to the meaning of the words. Before departing, close to nine o'clock, some houses had been searched three times. Mr. O'Reilly was brought to Enniskillen and no charge was made. The hurley belonged to his son who was a student in St. Patrick's College.

Several doors were burst in and in some cases the windows, when a reply to open was not quickly complied with... Some of the searchers said that "if the Ulster Bank premises were burned, some residents would be shot". Mr B. Rudden was placed under arrest for some time but was later released. The Ulster Bank manager was interviewed as to who put up the notices (boycott) connected with the bank around the town, but he could give no clue...

Another report illustrates the ongoing harassment of the town's people:
On a Sunday afternoon in November, Ballyconnell was again a target of the authorities when at about 1 p.m., as people were returning from Mass and divine service, a motor lorry carrying soldiers and a motorcar with police entered the town from the Belturbet side, some shots being fired on Daisy Hill. They passed on through Church St and proceeded to the townland of Derryginney, where they inspected and went through many fields, it is alleged, in quest of drilling but no persons were about. They then returned to the town and entered the premises of Mr John Drum and inquired for parties supposed to be there... they then visited Mr Ed. Fitzpatrick but no one was about except Mrs Fitzpatrick. They then proceeded to the townland of Lahernahone and searched a cowshed, digging up some manure, when they proceeded to knock down two sides of the boarded shed. They then went to Templeport and visited Mr Chas. Baxter's place where Mr P F Baxter, Co. Cavan Organiser of the Farmers' Union, was brought to his room and searched, but nothing of an incriminating nature was found. The constabulary then proceeded to Swanlinbar, the military returning again through Ballyconnell and holding up pedestrians and motorcars.

(iv) Annie Crawford

The ongoing raids by the police and military on Ballyconnell found no evidence of local rebel activity. Much of this is thanks to Annie Crawford, then a young assistant in Ballyconnell post office, who supported the interests of her community. The military authorities in Enniskillen or Belturbet would notify the local RIC of an impending raid on the town. Annie Crawford, on receiving this information by wire in the post office, would bring the message to John Drum. Delivering this sensitive but vital information was done under different guises. John Drum's daughter Ellie would then be sent to the various establishments and Volunteer outposts to inform them of the impending raid. Everyone would then be ready for the British forces the next morning. Anything that might be seen or taken as incriminating was hidden. Shops would have little on display to reduce any losses from looting etc. by the forces of the Crown. Being forewarned was more effective than being forearmed in these situations.

Proof of the success of Annie Crawford's good work for her community was evident as reported by the *Anglo-Celt*:

On a Monday in November 1920, three lorries and a motorcar conveyed military and police from Enniskillen direction when the premises of Mrs Angela Dolphin, The Hotel, Ballyconnell, were visited and a thorough search of the premises made, every room and the shop being visited. They then proceeded to a barn and outhouses, the thatched roof being tested with bayonets. Nothing was found. Mr Moran, a veterinary surgeon who was staying for the night at the hotel, had to show his papers and Mr Michael Kirby, assistant County Surveyor who resides there permanently, was closely questioned. During the search, the officer in charge was very courteous and several times inquired of his plain-clothed guide "if we were in the right house as they could discover nothing of importance". As the force departed, a framed picture of the Dáil in session was carried off. A visit was next paid to Mr O'Kane, from whom the key of the Town Hall was demanded... A thorough search was made and a dozen hurleys, the property of the local GAA club, were carried off. While the raids were in progress, the lorries were drawn up on the Market Square. Fowl belonging to Mr John Drum and Mrs Kells were taken. The fowl created much noise and some eventually escaped. This fowl-raid had its humorous side as a young man who is employed in the post office donned his uniform and cap and proceeded to interview the military, only to discover that his fowl had been commandeered. Some of the military remarked that they would have a square meal the next day.

On the following Wednesday morning at 2 a.m., a further descent was made on the town from the Belturbet side, the force driving through Church St and out to the burned courthouse. They entered on foot and proceeded to Miss Toomey's premises, where a thorough search was made. They then opened the shed where her motorcar was kept and submitted it to a close examination. They then proceeded to O'Reilly's, Drum's and Fitzpatrick's, inquiring about people staying there. Nothing was found. They visited the drapery shop of John Thomas Robinson, where a general search was made, he being held up attired in his nightshirt. Mr Robinson was a prominent member of the Orange Order and a member of the Masonic body.

Annie Crawford was the daughter of Robert Crawford, footman to Lord Benison, a popular Church of Ireland family who was supportive of Home Rule and Sinn Féin. When the Free State was founded, Annie Crawford was appointed postmistress at Ballyconnell, in spite of some controversy. She remained as postmistress until her death in December 1968.

The military paid a visit to Ballyconnell to wish the townspeople a "Happy New Year" and returned again on 11 January to search Drum's premises. During these early days of 1921, crime was noticeable and acted upon by the local Volunteers. Cattle were stolen from Lord Benison. Dr O'Rourke's house was broken into and coats taken. One business premises was entered during the night and property to the value of £50 was taken. The matter was placed in the hands of the local Volunteers, who raided two houses within a mile of the town and with the exception of a few articles all was recovered. A confession was secured from one of those implicated and he was given 24 hours to leave the country, which he did. A Corlough farmer was held up and robbed of £3 on his way home with medicines.. "The four men were known and will be brought to justice by the Volunteers," reported the *Anglo-Celt*.

On the evening of 13 January, a motorcar with armed men coming from the Derrylin direction fired shots along the road. In Ballyconnell there was a regular fusillade. After the discharge of shots they departed. This incident was not attributed to any one organisation. It may have been a cheeky visit by Ulster Volunteers from Fermanagh.

The *Anglo-Celt* reported:

> On 1 February, a large force of military entered the town and all males were lined up on the Fair Green, sentries being posted in the fields. Everyone, including persons coming to the pork market and every house was searched.
>
> Miss Toomey of Breffni Hotel was ordered to clear out her stock as the place was being commandeered as an RIC barracks. Shots were fired at a deaf man for not stopping when an order to halt was given. Rev. C. Magee PP was ordered to the round up but, on interviewing the officer present, was allowed to proceed. It is said that the raid was carried out with good humour by all parties. People assisted with the removal of Miss Toomey's goods to the Market House, which Mr O'Kane placed at her disposal. At noon, 30 RIC men arrived in lorries and took over the premises... Mr Hall NT was detained for having a shotgun. He was freed later. On the same morning, Bawnboy Workhouse, village and area were surrounded by military and buildings searched. At this time a number of Co. Cavan men who had been imprisoned were released from Ballykinlar Camp, while others from various parts of the county were being arrested for detention.

(vi) Military and Belfast boycotts begin

In April 1920, Crown forces entered two business premises in Ballyconnell and informed the occupiers that they were about to put up a notice in their windows and if any person attempted to remove it, they were to be notified. The notice read:

> ### NOTICE
> If any member of the RIC or Black and Tans of Ballyconnell Police Barracks meets with any injury or is caused any bodily harm or is threatened, or any attempt is made to do the same to any Loyalist or other person is harmed through being intimate with any member of the above-named forces, we the Black and Tans have decided that Ballyconnell must suffer, especially those who would encourage such an offence. If any person is found damaging or defacing this notice they will be severely dealt with.

The military and police authorities were using the situation to threaten the people of the area. They obviously carried out such threats as per the notice.

The West Cavan Executive of Sinn Féin countered this action with a notice published in the *Anglo-Celt* on 3 July 1920:

MEN and WOMEN of WEST CAVAN

The railway workers of Ireland have refused to handle munitions of war intended for the annihilation of Irish homes and Irish manhood. For this patriotic action the dependents of those men are deprived of £2,000 in wages weekly. Are the people of West Cavan going to stand idly by and see the families of those noble workers starve? They have saved your homes from destruction – save theirs now from starvation.

Arrangements are being made for a chapel collection on Sunday, 4th July, and we appeal to the people of West Cavan to show by their generous contributions their heartfelt appreciation of Ireland's dauntless workers. By Order

WEST CAVAN SINN FÉIN EXECUTIVE.

PS: All Clubs are hereby authorised to make the necessary arrangements for the collection and entering of all subscriptions, which will be published in due course.

The actions of the RIC and military led to a boycott of the handling and transportation of goods being conveyed to the military. This was an obvious reaction to the oppression being continually inflicted on the ordinary people throughout the nationalist part of Ireland. This was accompanied with a boycott of Belfast goods.

After the war, former Protestant employees of Harland and Wolff and members of the UVF who had volunteered to fight in France returned to Belfast to find Catholics in their jobs, which they wanted back. This coupled with their suspicions that all Catholics were republicans meant that Catholics were forced out of their employment. This led to serious economic repercussions for the north east with the boycott of Belfast goods in many parts of Ireland and surprisingly from some parts of the six counties.

A report in the *Anglo-Celt* in August 1920 said:

> The men expelled from work in Belfast are still out of employment, the shipyards being still closed against them. A statement was made at the end of last week that there were no objections by those who had driven their comrades from earning a living to their coming back if they gave their word they were not Sinn Féiners, but it was subsequently ascertained that the "Queen's island men" had to be "satisfied" of this.

To prevent the likelihood of another attack the Catholic workers remained away.

In support of the ousted workers in Belfast, a collection at Cavan Cathedral raised £130 and collections in Dublin had given £2,000.

A strike of the Amalgamated Society of Carpenters, Cabinetmakers and Joiners was called by the executive council in England in support of the members expelled in Belfast, but very few men in Belfast responded. They sent a delegation to England which was not received, as they were not accredited. Sir Edward Carson was engaged to take legal action against their council.

One local example of the Belfast Boycott was when Inglis's bread van was stopped and put across the bridge into the canal at Ballyconnell in August. Various reports of meetings on the growing boycott and other related issues were held throughout the country as the boycott of Belfast goods spread throughout Ireland. Worker pickets were at railway stations to see that no Belfast goods passed through.

At Roscommon fair, volunteers prevented Belfast buyers from doing any business and in Dublin markets Northern Bank notes were refused.

The Protestants of Oldcastle, Co. Meath, condemned the bigotry of Belfast and a subscription list was opened on behalf of the sufferers. Over much of the west and south of Ireland, Protestants acted similarly.

At a meeting of Protestants from all parts of the county held in Longford, resolutions were passed expressing keen appreciation of the invariable good feeling which had always existed between all creeds. One resolution expressed the hope that whatever the outcome of the present troubles, this Christian spirit might continue to grow. A protest was made against any person in Belfast or elsewhere being made to suffer on account of religious opinion.

In relation to the Belfast boycott on the August Fair Day in Cootehill, the *Anglo-Celt* reported:

> Houses of those who had refused to sign the boycott against Belfast merchants until the dismissed Catholic workers were reinstated were picketed by young men... The owner of one drapery house in the town said they had always dealt with Belfast, and since the boycott began they tried to get goods in Dublin, but no firm would open an account for them.
>
> A Catholic licensed trader who had signed a document against trading with Belfast firms, and who eventually accepted Belfast goods,

was a victim of a severe boycott during the fair and was fined £5 by a court set up by the Vigilance Committee.

In Clones, trade unionist members held up Belfast bread, preventing delivery and distribution and Belfast banks were given ultimatums to transfer accounts to other banks unless the Catholic ship workers were reinstated by a certain date. A countermander to the Belfast boycott was undertaken by the UVF in the Clones, Newbliss, Drum area of Co. Monaghan to protect, in the main, bread supplies. The action was not needed as the deliveries were already stopped before reaching the area.

Resolutions were adopted and passed by many Urban and Co. Councils throughout Ireland, boycotting Belfast goods until the Catholic shipyard workers were reinstated. One such council was Omagh where on one occasion, eight Belfast salesmen were ordered back to Belfast after alighting from the train.

The boycott of Belfast goods was also extended to Britain from where substantial financial assistance was gathered by the trade union movement in support of the victims of the shipyard tactics. Newspaper reports continued:

At a meeting of the Queen's island men in Belfast, resolutions were passed giving to every department of the ship workers the right to determine what men might be allowed to return to work, after the Chairman (Nick Gordon) stated that: "revolutionary and unprincipled men have combined, and are now attempting to stop supplies coming into the port of Belfast, and are also seeking government assistance to aid them. Should this policy be carried out it would mean that no material would be available for the great industries of Belfast, and as a consequence, all the workers would be thrown out of employment. We trust that the government will not yield to this, the demand of the enemies of our country".

The Belfast boycott resulted in its premier product names such as Gallaghers tobacco and Bass Ale and many Ulster branded goods being practically absent from the southern Irish market for over 40 years. Limited quantities of Bushmills Whiskey, Beleek pottery and Ulster Linen came south.

(vii) The first garrison attack.

The first major attack by a company of Volunteers in Co. Cavan took place on the night of 24 September 1920, when a company of 80 men made a well planned attack on the RIC barracks at Arva. The attacking party approached the town in military formation carrying rifles, while others arrived in motors. Pedestrians were cleared off the streets. All roads leading to Arva were blocked and barricaded by fallen trees. The Volunteers commandeered three houses, one being that of the local teacher who lived next door to the barracks. There, all the residents were made safe in rooms on the ground floor. The Volunteers then cut through the roof and into the adjoining roof of the barracks and the chimney was blocked so that Verey lights could not be sent out. Explosives and petrol were then thrown into the roof space while a vigorous external attack was made from both front and rear of the station. The garrison made a stout defence for about 20 minutes before surrender in a body and were removed to another adjoining house and placed under arrest. One constable was slightly injured. The Volunteers removed all the arms and ammunition from the derelict barracks, some of which were suspected of being belonging to the Ulster Volunteers. The police were allowed to return to the barracks to retrieve their personal belongings, before it was fully razed by an explosion of hand grenades, believed missed by the raiding Volunteers. The local Volunteers were ready in case the houses adjoining the barrack were threatened by fire. Damage to adjoining buildings was minimal except for bullet marks.

There were no reprisals on foot of this raid. Some weeks after this, it was announced that two of the RIC members in the Arva station on that night had resigned from the force after giving 22 and 14 years of service.

This official military action by the IRA was a joint venture by Cavan Town Company, Ballinagh/Drumkilly Company and the North Longford Brigade under the command of General Seán MacEoin.

CHAPTER 7

SELF-DETERMINATION OR PARTITION

(i) The Partition Bill

When Seán Milroy (Sinn Féin Director of Organisation) escaped from Lincoln Jail in February 1919, he remained in Britain where he became involved in promoting the Irish Self-Determination league. The league was based mostly in London with small branches in Liverpool, Manchester and Glasgow. Membership grew to about 20,000, the majority being Irish emigrants and trade unionists. It appears that the league was set up to bring the attention of the British press to the situation in Ireland and to sell shares in the Dáil Loan.

A mass meeting of the League was held in the Albert Hall London in November 1919 chaired by Lt. Commander Kenworth MP who addressed the 8,000 people present:

> If we are to bring any settlement and peace with honour to the world, a number of questions will have to be settled, and among those questions, Ireland is the most insistent. Let our critics remember that the only white race that is being held down today by force of arms is the Irish race, and let us English, who gave our best in the war for the freedom of small people, bow our heads in shame. Ireland today is being held down by an army of eighty thousand soldiers. I am speaking as an Englishman without one drop of Irish blood in my veins, and as a Protestant, when I say we have got to remember that today in Ireland, British rule differs little from the German rule in Belgium, against which we were fighting. We have heard a great deal of the Irish problem, but there is no Irish problem – the only problem today is the English problem. Every means has been tried to settle the Irish question by England – except one, and that is to leave the settlement to the Irish themselves... I deny there is any military necessity for the military display in Ireland at the present time and I also deny that Ulster is hostile to the idea of self-determination, as seen in the great strike in Belfast when Orangemen, Sinn Féiners and nationalists stood shoulder to shoulder.

Robert Williams of the Transport Workers Union moved a resolution condemning "past and present misgovernment of Ireland by the ruling classes." The meeting concluded with the singing of 'The Red Flag' and 'A Soldier's Song'.

David Lloyd George addressed parliament in December 1919 on the Irish question and introduced his scheme for permanent partition instead of the Home Rule Act of 1914. The IPP members did not attend. Opening the debate Lloyd George referred to the earlier unsuccessful assassination attempt made on Lord French, the British Viceroy of Ireland. Speaking on the act on the statute book he said:

I should like to review shortly the present position with reference to self-government in Ireland. The first fact the House will take note of is there is a Home Rule Act on the statute book. Unless it is either postponed or repealed or altered, it comes automatically into operation when the war ceases [the war had actually ended 13 months earlier]. We may be asked, "Why not allow it to come into operation?" I am afraid that it is no answer to that question to say, because no one wants it. But there are two reasons why the act of 1914 is inapplicable. The first is that it is not workable without fundamental alterations... The second is that when it was placed on the statute book, its promoters gave an undertaking that it would not be brought into operation until an Act of Parliament had been carried dealing with the peculiar position of Ulster. That was a definite undertaken given, with the assent of the Irish nationalist representatives. It was given by Mr. Asquith. Therefore, we cannot contemplate the allowing of the act of 1914 to come into operation without changes adapted to the changed conditions of 1919 and the changes which would deal with the case of Ulster, which has been recognised by the leaders of all parties in this House.

Now, what is the problem that we have to meet? There are two basic facts which lie at the base of any structure that you are going to build up in Ireland. The first is this, that three-fourths of the population of Ireland are not merely governed without their consent but they manifest the bitterest hostility to the government. That is the fact. It is the one country in Europe, except Russia, where the classes who elsewhere are on the side of law and order are out of sympathy with the law. What makes this more serious is the fact that it is not due to material grievances. I remember when it used to be argued that if you improved the social and economic conditions, if you got rid of agrarian trouble, improved housing, if you created a peasant proprietorship and built railways, constructed harbours and did everything possible in order to make Ireland as prosperous as conditions would allow, all this objection to British rule would vanish. What has happened? Ireland has never been as prosperous as she is today.

The MP, Mr J. Jones shouted: "She has never been so national." Ignoring this comment, Lloyd George continued:

The vast majority of the cultivators of Ireland are the possessors of their own soil; houses and comfortable cottages for workingmen have been built at the expense of the British taxpayer. Men who travelled through Ireland a generation ago and revisit that country would not know it today. It is completely transformed.

The fact remains that Ireland has never been so alienated from British rule as it is today. Therefore, the grievance such as it is, is not a material one. Irishmen claim the right to control their own domestic concerns, without interference... They have fought for it for hundreds of years. They have never held it so tenaciously as they do today. Now what is the fact – it is also a fundamental one – is that there you have a considerable section of the people of Ireland who are just as opposed to Irish rule as the majority of Irishmen are to British rule. Both these facts must be taken into account. The first, perhaps, disagreeable to one body of members of the house; the second equally disagreeable, perhaps, to another body. It is not our business to seek for agreeable facts for anybody but to seek for the facts, whether they are agreeable or otherwise.

In the north east of Ireland you have a population, a fairly solid population, a homogeneous population, an alien race, alien in sympathy, alien in religion, alien in tradition, alien in outlook from the rest of the population of Ireland, and it would be an outrage upon the principle of self-government to place them under the rule of the rest of the population. In the north east of Ireland, if that were done, you would inevitably alienate the best elements from the machinery of law and order. I do not say that it would produce exactly the same results, but it would recruit exactly the same conditions which you are trying to remedy in the south and west. This point is so important, and has been challenged on such scale, and the case for it has been so little stated outside the United Kingdom, that I think it vital that I should dwell for a short time upon it. It is not because I attach less importance to it than I do to the first proposition; it is because the first proposition is accepted outside, in the dominions, in the United States of America, in European countries. The second has not been stated and it is not known.

I shall state it, not in my own words, but from two quotations from witnesses who certainly are not biased in favour of the north-eastern part of Ireland. The first is a quotation from a very remarkable letter written in June 1916 by Fr O'Flanagan, a very able Irish Catholic priest. I believe that afterwards he became Vice-President of Sinn Féin. I do not know whether he holds the position still, and no one can doubt at any rate that he is in sympathy with the nationalist claims of Ireland. This is what he says upon this particular subject.

"If we reject Home Rule rather than agree to the exclusion of the Unionist part of Ulster, what case have we to put before the world? We can point out that Ireland is an island with a definite geographical boundary. That argument might be all right if you were dealing with a number of island nationalities that had definite geographical boundaries. Appealing as we are to continental nations with shifting boundaries, that argument can have no force whatever. National and geographical boundaries scarcely ever coincide. Geography would make one nation of Spain and Portugal; history has made two of them. Geography did its best to make one nation of Norway and Sweden; history has succeeded in making two of them. Geography had scarcely anything to say upon the number of nations on the North American continent; history has done the whole thing. If a man were to try to construct a political map of Europe out of its physical map, he would find himself groping in the dark. Geography has worked hard to make one nation out of Ireland; history has worked against it. The island of Ireland and the national unit of Ireland simply do not coincide. In the last analysis, the test of nationality is the wish of the people. A man who settles in America, transfers his love and allegiance to the United States. The Unionists of Ulster have never transferred their love and allegiance to Ireland. They may be Irelanders, using a geographical term, but they are not Irishmen in the national sense. They love the hills of Antrim in the same way we love the hills of Roscommon, but the centre of their political enthusiasm is London, whereas the centre of ours is Dublin. We claim the right to decide what is our nation; we refuse them the same right. We are putting ourselves before the world in the same light as the man in the Gospel who was forgiven ten thousand talents and proceeded to trouble his neighbour for one hundred pence. After three hundred years, England has tired of compelling us to love her by force. We are anxious to start where England left off and to compel Antrim and Down to love us by force."

That is a very remarkable letter; I quote it not merely because it is a forcibly, pregnant, eloquent statement of the case, but because no man can say that it comes from the lips of a reviler of Ireland or one who has no sympathy with national or Catholic Ireland. I think that I must trouble the House with one other short quotation, because it is so much better this testimony should come from the lips of one whose right to speak on this subject cannot be challenged and whose sentiments towards Ireland cannot be disputed, even by the strongest nationalist. Now, I will give another quotation from a very able Irish priest, Professor of Theology in Maynooth College, Fr McDonald.

"Were Ireland made a republic, fully independent of Great Britain, it seems to me that she would be bound to allow Home Rule for the north-east corner on the principles underlying our claim for Home Rule in the United Kingdom, which I regard as well founded. The Protestants of Ulster differ from the majority of the race of the island, not only in religion, but in race, mentality and culture generally. They are at once homogeneous and heterogeneous, homogeneous in their districts and heterogeneous as compared with the rest of Ireland. A minority in Ireland, they are a majority in the north-east corner, and therefore, on the principles we have been advocating, are entitled to Home Rule."

These two quotations state the case in favour of the treatment of Ulster. If they unite, they must do it of their own accord. To force union is to promote disunion. There may be advantage in union. I do not deny that geographically the conditions are such as to make it desirable. There is an advantage in the mingling of races and of religions, so as to constitute a variety of ideas, so as to have a different outlook, and there is undoubtedly an advantage in having industry and agriculture working side by side in the same parliament, but that is a matter for these populations themselves. Lord Durham attempted to force Quebec and Ontario, Lower and Upper Canada into the same parliament. That plan had to be abandoned; separate parliaments had to be given them.

You only have to look at what happened in the late war to realise what would have happened if Ireland had been a separate unit. A hostile republic or even an unfriendly one might very well have been fatal to the cause of the Allies. The submarine trouble was difficult enough in all conscience. There were many moments when we were full of anxiety. Our experts were full of anxiety, not of fear, for they were men of great courage, but because they knew the difficulty. But if we had there a land over whose harbours and inlets we had no control, we might have had a situation full of peril, a situation which might very well have jeopardised the life of this country. The area of the submarine activity might have been extended beyond the limits of control. Britain and her allies might have been cut off from her dominions and the United States. We cannot run the risk of a possibility such as that, and it would be equally fatal to the interests of Ireland. Irish trade interests are intertwined with those of Great Britain. Britain is Ireland's best customer. If Great Britain, with all its infinite resources, found it difficult to govern a hostile Ireland, I cannot see how Ireland could control a hostile north east.

There would be trouble, there would be mischief, there might be bloodshed, and then the whole black chapter of misunderstanding between Great Britain and Ireland would be rewritten all over again. We must not enter upon that course, whatever the cost, and I think it is right here, in the face of the demands put forward from Ireland with apparent authority, to say that any attempt at secession will be fought with the same determination, with the same resources, with the same resolve as the northern states of America put into the fight with the southern states. It is important that it should be known, not only throughout the world, but in Ireland itself. Subject to these three conditions, we propose that self-government should be centered upon the whole of Ireland.

Our plan is based upon the recognition of these three fundamental facts – first, the importance of not severing Ireland from the United Kingdom; secondly, the opposition of nationalist Ireland to British rule; thirdly, the opposition of the population of north east Ulster to Irish rule. The first involves the recognition that Ireland must remain an integral part of the United Kingdom; the second involves the confirming of self-government of Ireland in all its domestic concerns; the third involves the setting up of two parliaments and not one in Ireland.

That this is the first proposal that we recommend to parliament and that his government had considered four proposals. Three had been abandoned; they were: excluding the whole province of Ulster from a scheme of Home Rule for the rest of Ireland; the six-county plan and county option. The British government had now decided to construct a Unionist province on a six county basis and to set up two parliaments, one for the strictly Unionist parts of north-east Ulster and the other for the remainder of the country. The two parliaments were to be linked by a Council of Ireland, to which each parliament would send 20 representatives, and which would look after matters of common concern. The British kept control of foreign affairs, the navy and army, customs and excise, income tax and trade outside of Ireland – in other words, it was mainly the provisions of Home Rule all over again.

The Irish parliament was to have control of the subjects given in the 1914 act: education, local government, land, agriculture, roads and bridges, transportation including railways and canals, old-age pensions, insurance and municipal affairs, local judiciaries, hospitals, licences, all machinery for the maintenance of law and order, housing and labour questions. The police would be a reserve service for three years, but neither the postal service nor the higher judiciary would be transferred until the two legislatures had agreed a united Ireland.

As to the finance of the scheme, the government proposed that for two years Ireland's taxes should remain as they were at that time and that £23.5 million of the total sum should go to her local services while £18 million would be for imperial contribution. At the end of two years, a joint exchequer board would settle the future financial arrangement. Each of the new governments would be given an initial grant of £1million, and would also be given the Irish land-purchase annuities as a development – a total grant of £3 million a year. The income tax, customs and excise would be collected by the imperial government, but the Irish legislators could, if they like, levy an additional income.

The Prime Minister pleaded for a fair hearing for these proposals which he said, would be embodied in a Bill at the earliest moment.

Sir Edward Carson during the debate, said:
The whole reason why the Act of Union had not succeeded was because Irishmen themselves, out of hatred for England, and for historic reasons, mainly connected with religion, had refused to take part in the government of their own country and the imperial parliament. For the previous 25 years there had not been a single

government which would not have been willing to trust men such as the late John Redmond and some of his colleagues with important positions in the Irish Executive if they had been willing to accept them. He was sure that there were a number on the opposition side of the House who imagined when the Bill was passed, there would be Utopia in Ireland, and that policemen would never be shot again, but he said that shooting had been going on as long as he could remember.

In essence Carson believed that the new legislation would not make things any better in Ireland than if it continued to be governed directly from Westminster.

Carson continued:

As a southern Irishman himself, he looked with the greatest apprehension at what would happen to the large body of loyal Unionists in the south and west, whose fate they were preparing to hand over to a parliament in Dublin. He had seen three Home Rule Bills passed in his time. Each of them was a perfect solution of the Irish question. When the first Bill was passed, it was to bring in a union of hearts, such as the world had never known before. When the second bill was proposed in 1893 by Mr Gladstone, the first perfect Home Rule Bill was denounced as one which would have brought great misery upon Ireland, and when the third Bill was brought in 1912, we were told that if the two previous ones had passed it would have been nothing but ruin and chaos in Ireland.

What the Prime Minister told us of the last Home Rule Bill, which is now an act upon the statute books, was that one of the facts that we must take into consideration was that only five years had elapsed since it was passed, and although it never attempted to be worked, there was not a single soul in Ireland who wanted it. And what was more, he told them, it could not be worked, and he is right. As to the present bill, he would give no opinion until he saw it in print. This was the first Bill which made the admission of Ulster's right to be treated as a separate unit. He believed that to be a great advance towards a settlement. There was no shutting their eyes to the fact that the north is as different to the south in its race, religion, ideas and views as it is possible to be. The war has emphasised the fact. They could find no difference between north-east Ulster and any other part of Great Britain.

We have thrived under the union; we are in sympathy with you; a part of you, we are prepared to make any sacrifice that you make, and under these circumstances, keep us with you. They never made any other demand, and he appealed to the government, as the bill is not yet brought in, to keep Ulster in that united parliament. He could not understand why they should ask them to take a parliament which they had never demanded, and which they did not want. Of course, if this parliament turned on a system of devolution, then, of course, Ulster could not object, and would not object to the same treatment that Great Britain was getting.

He concluded by saying that his action would be determined after he had taken counsel with his Ulster friends.

During the debate Arthur Henderson of Labour said:

If he could get a measure that found acceptance with the majority of the Irish people, the same beneficent results would follow as in South Africa. Labour was sending a deputation to Ireland, which would consult with the organisations there referred to by Carson and, in conference with groups all over Ireland, would endeavour to ascertain exactly what their views were before coming to a final conclusion on the proposals brought before them.

The scheme conflicted with the sincere aspirations of the majority of Irish people for self-government. These proposals could be regarded as a half-hearted and unsatisfying compromise, which went no distance to meet the claims that had been set forth over and over again in the House. The government might have devised a scheme of Dominion Home Rule minus any army and navy and given to the respective counties what was known as county option. A second course, and the one which he would have preferred, was that they might have summoned an Irish parliament under the act of 1914 and left to that parliament the working out of its own constitution. That method would not only have commended itself to Ireland but to the dominions and the United States, who were watching what the British people were going to do after talking so much about self-determination ... They had shown their mistrust of the Irish people over and over again and the evidence lately was that they were getting back to the worst form of distrust. The demand for an Irish Republic was the result of their opposition to the granting of a reasonable form of self-government. If the demand had grown, the responsibility for the increased demand rested with those who had resolutely opposed the claim of the Irish nation.

These proposals would be regarded in Ireland as a triumph for the dictatorship of the minority, and he was as much against the dictatorship of a minority in Ireland as in Russia. In the name of

Labour, he declared that he had not lost faith in the principles of self-government or self-determination, and when the time for the final test comes so far as their attitude on these proposals was concerned, the test would be made in harmony with the fundamental principles to which he had referred.

Lord Henry Cavendish Bentinck also spoke. He said:
That coercion led to crime and crime to coercion. Although Ireland was governed by a Liberal Prime Minister and a Liberal Chief Secretary. Ireland was not at that time governed on Liberal principles, but on the principles of Fitzgibbon, Earl of Clare. Fitzgibbon believed thoroughly that the majority of Irish people were all bad, but the minority were good, and that Ireland should be governed in the interest of the minority. He declared that the British government thoroughly believed in minority government and he was afraid it was minority government which had inspired the speech and proposals put forward by Lloyd George.
These proposals were inspired by thorough distrust of the majority of the Irish people. The proposal put forward was unsound and artificial. He, however, wished it well and hoped it would be accepted by the Irish people, but he felt it had very little chance. The reason they had always failed to solve the problem of Irish discontent is that they never approached the Irish problem in the spirit of the British Constitution – viz., majority rule. It was in that spirit that they had solved all their imperial problems in Canada, South Africa and Australia. Before the days of Lord Durham, there were exactly the same racial animosities in Canada as existed in Ireland. In Canada a minority, as in Ulster, made the charge of disloyalty against the majority. The Canadian problem was solved not by the establishment of two parliaments but by the creation of a Dominion Parliament.

(ii) Church of Ireland and media reaction

The above extracts from Westminster in 1919/20 were a major step in killing the Home Rule Act of 1914 and a first move towards partitioning Ireland in the interests of the minority. The reaction to these proposals and their acceptance by the Unionists is aptly taken up in an editorial in the *Church of Ireland Gazette* of 12 March 1920:
Wednesday, 10th. March 1920 was a sad day for Irish Unionists. It witnessed the acceptance by the Ulster Unionist Council of Mr Lloyd

George's Home Rule Bill. Probably the Ulster representatives will press for certain amendments in committee, but the die has been cast, and the spectre of partition has now become a thing of flesh and blood. Irish Unionists, who are also Irish churchmen, cannot but look to the future with consternation. The partition of Ireland creates a more or less homogeneous state in the north-east corner of Ireland and leaves a large and important body of Unionists under the jurisdiction of a parliament which it is proposed to be set up in Dublin. United we stand, divided we fall and the divorce of southern Unionists from northern Unionists is a calamity. Ulster had no alternative. Sir Edward Carson never wanted Home Rule, and he does not want it today, but what could he do? He was forced by circumstances and the coalition government to save what he could from the wreck of the Irish union and if in the fulfillment of his duty to Ulster he was forced to abandon the southern Unionists, who can blame him? We do not blame him and we do not blame the Ulster Unionist Council, but we would not be Unionists if we did not deplore the collapse of the union, and we would not be Irish if we did not protest against partition to the end. The Unionists of the south and west have never faltered in their loyalty to the British Empire and the British Throne. When the war clouds burst over Europe and the call to the colours went forth throughout our island, southern Unionists went to battle and sent their children to battle for the Empire's cause. They have a claim upon the Empire, and that claim is that they shall be allowed to retain their citizenship, which is their most cherished possession. Permanent partition will rob them of that possession and the present bill for the "better government of Ireland" can have no other result if it passes into law and is imposed upon our country.

Permanent partition is a thing of evil. It is repugnant to every Irishman and Irishwoman who has the good of the country at heart. When the women came to Solomon to seek his judgment as to which of them should have possession of the child, she who owned the child and loved it would rather lose it than see its body cut in two. The partition of Ireland means the doom of Ireland. Nobody who read Sir Edward Carson's speech on Wednesday, or the account of the businessmen's meeting in Belfast on the same day, can hope for a moment that Mr Lloyd George's dream of an eventual rapprochement between Ulster and southern Ireland can ever be realised. No. Ulster will govern itself sanely and well. It will flourish and prosper and its councils will work and act for the welfare of the province. And southern Ireland? Who can doubt what can happen here? Sinn Féin will either capture the southern parliament or ignore it. In either case, the result will be the same. Those who are 'out' for a republic 'free and independent' of Great Britain and the Empire will redouble their efforts to secure that end. The measure of self-government which Mr Lloyd George's Bill affords means little to them. They will continue their striving for a republic and treat all overtures of Home Rule with contempt. Can any loyal Irishman contemplate such a position of affairs with equanimity? Sinn Féin is openly hostile to Great Britain. It makes no secret of its hostility. If and when it assumes control of the destinies of southern Ireland, is it likely to transform that hostility into friendship and fall into Ulster's and the Empire's arms? Southern Unionists recognise that the vast majority of nationalist Irishmen have as little real sympathy with Sinn Féin ideals as they themselves, but Sinn Féin has the power and at present its star is in the ascendant.

The Bill is not yet law; therefore there is still a glimmer of hope that it may be defeated. The duty of every Irishman and especially of every Irish churchman is to work to its defeat and to spare no effort towards that end. The ranks of southern Unionists now will be swelled by the exclusion of Cavan, Monaghan and Donegal from "Ulster". Unionists should immediately unite and make their voices heard ... they do not want partition, permanent or otherwise. They dread an Irish Republic, because they know the leaders of Irish republicanism hate the British Empire and would fain destroy it. They want to live in peace and friendship with their fellow Irishmen and to enjoy the rights and privileges of their British citizenship, which constitutes their birthright ... Will the people of Great Britain – the people whose sons died side by side with young Irishmen in the trenches of Flanders and on the shores of Gallipoli – leave southern Ireland to its fate? We cannot believe that public opinion in Great Britain will consent to the imposition of this iniquitous Bill upon an unwilling Ireland. Ulster has refused to accept any responsibility in the matter and we agree with Ulster. The onus of decision rests on the British House of Commons and ultimately, on the British people themselves. If they persist in the partition of Ireland, they will be compelled to face the fact of an Irish, or rather a three-quarter Irish Republic.

In July of that year, another comment in the *Church of Ireland Gazette* was published. It addressed partition in a more reflective way. It took a regretful stance that partition was ever entered into, on the grounds that the church's own communion and community would be divided and not for the common good. What was said had been inferred before; however, this honest and far-reaching statement has historically been proven correct.

Not only will partition mean constant friction between "Ulster" and Ireland, but it will mean constant friction within the frontiers of Ulster itself. The proposed Ulster state has not been defined on any intelligible democratic principles. There has been no plebiscite of the province of Ulster – for obvious reasons; there has been no county plebiscites such as have been granted to the districts of Slesvig. The frontiers have been defined on the lines which politicians of one way of thinking imagine they can control and dominate in security. Within several Ulster counties, there will be powerful nationalist majorities who will permanently question the right of a parliament in Belfast to govern them and refuse to submit to an authority which has been designed to represent them. How, in the event of partition, the nationalist   majority of Derry City, with the frontier of "Ireland" on the other side of the Liberties, is to be kept in subjection, we fail to see. Partition means perpetual inflammation of the most acute kind and the existence of an Irish irredenta within "Ulster's" frontier and an "Ulster" irredenta inside Ireland's.

Under the provisions of the Treaty of Versailles, the people of Slesvig or Schleswig had a plebiscite in March 1919, which split the territory, north and south, between two countries. Southern Schleswig, where there is a sizable Danish ethnic minority, voted to remain in Germany rather than returning the territory to Denmark. Northern Schleswig, with its ethnic German minority, united with Denmark. The region was one of dispute for many decades between the old kingdoms of Denmark and Prussia.

In September 1920, there were many pertinent political questions and comments on Ireland in UK papers. The Press Association announced that "the Cabinet has decided to appoint an additional Under-Secretary for Ireland. His duty will be to deal with all problems that may arise in the six counties". It cited the *Irish Bulletin*, a news-sheet that the Dáil published periodically to counter British propaganda in Ireland. The *Bulletin* stated "that the authorities in Ireland, acting in conjunction with certain members of the British cabinet, had decided to break the republican movement in Ireland before the British parliament reassembled on 19 October". The recess period, it stated, was selected in order that during the operation of the plan, those directing it should be free from criticism and that parliament when it reassembled would be presented with the accomplished fact of a broken republican movement in Ireland and a cowed people. The *Bulletin* outlined how this was to be brought about, and added that the futility of the policy was evident to those who understood the existing situation in Ireland.

(iii) Lloyd George's speech at Caernarvon

On 9 October 1920 Lloyd George gave a very lengthy address at Caernarvon, which showed his unwillingness or inability to open direct dialogue with nationalist Ireland. He openly uttered his personal contempt for the Irish people. In so doing he used the peaceful and law-abiding conditions prevailing in Caernarvonshire to compare with, in his words, the "lawlessness in Ireland" – shooting policemen and soldiers and the burning of courthouses – an attempt to tell the Welsh people how dark life was in Ireland and that arming the security forces in Ireland was well justified. He spoke praising Arthur Griffith and in the next sentence castigating him for not condemning the atrocities in Ireland. The Prime Minister went to extraordinary lengths to tell his wonderful Welsh people of the murders of policemen, which were called "reprisals" in Ireland, while stating they were the facts:

> How are we going to improve on this condition and put things right in Ireland? Undoubtedly you must restore order there by methods very stern. You cannot permit the country to be debased into a condition of complete anarchy where a small body of assassins – a real murder gang – is dominating the country, and terrorising it and making it impossible for reasonable men to come together to consider the best way of governing their country. They are intimidating, not Unionists, not Protestants, but men of their own race, men of their own faith, who would only be too anxious to discuss the sanest and best method of restoring order and good government to their country if they are left alone. Therefore, it is essential, in the interests of Ireland, that that gang should be broken up. Unless I'm mistaken, we shall do it.

Lloyd George continued to speak at length on Gladstone's Home Rule Bills and Dominion Home Rule. He then referred to a letter written by Lord Edward Grey.

Lord Grey is opposed to full Dominion Home Rule, because he says and says rightly:

"that you cannot give to Ireland the right to organise a separate army and navy". I should have thought that was common sense, but the proposal which he put forward, and which goes very far, Mr de Valera has repudiated with indignation – I might say with insult. He will not look at it. Dominion Home Rule means that they can organise their own army and navy. As Lord Grey points out, "they can organise their own submarine bases". They have got full command of all the ports of Ireland and Lord Grey says "he could not consent to that".

But, as Mr Asquith agrees to that, I put to him a question in the House of Commons. I said: You are talking about Dominion Home Rule. The Dominions have got armies and navies of their own, their ports are entirely in their control ... You cannot have an army of five or six hundred thousand men in Ireland commanded by Mr Arthur Griffith and Mr Michael Collins, who vowed the destruction of this country, and only an army of one hundred thousand here ... They won't be so foolish as to spend money on a navy. You do not need to spend much on submarines. They are vicious little craft. They are dangerous and perilous, but they are not expensive ... Do you know that Ireland was our worry during the war? We did not tell you much about it. It was no use; it would only have encouraged the enemy... Ireland was a real peril. They were in touch with German submarines. There it stands at the gateway of Britain... I saw a map – a German map – a map circulated to show how Britain was having her fleet destroyed, and the coast of Ireland was black with British ships that were sunk in the Atlantic, in the Irish Sea, in the St George's Channel. It is girdled with British wrecks. Yes, the British seamen are there too! And we are to hand over Ireland to be made a base of the submarine fleet, and we are to trust to luck in the next war. Was there ever such lunacy proposed by anybody?"

[See appendix 1 for full Lloyd George speech]

Asquith responded to Lloyd George's Caernarvon speech, declaring that the Coalition Government was bereft of policy on Ireland:

Ireland represents today the one issue of supreme importance, involving both the safety of the Empire and the honour and good name of Great Britain. The only Irish policy which the Prime Minister has to offer is a repudiation, root and branch, of Dominion Home Rule, and a condonation (for it will be universally understood) of the hellish policy of reprisals. The attempt to answer murder by murder and outrage by terrorism is not government but anarchy.

Arthur Griffith on behalf of the Irish people replied to Lloyd George:
The English Premier is a master at misrepresentation, but he will not succeed by distortion and falsehood in obscuring the issues at stake – issues that have been defined in his own words. "The rights of nations, however small, are as sacred as the rights of the biggest Empires." The issue is: Is Ireland's claim to national independence right or wrong? If it be right, the English government has no authority in Ireland. If it be wrong, let England try and disprove it, not by murdering Irish civilians, sacking Irish towns, burning Irish homesteads and factories, imprisoning Irish citizens, blocking Irish ports, and torturing Irish captives, but by argument before the great civilised world. In December 1918, the electors of Ireland, peacefully and constitutionally, in strict accordance with the principle of self-determination laid down by the United States, explicitly accepted by the English Premier on behalf of England, voted for their country an independent status, by a majority twice as great as that in virtue of which Mr Lloyd George holds office as Premier of England.

The reply of the English government to the lawful and peaceful expression of a nation's will, has been: Since New Year's Day 1919, 38,720 armed raids on private houses and Irish citizens; 4,982 arrests and imprisonments; 1,604 armed assaults; 102 sackings and shooting up of towns, and 77 murders of unarmed inoffensive civilians, including children from 10-15 years old. For these outrages upon civilisation and the consequences that have followed, the government of England is solely responsible.

Griffith referred to a speech in the English House of Commons in regard to Russia when the British Prime Minister said: "You must set up a government which the peoples want; otherwise it would be an outrage upon the principles for which we fought in the war."

The people of Ireland showed by the ballot the form of government they wanted, and the Prime Minister of England is now engaged, in his own words, perpetrating an outrage upon the principles for which the war was fought. This day 29 years ago, I followed the coffin of Charles Stewart Parnell to its tomb. Callous and short-sighted English politicians thought that on that day that it was the Irish nation they had struck dead. They find today the Irish nation throbbing with tenfold increase of life, and they face the apparition with disgusting calumny, in the stupid belief that by slaying the Irish leaders of today they can slay the indestructible Irish nation. What can be the estimate of the intelligence and courage of the English people possessed by a Prime Minister who seeks to terrify them with the grotesque fable that a free Ireland, with a population of one of England's 10, would raise up an army to destroy England?

If there be any reason left in the English people, and real desire for peace with honour and security, not such malignant absurdities, but proposals such as those made by Brig.-Gen. Cockerhill MP, would be their guide out of the Serbonian bog into which their government has led them.

On the following weekend an article by Arthur Griffith was issued in the *Sunday Times*:

I would like to say to the English people: For hundreds of years a government, to use Mr Lloyd George's words, has been striving to choke the voice of the Irish nation in its own blood. But you will never succeed in doing that. This policy in Ireland continually acts upon yourselves. You have made a country which is your neighbour, and might be your friend, you have made that country by your policy an enemy. That country must by the very nature of the case continue to be your enemy while you continue that policy, because that policy is directed against its life, and it must fight for its life. Abandon that policy freely, admit that Ireland has a right to choose her own government, and Ireland ceases to be your enemy. Some of your politicians refer to Ireland as an enemy on your flank. When you deal with Ireland as nation with nation, there will no longer be an enemy on your flank. She will be a country on your side whose interest and will, it will be, to live in peace and amity with you. As to the temporary shifts and expedients you are making in Ireland, by changing at intervals the personnel of your representatives here at Dublin Castle, these mean nothing. With Dublin Castle plus ça change, plus c'est la même chose.

General Cockerill's proposals to which Arthur Griffith referred, were "that the future relationship of Ireland to Britain and the Empire was a matter for negotiation under conditions that could not wound the susceptibilities of the majority of the Irish people. Griffith commented "Of the ordinary kind of negotiations Ireland has had more than enough, and he puts forward as his plan the normal means of negotiating a convention between nations at peace, and stipulates that the procedure should be that of an international conference. He is represented as being prepared to recognise, for the purpose of this international conference which he proposes, the government of the Irish Republic. His scheme provides for an equal number of fully accredited plenipotentiaries, and he lays down that once the provisions of the new constitution have been agreed upon, they should be submitted for final acceptance or rejection, but not amendment, to the parliaments of the contracting peoples."

Brig.-Gen. Cockerhill was the Unionist MP for Reigate and had spent almost 30 years on active military service. He was a native of Newquay, Cornwall and acted as British technical delegate to the Hague Conference in 1907.

Lloyd George in his Caernarvon speech caused further aggravation when he referred to Sir Horace Plunkett, Liberal Unionist and father of the Irish Co-Operative Movement, by asserting that "he did not represent anybody, and could not even speak for his creameries (of which 25 had been burned down already). He said that Plunkett had his views, but they were his own, and that he represented no party except a very small handful of very devoted admirers." Sir Horace Plunkett issued the following statement to the *Freeman's Journal* in response to the Prime Minister's tirade:

The prose poem with which Mr Lloyd George has delighted every enemy of Ireland is a poor thing compared with the 'Hymn of Hate', but it is, at any rate, according to plan. The Prime Minister says I don't represent the creameries. If there is anything in Ireland I do represent – and I say this not without a little personal pride which I hope he will forgive – it is these particular victims of the reprisal policy, which the champion, in other days, of the Boer farmers has blessed. I trust the Co-operative Union, with whom in this matter British Labour will be in entire accord, will lose no time in calling a halt to this part of the punitive expedition's procedure. For, after all, the organisation of food production in Ireland cannot be destroyed without injury to the British as well as the Irish people.

Press comments made in British newspapers at that time outwardly condemned their own government's Irish policy and that of the Prime

Minister himself. General Sir F. Maurice in the *Daily News* said:
"The creation of this new force is producing a peculiarly revolting form of guerrilla warfare, in which the chief sufferers are women and children. This must be stopped at once. The way to stop it is to disband the 'Black and Tans', who ought never have been created. The people to blame are those who created such a force and gave it such powers."

The *New Statesman* said:

For all the outrages... which are part and parcel of the policy of reprisals, the guilt lies directly at the door of the Prime Minister himself. He can put an end to it tomorrow if he chooses, and his guilt is incalculably deeper in that his refusal to end it is a matter not of principle but of personal considerations. We are earning a depth of hatred which a generation will not wipe out – and which in truth we do not deserve. For there is no question but that the country is overwhelmingly against the Irish policy of the government. It may not be sure what it wants, but it knows very clearly that it cannot and will not approve of any attempt to rule Ireland by Balbriggan methods. *

The *Daily News* commented:

The suspicion is rapidly growing in this country and abroad, as well as in Ireland, that British authority is secretly conniving at the barbarous reprisals now being systematically and openly carried out... It is a dangerous suspicion. If it is not killed by prompt action, it will foul the name of Britain in the world's regard as the honour of Germany was dragged in the dirt at the beginning of the war through the atrocities of her soldiers in Belgium. What will perhaps appeal with stronger force to the government is the serious possibility that unless they control the soldiers and police in Ireland, the soldiers and police will soon control them. We do not care to contemplate the full consequences of any further loosening of the reins of control. Ireland would become bedlam, but that might not be the limit of the calamity.

An editorial in the *Manchester Guardian* stated:

The Castle authorities profess to make inquiries into each alleged outrage. But nothing happens. Nothing is published. Nobody is punished; nobody, so far as appears, is even reprimanded. And so the black game of reprisals goes on, and so the Irish administration – the representatives and agents of the government of this great country and its mighty dependencies – day by day covers itself and us with great discredit. Of course there has been provocation – terrible provocation. But reprisal in

*(This refers to the burning of Balbriggan, Co. Dublin by the Black and Tans.)

kind is not a tolerable form of action on the part of any government calling itself civilised.

A correspondent called Londoner, writing in the *Evening Standard*, said:

I find a curious contrast between the calmness with which events in Ireland are reported in the papers and the extreme uneasiness with which the constant alteration of outrage and reprisal inspires some of our more thinking public men. I am not referring to ministers but to those men of both political parties who have been distinguished by their efforts to secure an Irish settlement. They are frankly horrified by the whole business of reprisals. The present policy of drift is certainly not producing encouraging results.

The London Times of 11 October had this point to make:

We know also that influences to which the Prime Minister and some of his colleagues were susceptible would seek to impede peace in Ireland. At Llandudno, the Prime Minister sought to ridicule the press that he is in the pocket of Sir Edward Carson. We have never charged him with being in any man's pocket, but we now say, without fear of truthful contradiction, that he is the self-constituted prisoner of the forces associated with the name of Sir Edward Carson, not because he admires or believes in the ideas they represent but because he is persuaded that were he to flout them they would expel him from office.

Most Rev. J. A. F. Gregg DD, at his enthronement as Church of Ireland Archbishop of Dublin, at that time, declared:

The present situation is a moral outrage and the policy of repression can never be the last word of British statesmanship in Ireland. Our race pleads for mediation, conference and peacemaking as a solution to the present impasse. The church can never allow itself to be a stranger in Ireland. It is not required to ally itself with any government or party in the land, and must refuse to be a ruler or divider. The church must be aloof from the political arena, and must stand before all for righteousness and peace. The unhappy condition of Ireland must be brought to an end by the political government, and by all patriotic Irishmen; the call for rebellion must cease if repression ceases. The call today is for an amalgamation of politics.

There is nothing impious in pulling down a church that is no longer required.

CHAPTER 8

LOCAL ELECTIONS AND
THE DÁIL COURTS

(i) Popular support

The 1918 general election to Westminster has been regarded by many
historians as Ireland's defining act in establishing self-determination. Ireland
had to fill 105 seats from 103 constituencies, which Sinn Féin would contest
on its Election Manifesto of October 1918. It would act:

by withdrawing the Irish representation from the British Parliament
and by denying the right and opposing the will of the British
Government to legislate for Ireland;

by the establishment of a constituent assembly, comprised of persons
chosen by Irish constituencies as the supreme national authority to
speak and act in the name of the Irish people and to develop Ireland's
social, political and industrial life for the welfare of the whole people
of Ireland;

by appealing to the Peace Conference for the establishment of Ireland
as an independent nation;

Sinn Féin, it is set forth, stands less for a political party than for the
nation; it stands by the proclamation of the Provisional Government of
Easter 1916, reasserting the inalienable right of the Irish nation to
sovereign independence; reaffirming the determination of the Irish
people to achieve it and guaranteeing within the independent nation
equal rights and equal opportunities to all its citizens;

Sinn Féin will oppose at the polls every individual candidate who does
not accept this principle;

Sinn Féin goes to the polls handicapped by all the arts and
contrivances that a powerful unscrupulous enemy can use against us;

Conscious of the power of Sinn Féin to secure the freedom of Ireland,
the British Government would destroy it;

Sinn Féin, however, goes to the polls confident that the people of this
ancient nation will be true to the old cause.

Sinn Féin had grown in strength throughout Co. Cavan, which was evident when Arthur Griffith's and Peter Paul Galligan's nomination papers were presented, in their respective electoral areas, to contest the 1918 general election.

According to the *Anglo Celt:*

At the Courthouse in Cootehill, Mr. Travers R.Blackley, J.P., Sub-Sheriff sat as Returning Officer to receive nominations for the East Cavan Constituency.

Rev. P O' Connell, PP Cootehill was accompanied by Mr. E. J. Duffy solr. Kingscourt (election agent) and Mr. H. Fitzsimons, Virginia (director of elections) and handed in the nomination papers for Mr. Arthur Griffith, Sinn Féin, who was the only candidate nominated. Arthur Griffith was proposed by Fr. O'Connell and seconded by John Lennon; the other assenting electors were Peter Reilly, John McCaul, Thomas Shields, Bernard Boyle, and Patrick Woods, all Cootehill. Twenty-six nominating papers were handed in. At 2p.m. the Returning Officer declared Mr. Griffith elected for East-Cavan, retaining the seat he had won in the by-election five months earlier.

Griffith was also nominated to contest the Tyrone West seat for Sinn Féin, which was contested and which he won by defeating the unionist candidate William Millar.

At the Co. Council Chambers, Cavan Courthouse, Mr. T.C. Burrows DL, Crossdoney, High Sheriff with Mr. W. H. Halpin, Solr, received nominations for the Parliamentary Constituency of West Cavan. Mr G.V. Maloney election agent and Mr. Paul McShane represented Sinn Féin. The only papers handed in were on behalf of Mr. Paul Galligan, and at 2p.m. Mr. Burrows from the balcony of the courthouse declared Mr. Galligan returned unopposed. Mr Maloney proposed a vote of thanks and seconded by Paul McShane to the High Sheriff for the courtesy displayed in connection with the nomination. Mr. Burrows acknowledged. The crowd present sang 'The Soldier's Song'.

The paper accepted in nominating Mr Galligan was proposed by Mr Paul McShane, Cornafaen and seconded by Thomas Smith Co C Pottle, Cavan. Assenting electors were P. J. Bartley Mountnugent, H. J. O'Reilly Scrabby (Gowna), T. O'Reilly DC and John Drum, Ballyconnell, Michael Reilly, Lahard, Peter Corr, Legaginny, Patrick Reilly, Atbara, Cavan and Owen McLaughlin DC, Belturbet.

In total 35 nomination papers were handed in.

From the nomination papers handed in for both candidates in Co. Cavan, it was apparent that some 500 people in the county were strategically placed to influence the electorate to vote for Sinn Féin. Obviously there was no contest.

(ii) Local elections 1919

The next electoral contest for Sinn Féin after the 1918 general election was the local elections of 1919. By regulation of the Local Government Board, these elections were due to be contested throughout Ireland in June 1919. Sinn Féin was well ready to contest every electoral division. Cavan Co. Council appointed the then Co. Secretary, Mr William Finlay, as returning officer for the local elections which were fixed to take place on 4 June. Thomas O'Reilly was the sitting councillor for the district of Ballyconnell and he was proposed by John Drum and seconded by Thomas Dolphin to contest the seat. His nomination was handed in to the Returning Officer on 6 May. As this would appear to have been within the last days for nominations and as there were no other candidates nominated for Ballyconnell, Thomas O'Reilly, like 13 other unopposed Sinn Féin candidates in the county, was in a position to be declared elected.

Two days after receiving these nominations, Cavan Co. Council, in accordance with instructions from the Local Government Board, passed a motion to nullify the local elections as called. This led to a court application by Sinn Féin before the Master of the Rolls, Chancery Division, Dublin which was heard on 23 May. This was perhaps brought as a test case to embarrass the establishment. This action had to be obviously taken by Sinn Féin as an extension of its campaign of civil disobedience by challenging the British establishment in the very courts which Sinn Féin by its own policies was attempting to bring down.

Aidan McCabe, a solicitor based in Cavan, instructed King's Counsel on behalf of the plaintiffs, Thomas O'Reilly, John Drum and Thomas Dolphin. They applied for an interlocutory injunction, claiming "a declaration that the resolution of Cavan Co. Council passed at a meeting on 8 May 1919 whereby it was resolved that no further steps be taken in the conduct of the local elections is invalid and of no effect and not binding on the Returning Officer appointed by said Council at a meeting on 6th. February 1919 and that the said Returning Officer is not precluded thereby from proceeding with the election of County Councillors in accordance with the requirements of the statutes". They also applied for an injunction "restraining the defendant from acting on the resolution of 8 May and for an order that he be directed to proceed with the election already entered on by him and for a declaration that the plaintiff, Thomas O'Reilly is entitled to be declared elected on June 4, 1919 as County Councillor for the said Ballyconnell electoral division." (See Appendix 2 for hearing record)

This case was an attack to discredit local government in Ireland which in the view of Arthur Griffith was rife with political cronyism and nepotism. Local government, as we know it today, was established in Ireland in 1898 and such cancellations of local elections was an attempt to survive the obvious political changes which Sinn Féin was espousing and leading. The local elections went ahead in Co. Antrim.

Taking on the establishment in a case like this was courageous. However, Sinn Féin had no option but to follow on its 1918 general election success. Everything was going right for Sinn Féin to contest each local government division on the traditional "first-past-the-post" basis. As things were, it was likely that in the vast majority of local government divisions, there would be an assured victory for Sinn Féin. A bill was before parliament to change the voting system to proportional representation in Ireland, and so this led to the cancellation of the election. While the court action against the returning officer failed, it was in essence won on the issue of costs being reserved. It showed up uncertainties within the establishment on many fronts. It was not easy to take on the establishment. The local elections were eventually held in 1920. Proportional Representation was introduced purely in the interests of the Unionists attaining some representation. Due to public apathy, Sinn Féin and Labour claimed many uncontested seats.

(iii) The Dáil Courts

Sinn Féin and the fledgling first Dáil were forced to make the Parish Arbitation courts public in June 1920. Dáil Eireann had to place the courts under its public control due to much land agitation throughout Co. Mayo with many disputes between farmers and cattle drovers (dealers). Land Commissioners appointed by Sinn Féin succeeded in calming down this agitation and in particular surrounding the Fountain Hill Farm, a 250 acre estate at Kilmaine, south Mayo which was rented by Hyland and Murphy from the Magdalene Asylum, Galway. Nine adjoining farmers occupied the land and wanted legal access to extend their holdings and to sustain a living.

The Sinn Féin Land Arbitration Court ruled on the matter in the interests of justice. The farmers, having lost the case, refused to accept the court's decision and were detained on an island on Lough Corrib. This case was dealt with in Ballinrobe in May 1920. This land agitation in the west would continue to be a matter of some division within the Sinn Féin movement.

Austin Stack as Minister for Home Affairs directed this act of the new Dáil and he based the rules and costs on the model of the Arbitration Courts in Co. Clare and similar courts in Co. Cavan. The legal profession undertook their briefs for both plaintiffs and defendants in the Dáil Courts, before lay judges or arbitrators who had heretofore sat in the Parish Courts.

A Colonel Ashley put a very interesting question on the "Sinn Féin Courts" to the Attorney General at Westminster in early June 1920 when he raised the issue of legal representations in the courts. Ashley asked "what could happen to those barristers and solicitors who took part in 'illegal' proceedings." The Attorney General replied: "That is a matter in the case of barristers for the King's Inn and in the case of solicitors for the Incorporated Law Society". To which Colonel Ashley responded: "Am I to understand that the Crown has no power to deal with barristers or solicitors who have taken part in treasonable and illegal proceedings?" There was no reply.

This unanswered question in the British parliament was indicative of Arthur Griffith's and Sinn Féin's policy of civil disobedience working in destabilising the British administration in Ireland.

These courts, when disrupted by the British military or the police, were often quoted as being recognised by the Lord Chancellor. For example, a solicitor from Enniskillen who came to Co. Cavan to represent a client at Dowra court, said: "he was pleased to be present" and referred to the Lord Chancellor's recognition of the proceedings.

Each arbitrator appointed to sit in a Parish or District Court had to be a member of Sinn Féin by firstly signing a formal declaration or oath of allegiance:

> I_____ do solemnly swear (or affirm) that I do not, and shall not, yield a voluntary support to any pretended government, authority or power within Ireland, hostile or inimical thereto, and I do further swear (or affirm) that to the best of my knowledge and ability that, I will support and defend the Irish Republic and the government of the Irish Republic, which is Dáil Éireann, against all enemies, foreign and domestic; that I will bear true faith and allegiance to the

same, and that I take this obligation freely without any mental reservations or purpose of evasion.

So help me God.

The first Dáil Courts reported openly in the *Anglo-Celt* (7 July 1920) were from Ballyconnell which sat in the Town Hall or Market House before Tom O'Reilly, Chairman, John Drum, Patrick McGinn, and Frank Dolphin as the court secretary, representing the Catholic parish of Kildallan and the Church of Ireland parish of Tomregan. It was said during the proceedings that a member of the Volunteers served a summons. While the proceedings appeared to be petty in nature, they showed some interesting aspects of community life and above all the respect which the court had within the parish.

The court list in Ballyconnell included:
Ned Farmer had lent his spade and wanted it back or 10/- in lieu.
The second case brought, was by Patrick Donohoe, Tailor, Main St, who wanted his house repaired and put in proper condition, against his landlord, J.F. O'Kane.
The third case was brought by Joseph Armstrong, general merchant, who was claiming £1 from Sammy Bradshaw for taking his hay.

All the cases were referred to the next month's court for interim consideration and resulted in Ned Farmer getting his spade back, J.F. O'Kane being ordered to repair Donohoe's house forthwith, and O'Kane told to bear two-thirds of the cost. (The impartiality of the Arbitration or Dáil Courts has to be noted here, as in this instance, O'Kane was a founding member of the Volunteers in Ballyconnell in 1914.) The damage to the roof of Donohoe's house was the result of an earlier IRA attack on the adjoining RIC barracks.

The case of Armstrong v Bradshaw was interesting as this brought before the court both Catholic and Protestant. Armstrong had purchased meadow from the trustees of the Methodist Church body, which was close to Bradshaw's house. Aaron Kells, the caretaker of the Methodist Church, let the grass/meadow without authority to Bradshaw and so the dispute arose. Representatives of the Methodist trustees were requested to send a report to the court, which they did, confirming Armstrong as being the rightful owner of the meadow. The court decreed accordingly for Armstrong and ordered the caretaker to refund. Contrary to some thinking, this showed the respect and trust that members of the Protestant community had in having matters dealt with through the Dáil Courts.

The Dáil Court sat in Ballyconnell a week later when it dealt with a case brought by Owen Maguire, Callaghs. He sued Andrew Huggins (a Protestant, who was represented) also of Callaghs, for damages for allowing the soil of the mountain, which he held a title to graze, to be dug and cut away. Maguire deposed that he had rightful title, and Huggins who was baliff and agent "brought in the country" to cut it out. The dispute was about who could cut turf and what depth of bog had to be left. The court ordered that Huggins be notified by the clerk of the court and in future persons cutting turf be informed by him to leave one foot of bog over gravel and failing this a heavy fine would be inflicted and persons transgressing would be precluded in future from cutting turf there. On a complaint, the arbitrators would inspect the place. Maguire's claim for damages was not allowed.

Another case was brought by a farmer who applied for possession of a house against a labourer whom he alleged had agreed to work for 2/6 per day and had been given ground for crop but who went to work elsewhere. A Volunteer served the summons, but the defendant did not appear. The court decided that possession should be given up in 14 days, that eight weeks' rent be paid for the house, and that two independent men value the crop, complainant to pay the compensation to the defendant. The defendant turned up an hour late and gave notice of appeal.

The next Dáil Court proceedings reported in the *Anglo-Celt* were from the Town Hall in Cavan where on the 10 July many cases were heard and disposed off with all plaintiffs and defendants named. The arbitrators were E. Brady UC, Cavan, Charles Reilly DC, Drumberrish and B. Smith jnr, Alacken, and the legal representatives present were solicitors M.Tierney and Aidan McCabe. There was a large attendance of the general public who followed the proceedings with interest. At the same time the bi-monthly Petty Sessions were to be held in the Court House, Cavan. T. McGuinness JP was the only magistrate in attendance and he adjourned the cases listed for hearing.

As these reported proceedings happened within days of the establishing of the Dáil Courts, the old Parish or Arbitration Courts had put down solid roots throughout Co. Cavan. This was further evidenced when a District Appeal Court, under Dáil Eireann, sat in Templeport in August with Peter Paul Galligan TD as chairman and J. Kellegher and John "The Leaguer" O'Reilly appeal judges. District Appeal Courts were normally held every quarter.

In the first case before this Appeals Court, a defendant asked for an adjournment as his solicitor was grouse shooting that day. Paul Galligan TD in response said: "That means a solicitor can hold up this court. We are here to do our business, and are not like the RMs who are paid nice salaries." The plaintiff objected to the adjournment, which was granted. The defendant had to pay the plaintiff her costs for the day.

This court also had a protracted land dispute before it, a case that was heard several times before the British courts, which was overturned on the presentation of new evidence. The plaintiff was fined £2. In another case, a defendant had a lay advocate to speak for him in a case concerning the death of a stirk. Such lay advocacy opened the courts to all, regardless of their means.

The Dáil Courts, were established and held within every parish in Co. Cavan. In neighbouring Co. Monaghan, it was not until August 1920 that a convention was called to appoint arbitrators to the Dáil Courts, parish and district, in Monaghan town for North Monaghan. A second convention was held in Castleblayney to select arbitrators for South Monaghan. Eoin O'Duffy acted as secretary to both conventions on the direction of the Dáil Minister for Home Affairs. He outlined court procedure saying: "It had decreed that the judges should be elected by the people and not on the Dublin Castle system. Popular elections were not possible at present and the conventions were being called to temporarily select arbitrators. In December a ballot would be held to elect judges. Judgements should be based on absolute justice irrespective of creed, class or politics. The courts had already achieved excellent results elsewhere, particularly in connection with land disputes. The British government had hoped that the land crisis would destroy the Sinn Féin movement and create a social revolution."

Throughout the country the Dáil courts were in full swing from July 1920. A report from Co. Mayo is indicative of the respect which the Dáil courts were achieving among the people and the legal profession by their rulings. The British Courts were practically abandoned.

At Mayo Assizes, before Mr Justice Pim, of the 130 jurors summoned only 19 attended; The absentees were fined £2 each. Most cases had to be adjourned because of the non-attendance of jurors. Also in Mayo, Lord Justice Rowan had practically nothing to do at the Record Court as over 80 of the 99 appeal cases before him were withdrawn. This was because on the previous day a Dáil Court decided almost all of the appeals listed for hearing at the Assizes. Barristers and solicitors attended the Dáil Courts.

At a Dáil Court in Listowel, parties were fined for poisoning the River Feale and ex-soldiers were ordered to leave the country for a certain period for window breaking. A similar order was made against persons for taking porter from the railway.

In Co. Kildare several courts were held. A man pleaded guilty to taking oats. Men who pleaded guilty to cutting up a road to stop timber haulage were fined 5/- each. A young man who made use of statements reflecting on Volunteer officers was fined £1. A labourer who was found guilty of burglary was ordered to leave the district.

In Co. Longford, a clergyman was granted an injunction by district arbitrators, restraining certain parties from trespassing on his turbary.

It was also reported that Volunteer Courts, which dealt with criminal cases, were being held in various parts of the country. In the majority of these criminal cases, the Volunteers so appointed investigated the criminal matters and issued summary justice on the spot by, in most cases, ordering the culprits to leave the district or the country. The *Impatial Reporter,* reported on "The first of the Dáil Éireann Crimes Courts held at Cootehall, Co. Roscommon where men were charged with the robbery of various sums of money from Cootehall and Knockvicar Post Office." The president of the court said that the prisoners would remain in custody until the rest of the money was restored. The same issue also reported on the recovery of valuable articles, stolen from the home of Capt. De Stackpole at Longwood, Co. Meath. The Volunteers had arrested a man who indicated the hiding place of the articles. "The liberal reward offered was refused." The Sinn Féin courts were obviously impressing some of the Unionists in the six counties.

Not all members of the legal profession were in favour of the Dáil Courts. Mr Serjeant Sullivan, known as A. M. Sullivan, Serjeant-at-law, who was leading counsel for the defence in Sir Roger Casement's trial in 1916, was a prominent member of the legal profession who was not of like mind to many in his profession regarding the Dáil Courts. He wrote a lengthy letter to *The Times* of London from Altona House, Dublin, saying among other things:

> No counsel will soil himself by lending the sanction of his participation to the performances of a body which repudiates and denounces those principles of justice which constitute his creed. The slaves who are bullied into submitting to the Sinn Féin Courts are obliged to subscribe to the lie that the Irish Courts, of which every member of the Bar is an officer, are enemy organisations for the oppression of Ireland. No man, unless afflicted with the mind of a prostitute, could believe in this declaration and still desire to be a member of the Irish Bar. It is quite clear that no man of honour can be an officer of both systems. It is not consistent with the duty of a barrister that he should assist in depriving the Irish people of the protection of their own public courts.

The institution of these sham tribunals is an evasion of the liberty that it is the privilege of the Irish Bar to protect. Ireland may well be proud that, in spite of the murder society, the police have stood true to her. To the criminal mind that murders policemen, the destruction of the administration of justice and of the rule of public law is naturally desirable. Murder and justice cannot co-exist. An attempt is therefore made to terrorise litigants into deserting the Irish Courts. Ireland looks in vain for the service of her sons to rescue her from degradation. They shrink before the error and whine about the defects of British government. The Downing St. poltroons do nothing. Of this growth of savagery and decay of civilisation the Irish Bar may be the victim but it must not be the slave.

It was quite obvious that the Dáil Courts were taking over from the British court system in Ireland. The legal profession followed by representing their clients not just in law, but with common sense, and for their own "bread and butter". Those like Serjeant Sullivan who despised the potential and wishes of a newly emerging state and its chosen courts' system were soon to be a minority. They obviously were thinking the Dáil Courts were merely "bog law", while they attempted to cling onto the coat tails of a fading aristocracy embedded in the past. As regards his comment "no counsel will soil himself", the fact is, if counsel did not, he would have a very weak practice before long.

A. M. Sullivan was a well-known lawyer and served mostly as a KC on the Munster Circuit. A moderate nationalist and supporter of the IPP, he abhorred Sinn Féin and republicanism and was often a prominent prosecutor on behalf of the Crown during the war of independence. He relocated to England in 1921 and established a career at the English Bar.

When the Parish Arbitration Courts were set up from 1917, it was acceptable for legal representatives or lay advocates to quote Brehon Law, Canon Law or American law, but any mention of the Acts of the Realm were seriously frowned upon unless absolutely necessary. When the Parish Arbitration Courts were set up, their function was political and in the interests of good conduct within their respective communities. While there are few records of these earlier courts, many families, and in particular Protestant families approached them to deal with entailed wills. As mentioned earlier, entailed wills were complex in that the immediate occupier could not dispose of the property, but had to carry full responsibility for its maintenance. This was an Anglo-Protestant method of retaining and ensuring property ownership within the family.

Ellie Drum, daughter of John Drum, recalled an "in camera" function of a Sinn Féin Court in the Ballyconnell area in relation to a substantial Protestant family farm which had been divided between the only two sons in the family. A condition of this division was that the lands and farmsteads were laid out so that both families had to cross each other's front streets daily to get to their lands and outhouses. This was done to ensure that they could never fall out, as they had to meet and greet each other daily. The practicalities of farming or of the brothers and their spouses agreeing on all things were not considered. The lands could not be sold without the other party's consent. Therein lay the problem. One son did not have a male heir to inherit. He wanted to sell his farm to provide a dowry for his daughters. His brother could not afford to buy the property. The Sinn Féin arbitrators were approached for consideration and the matter was settled.

Another example was a Protestant business family where the property was entailed for generations. The father, on making his will, did not accept the advice of his witness John Drum, a court arbitrator, who was a close neighbour and friend. The then owner did not want to leave his property directly to his eldest son, as he was a bit wild, and so willed it to his son's heir or grandson, who was not yet born. The son at this point was not even married. However, the son married and in a few short years he died suddenly without an heir. The question was who would inherit. The matter went to the High Court in Dublin and the property, on the issue of blood-line, went to the younger brother who was studying theology at Trinity College and nearing ordination. The widow of the deceased had no rights and could not claim on the estate. Fifty years later and with still no issue, the property, the business and the name ceased.

Sinn Féin arbitrators undertook other related issues by advising people and families to make wills, to establish rightful ownership to owned or leased titles in order to avoid litigation in later years.

The original proposal in the formation of the Parish Courts was that one of the arbitrators could be the parish priest or curate, which was not evident in Co. Cavan. The priests of Kilmore were probably banned from partaking in these Courts on the instructions of their bishop. The clergy's involvement in the parish or Dáil Éireann Courts was evident in Co. Mayo when the parish priest of Shrule, Fr Lydon, presided at a Sinn Féin conference in Ballinrobe to elect justices to preside at the courts, which resulted in two curates, a Fr Carney and a Fr Burke being elected to sit as arbitrators.

A further newspaper report from 1920 showed that: "North Fermanagh

Appeals court sat in a well known mansion near Belleek. The five arbitrators were sworn in publicly with much ceremony, and included two well-known people, as well as a parish priest. Four solicitors, a barrister, seven clergymen and a great number of litigants and the general public attended the court. Volunteers were on guard inside and outside. Two of the appeal cases listed involved the ownership of large farms. In the Beleek area of Fermanagh every Catholic magistrate has now resigned his Commission of the Peace. Sinn Féin Arbritration Courts were also held at Derrylin and Gortaree."

In the summer of 1920, a letter of resignation from West Cavan to the Lord Chancellor said:

> We cannot consistently continue to administer the laws of a
> Government which instead of meeting the just aspirations of our
> people in their demand for independence seems bent on the destruction
> of their lives, liberties, and property, as is evidenced in the latest
> Draconian measures just enacted. The insult offered and outrage
> committed on our compatriot and distinguished prelate ---- Archbishop
> Mannix---- have irrevocably fixed our determination to do what we
> now do ---- resign our Commissioners of the Peace.
> Signed; Patrick Fay; Edward O'Reilly; John McGovern; Terence
> Hamilton; Philip Gilroy; P.A.McCorry V.S.; Thomas McNamara.

(iv) Courts disrupted

During the summer and autumn of 1920, the Dáil Courts were operating throughout Co. Cavan and adjoining counties, as was the wish of the people. However, in the developing political and military climate, it was likely that the RIC and military would disrupt these proceedings from time to time, as they were undermining the British Courts system. A Sinn Féin Court to be held at Carrickallen (Mountain Lodge) was stopped by soldiers one morning as several lorries of military and a few police arrived at the hall beside Carrickallen Chapel and held up and searched all passers-by. A detachment stopped at George McCabe's public house and arrested J.J. Hennessy, registrar of the court and took his papers. The solicitors, Messrs T. G. Duffy, Kingscourt; A. McBreen, Bailieborough and J. C. McKenna, Mullagh were stopped and asked for their papers. Duffy on behalf of the solicitors objected. The incident was reported as follows:

Mr. Duffy said:

The Incorporated Law Society, of which the Lord Chancellor is the head, had no objection to solicitors attending the Sinn Féin Courts. Mr. Duffy's papers were taken from him, an officer remarking that anything Mr. Duffy had to say would have no effect there. The solicitors said, D.I. Hunt was very courteous. A press reporter who did not produce a letter of authority from his editor was arrested and was taken away along with Mr. Hennessy by the military. While these things were happening at McCabe's, the military at the Hall broke down the door with a hatchet and searched the place, but found nothing... The military waited a considerable time at the public house, expecting the judge of the Court to arrive, and they questioned the bystanders as to his name...

In Arva, as the Dáil Court was about to commence, a lorry of British military arrived at the Temperance Hall. Two men who were at the door were covered with rifles and ordered back. All those present were ordered to put their hands up and a military sergeant searched everyone. The officer in charge then examined each one as to his business and told them the proceedings were illegal. A report on the incident continued:

He asked for the president and Mr. William O'Donnell came forward.
Officer - What is your business?
Mr. O'Donnell - We are holding an Arbitration Court.
Officer - Are you aware that these Courts are illegal.
Mr. O'Donnell - It is the wishes of the people.
Mr. O'Donnell was placed under arrest and later released. The officer said, anyone taking part in future would be liable to a month's imprisonment.
The officer was courteous.

The Sinn Féin Quarter Sessions (District Appeal Court) were under way in the Meath Council Assembly Room, Navan, before well-known men acting as adjudicators before six solicitors present, to hear 29 cases with 100 members of the public present.

As the second case was opening a party of South Wales Borderers, accompanied by RIC men, marched to the council assembly room and guarded all the exits. Two military officers, with a head constable of police and a party of military, entered the court. The head constable asked was the court proceeding and on being told that it was, he asked the adjudicators who they were. The court president replied that they were the elected representatives of the people. The head constable answered that they had no right to hold a court, and that he had come there to disperse it and seize all documents in connection with it. The president replied that under the circumstances, force would be worse than useless.

The military then searched the adjudicators, solicitors and litigants, taking all the names of those present. The entry sheet was taken, as were also the solicitors' briefs and the reporters' copy, the officer intimating that the copy would be restored as soon as they were examined by headquarters. The names of the two journalists in court were taken.

Similar disruptive measures were taken by the authorities against early sittings of a Dáil Court in the Central Rooms, O'Connell St, Limerick and at Thurles.

The Dáil Courts functioned very successfully throughout Co. Cavan and indeed in most parts of Ireland until the autumn of 1922. After the outbreak of the Civil War, many arbitrators found themselves on opposing sides. In some instances the courts survived into early 1924. In the absence of a police force, the Sinn Féin Clubs and the court arbitrators appointed senior volunteers to act as Irish Republican Policemen (IRP). Paddy Woods, a native of Co. Tyrone who had come to teach the Irish language in south Fermanagh and west Cavan under the auspices the Gaelic League, was appointed senior republican policeman in Ballyconnell. He commanded D.Company (Ballyconnell), Corlough Batt and he was also O/C. He was later a commissioned officer in the Free State Army until he resigned in 1929 to run the post office in Swanlinbar. As well as serving court summonses, the republican policemen investigated criminality, like theft and arson, and either brought the culprits before the courts or used summary justice by ordering those involved out of the district or the country for a time.

Chiefs of Republican Police were appointed by the Army Council of the IRA to districts in every county in Ireland, including the proposed six counties, to enforce the civil authority of the emerging State. In Co. Cavan the following were appointed:- P Smyth, Carrickallen; __ Connolly, Cavan Town; T McGee, Cootehill; Terence Reilly, Belturbet; John McCaffrey, Corlough and J. West, Crosserlough.

In Co.Fermanagh, Terence Corrigan, Enniskillen and T. Corrigan, Arney were appointed.

The strongest political recognition and condemnation which the Dáil Courts received was from the British Premier, Lloyd George, at the commencement of the Anglo-Irish Treaty negotiations on 13 October 1921. The fact that the Dáil Courts were being held openly for some time and were being opened in the name of the republic was an irritant to the British and could be construed as a concession to a republic. Lloyd George told his colleagues that "we shall have to scatter these courts". When the matter was raised with Arthur Griffith and Michael Collins, assurances were given that something would be done — a wise statement in the early days of negotiation, avoiding any confrontations at that stage. Obviously the Dáil Courts were working towards the formation of the new State and still hurting the British establishment.

In his study of the Anglo-Irish Treaty negotiations, entitled *Peace by Ordeal*, Lord Longford wrote:

> By July 1920 there were few places outside of Dublin and north-east Ulster where the King's Writ continued to run. And testimony in favour of the new courts was astonishingly general. Lord Montegal praised them, the *Chicago Tribune* praised them, the *Manchester Guardian* and *Daily News* praised them, the *Daily Mail* praised them; and even the *Irish Times* had no complaint to make of them, and plenty of fun to poke at their supplanted rivals. The commission appointed by The Society of Friends reported – Moderate people and many Unionists admit the only protection they enjoy is provided by the Sinn Féin police. By this time the Republican Administration possessed, as Bonar Law admitted- 'all the symbols and all the realities of a Government'.

Why did the British government not deal with the full Irish question, from the introduction of the Partition Bill in 1920? This would have avoided the suffering of the Irish people, the expense on the British exchequer and the legacy of the Black and Tans.

The answer lay with Lloyd George, Sir Edward Carson and James Craig. DeValera, as president of Sinn Féin, was still in America.

CHAPTER 9

CONCILIATORY UNIONISM

(i) Covenant broken

Sir Edward Carson in an interview on Irish unity and the power of agreement, as reported in many newspapers in the early summer of 1920, pointed to the Council of Ireland as a medium for bringing unity by agreement. On the suggestion of a government offer of a truce, he asked, "Who is to negotiate?" (He was probably asking, who would be representing Southern Ireland in such negotiations, while indicating that those elected in 1918 as representative of Sinn Féin would not be acceptable.) Government policy at the time, he asserted, was only one of drastic action to protect the lives of innocent and unoffending people. Carson was quoted:

> So far as Ulster is concerned, there is no part of the community which more earnestly desires peace and permanent settlement. When the present Bill was brought in they accepted the idea of parliament for six counties and a southern parliament, with a council representing both parliaments, which should have power by agreement to bring about unity at any time when the people in the north and south settled down and showed themselves efficient in government, and although at that time they would have preferred exclusion, they now feel the only way in which they can avoid being pawns in political controversies of the future in this country is that they should be allowed to set up their parliament and proceed with the expansion of their business in peace and without further interference.
>
> Too little regard has been paid to the provisions in regard to this council. We hear a great deal about self-determination and the setting up of conventions to bring about unity, but the council really means that the two parliaments, representing the constituencies of the whole of Ireland, can at any moment, by agreement themselves determine they will have a united Ireland. This is the only possible method of bringing about a real and genuine unity. Such unity can never be forced upon either of the constituent elements, without further hostilities, which would not lead to agreement but to disagreement — whatever label of unity you may pretend to put upon it...

The majority of Protestant people in Counties Cavan, Donegal and Monaghan had to be disappointed that they were now being excluded from the union which was contrary to their belief when they signed the Ulster Covenant eight years earlier. However, pragmatism and the issue of unmovable properties and estates were the influences which encouraged them to accept and adapt to the new situation, that they would now be part of southern Ireland. The proposed Council of Ireland from both parliaments would have been of some comfort to them looking forward.

At a 12 July demonstration in 1920 at Drum, Co. Monaghan, Lt. Col. Madden DL JP, (who was on the platform with Sir Edward Carson at Enniskillen, 18 September 1912) said:

> The country is in a state of terrible turmoil and a certain section were carrying on a war against the government and not a week was passing without accounts of murders of the RIC and Dublin Metropolitan Police. To say that these forces acted in a provocative manner to the people of this country was absolutely untrue... Referring to the Ulster Covenant, it had been torn to shreds in Belfast, and they knew it was mainly by the men of Belfast and surrounding districts that it had been torn to shreds, and on advice of their Members of Parliament. Belfast and the commercial districts thought they had made a bad bargain buy, in admitting the men of Monaghan, Cavan and Donegal into their covenant, and were determined to get out of it. Anyone going amongst them, as he did, could see the idea working in their minds. In 1916, by efficacious arguing, in which their leader excelled, he got their delegates to the Ulster Council to agree to the six-county cut and he regretted that he did not resign his position as a delegate instead of giving way as he did on that occasion, when he found the other delegates were so hypnotised by that great arguer, Sir Edward Carson, that they were prepared to agree to anything he asked. Having referred to the subsequent transactions, he said that they could believe him that Belfast had made up its mind long before 1920 that the covenant with all Ulster was a mistake, and, declared with emphasis I am going to say it, whether you like it or not that Sir Edward Carson has given us the most perfect example of legal quibbling that I have ever seen in my experience. The covenant did not mean what a plain man like me thought it meant, but something quite different. I say, away with our Belfast-made covenants; I want to hear no more of them. The best thing you and I can do is to consign the whole matter to oblivion and

try and forget that we ever entered into any covenant.

If a Northern Parliament is set up in Belfast the northerners say they will work it under protest, as they do not want it. On the other hand, the Sinn Féiners say they will not have anything to do with a Southern Parliament as they are out for a Republic — for the whole of Ireland, which Mr. Lloyd George has declared, on behalf of England, they shall never have. How are all these difficulties to be overcome? Well, I don't suppose anyone will listen to my advice, but if I had to advise, I would say to the Sinn Féiners, follow the lead of the northerners and stop burning police barracks and attacking the police, and when the Home Rule Bill is passed start your Southern Parliament in Dublin and show how wisely and well you can govern (hear hear). Should a Southern Parliament be started, I would say we should all owe allegiance to it and do out part to help in every way that we can carry on the business of the country and this is our country (applause). We must not presume that there will be oppression. We must not presume that wrong will be done to anyone. It looks like the British Parliament is determined to pass this Home Rule Bill and we must act the part of good citizens and hope that all will be for the best.

But if oppression and wrong came, we must stand up against it like men, and help will surely come to us. Shall we not have Ulster at our back if that should happen, aye, and England too? I refuse to look back at rebellious and broken covenants, but I ask you to look forward, as I do, to better days. God grant that peace may come and soon come, and that better days may be in store for all of us... Your policy and my policy is, therefore, quite clear, to go about our business and not interfere... We have always been on the side of law and order. It is one of our rules not to give offence to those who differ from us, but it is as well to remind those who do differ from us that though we are men who stand no bullying we are all anxious to put an end to dissension and to live in peace with our neighbours. Let us hope that before next year, peace and prosperity will again reign in our beloved country (applause).

At the same Orange demonstration, Mr. T. E. L. Clements DL, Rathkenny, Cavan (on whose lands the Ulster Volunteers drilled regularly) in referring to the action of Belfast as regards Cavan, Monaghan and Donegal said:

He did not think that any of their fellow covenanters could have sunk to the level necessary for the repudiation of the Solemn League and Covenant. They had been cast off by those who, even if they were not their friends, ought to have been loyal to the British Empire. For themselves and their property he honestly thought that there was no special danger. The time has passed when individuals could be penalised in their persons or property for their religious opinions, and it seemed impossible that Communism could ever gain a firm foothold in Ireland. Irishmen were not Communists. Sinn Féin itself was not for the establishment of a Red-Republic and if it were the members would soon find themselves opposed by practically the whole population of Ireland. His own opinion was that Sinn Féin was a clean fighter, seeking, mistakenly, but honestly, the welfare of Ireland. Concluding, he did not anticipate anything like the confiscation of property.

At a 12 of July celebration in Killeshandra, held at the rectory grounds and attended by members from Cavan, Leitrim and Fermanagh, Rev. R. D. Martin Rector and chairman said:

They were living in terrible times of crisis, but, as a Killeshandra man, he was glad to say that their district was one of the quietest in all Ireland (cheers). If the cow of a Roman Catholic took sick, a Protestant would sit up all night to help his Catholic neighbour, and the Catholic, of course, would do the same, so those were the relations which existed amongst them, here and around Killeshandra (cheers and a voice "It's the best way to live"). Continuing, the Rev. Speaker said it was the principles of the Orange Order to love thy brethren, and they were all brethren and Irishmen. Concluding he quoted the apostle's advice about being quiet, minding their own business, and if they did this, no matter what their politics might be, he was not one bit afraid of trouble in the country...

(ii) Peace Conference

In August 1920 an Irish Peace Conference was convened in the Mansion House Dublin as called by the Irish Dominion Home Rule League. This ad-hoc group of influential southern Unionists and nationalists wanted an Irish settlement sooner rather than later. Among those present were many Irish members of the House of Lords, nationalists, clergymen of all denominations, legal and other senior people of the establishment and the general public. The influential and prominent Unionist, the Earl of Shaftsbury, attended without a mandate. The international and Irish media were represented. Sir Nugent T. Everard was elected as Chairman. A Mr Fennell proposed: "That this Conference, in session assembled, before entering upon any business whatever, appeals to the Government, in the interests of justice, peace and the welfare of Ireland, to at once release the Lord Mayor of Cork, who is dangerously ill and weak and requests the Chairman and the Committee to convey this resolution at once, by wire, to the proper quarter."

The proposal was greeted with prolonged applause. (The Lord Mayor of Cork, Terence McSwiney, had been on hunger strike in Brixton Prison.)

After a formal agenda was adopted, Lord French moved:

"That this conference hereby records its conviction that the policy of the Government in Ireland is inevitably leading to civil war, and it is of paramount importance to take steps to secure peace in Ireland". He continued:

The acceptance of the resolution by the meeting would put on record a realisation of the facts as they were in Ireland today. In their policy the Government were deliberately adopting a species of anarchy with a view to bringing what they called law and order. It seemed that the policy of the Government was that by retaliating on the ordinary people of the country they would produce law and order. It was simply anarchy, and within the last two or three weeks valuable industries and towns in Ireland had been wrecked under this policy of retaliation. What that ultimately meant was that every industry and town in Ireland would be wrecked if that was allowed to go on . . . What that policy meant was the reconquest of Ireland, and that meant the destruction of any prosperity left in the country. Continuing he said those who called for any form of military retaliation were calling for the destruction of his own people and the assassination of the whole people...

Retaliation on one side produces retaliation from the other side, and it would go on in an endless circle until the country would be destroyed. A body of men had now got together and was not going to leave the present state of affairs unexposed, and arrangements would have to be made to carry on a propaganda to expose the meaning of the present situation in Ireland.

Major O'Connor, in seconding the motion, said:

On looking at the members and the representative character of the meeting, there could not be the slightest doubt in the mind of any impartial person that there was a large body of opinion in the country in favour of the resolution. They wanted peace and demanded from the government that they should do everything in their power to ensure that peace.

It could not be denied that in Ireland they had become a very pariah amongst the other nations of Europe. They were fast heading to the destruction of their national, social, economic, political and sectarian ties, which bound them to one another in Ireland, because what was in the power of the Government to give was withheld from them. An Irish Prelate stated a few days ago that they were heading for civil war, chaos and anarchy. Could that be denied? (Cries - " No".) In the city of Cork the other day he was attracted by a small placard, which held out to anyone advocating the only method which would bring peace to that country the penalties of treason. That was a monstrous thing, and would give the delegates an idea of the enormous distances which separate them. They had to contend with misrepresentation. The whole country, in fact, was suffering an amount of misrepresentation so bordering on mendacity that even the father of lies could not tell where the one began or the other ended. They wanted to stop that, but they could not do so until they got peace in the country.

Mr. Samuel Wray, Roscommon, said:

As a tenant farmer, who had purchased his holding, he asked the co-operation of his brother farmers in Ireland to aid in having the country settled on a solid peace. As a Protestant he had lived in most amicable terms with his Catholic neighbours. He could also say that amongst those engaged in the Sinn Féin movement he never found the trace of religious bigotry. He wished the brethern in the North of Ireland would take cognisance of that fact. He had been a Unionist, but for some years he had come to the conclusion that the settlement of the Irish question could only be brought about by giving to Ireland proper self-government and the charge of her own destiny.

Rev. Fr. Kearney, Co. Down, supported the resolution, observing that he fully recognised the possibilities attaching to the conference... He went on to refer to the causes of the disorder, which, he said were leading to anarchy. "It was bad enough to have reprisals amongst sections of their countrymen, but reprisals from government had shocked civilisation. Ninety per cent of the Unionist and Catholic population abhorred this fiendish work. The majority of the people looking beneath the surface saw in the ills of the country the failure of British rule and Coercion Acts, was there a nation on earth that could have borne the yoke of slavery more patiently?"

The next business before the conference was the consideration and discussion of, and, if approved, adoption of resolutions recording the outcome of the peace conference. "That it would be possible for the British Government to secure peace in Ireland, by an immediate and binding offer of full national self-government, to be accepted or rejected by specially elected representatives of the people of Ireland, upon whom should be laid the task of adapting the new institutions to the special requirements of Ireland or any part thereof requiring special treatment."

Lord McDonnell (former Under-Secretary of State for Ireland) proposed the following resolutions:

> That in the judgment of the conference the grant of full national self-government within the Empire could alone bring peace to Ireland, and that complete administrative, fiscal and financial independence was the decisive test and characterisation of national self-government;

> That the conference welcomed the acceptance by north-east Ulster of the principle of self-government, and repudiate the idea of coercion by armed forces of any part of Ireland, and that while expressing its unalterable repugnance for any form of partition of Ireland, it recognised that in any negotiations concerning the relations of north-east Ulster to the rest of Ireland the former must be accorded the status of a free contracting party; and that the grant of such full national self-government is quite compatible with the Prime Minister's declarations of the Government's Irish policy;

> That if we were to claim liberty for ourselves, we must give liberty to other people. It was not by the shedding of blood in the south and west of Ireland that Ireland could be conciliated; and neither by the shedding of blood in the six counties of Ulster, could Ulster be conciliated. There are other means of conciliation, which enable people to live in peace and unity.

Sir Stanley Harrington, who seconded, was interrupted during his speech by a voice from the gallery, which said, "Ireland is not a colony; we want a republic". Sir Stanley continued

It was quite true that the Irish Convention was tried in 1917 and, he was sorry to say, failed — not certainly through any faults of his patriotic friend Sir Horace Plunkett. Things were, unfortunately, very much worse now; hence many men considered that a final effort at agreement might yet be made. As a Home Ruler, he could never understand the objections to it, but he was delighted to see so many Unionists agreeable to the policy. To prevent any misunderstanding, the object of that Conference should be made clear. They did not want to supersede any party or to create a new one. Their function was to endeavour, for the sake of Ireland, to bring together the Sinn Féin and Ulster parties, recognising, as they must, the strong position of those two factors... Might I, Sir Stanley concluded, appeal to the Government to adopt conciliatory methods in dealing with the present situation so as to give the suggestion of this Conference every chance of success.

Later he suggested that if Dominion Home Rule was not accepted, three mediating statesmen should be chosen from Australia, Canada and New Zealand to draft a scheme.

John Sweetman, Kells, a former president of Arthur Griffith's Sinn Féin, mentioning that the only thing they had to consider was how were they to get peace, inquired whether they were to ask the British government for Dominion Home Rule. "There were two objections to that. Even if granted, would it be a solution of their present difficulties? He was convinced, in the first place, that the British Government would not give it, if they were asked. Secondly, even if they did give it, the vast majority of Irishmen would not accept it at that time. What then was the use of asking for it?"

Lord Shaftsbury then spoke:
He came here from Ulster (cries of "Welcome") and he just wanted to say this, that of course they would readily understand that he had no mandate to speak for Ulster, nor could he claim to represent any concourse of opinion in the province. Everything he said to them must be taken as an individual view representing his own opinion and no one else's. He wanted to say that he was wholehearted in support of this great and superb effort that they were making to bring peace to Ireland, to crystallise all shades of opinion and thought, and to put forward some concrete proposal that would find acceptance and bring peace to their country (appaluse). When he looked around him he

almost thought he could feel the spirit and the presence of those two great Irish patriots and brothers, the one who shed his life-blood on the battlefields of Europe in order that he might consolidate all classes and creeds in Ireland, and the other who died of a broken heart because he found his efforts at conciliation failed (applause). But he must in this meeting say that as an Ulsterman he should stand by Ulster, He wished to put in a plea for a spirit of understanding from that meeting with the spirit of Ulster. He asked them to have patience with her, and then he thought the time would come when all Irishmen would see eye to eye (applause).

There is nothing in this resolution that he could not ascribe to except one thing. He was not quite sure that they were right in saying that Ulster had accepted the principle of self-government. Were they not a little premature? She had accepted this Bill, it was true, and would work it as well as she could. Have patience with her. She had come a long way upon the road, and could there be any doubt that when once they saw peace and order established in the country, that there might not be a union of hearts or a disposition to come together and to think as united Irishmen on Irish affairs? He believed it would be so. He himself could only go this far with the meeting, and that they should pass this resolution as it stood. He went so far with them as they would enable Ulster and the people of Ulster to go with them. This resolution, he concluded, is exactly what I can subscribe to, and what I believe the people of Ulster will accept. Pass it as it stands and I am with you.

Sir Thomas Esmonde (also a former supporter of Griffith's Sinn Féin) said: "That he had listened with intense satisfaction to Lord Shaftsbury's most remarkable speech — and he could not resist the impulse which had come to him from that deliverance to strike a responsive chord on behalf of at least one southern Irishman. Lord Shaftsbury had thrown strong light and hope on a general situation. All they asked was sympathy and understanding. If the spirit of Lord Shaftsbury's speech should spread and permeate his own people, and if it brought together the northerners and the southerners he believed the dark cloud over their country would vanish into thin air."
Rev. Fr. McCotter PP Antrim, said:

He believed in Dominion Home Rule because he believed there was no means at the present time of obtaining government for Ireland of the extreme kind. The republican idea, as they all knew, was perfectly sane and sound in its own way. But who was to give a republic to

Ireland, he asked. He did not believe it possible... If Dominion Home Rule was put into effect by the British government immediately, and he believed that was possible, a majority of the Irish people would accept it. He considered the Earl of Shaftsbury's speech would do a lot of good in Ulster. He welcomed Lord Shaftsbury's statement as opening a new era in the Ulster question.

Serjeant Hanna KC, supporting the resolution, said:

He stood here as an Ulsterman and a Unionist. He had come to the meeting because the condition of affairs in Ireland for a considerable time past had forced on him the conviction that every reasonably minded man should at once take his place — if he had the courage — with the strong body of moderate opinion in Ireland at the moment to bring this terrible chaotic state of their country to an end. He said he knew the people of Ulster and could agree with what Fr. McCotter had said. He would ask them to take home with them to the other parts of Ireland what the Earl of Shaftsbury said: "Have patience with Ulster". As one born and educated in Belfast, and who had the centre of his practice there, Serjeant Hanna knew he was expressing the view of a great percentage of the people there.

They longed in their hearts for peace as much as those present that day. And there was no doubt that 99 per cent of those objected to reprisals as much as anyone present in that hall. They should remember, however, that there was a public opinion in Ulster that prevented men from expressing in public what was in the secret of their hearts, so that everyone might know what their views were. There might be people in other parts of Ireland who for the same reason did not express their views. In Belfast there were many people who wished to see this question settled, but they had not the courage to come out and say so in the face of people who knew them as strong Unionists. We in Ulster, should not take up such a stiff position, but we should meet our fellow countrymen in other parts of Ireland. Have patience with Ulster, and if you bide your time you will see that there are the most vital economic reasons why the people of Belfast and of Ulster should stand in with their fellow countrymen rather than with men across the channel.

The O'Conor Don recalled:

Mr. Lloyd George had sneered at them as only a puny body and of no importance, and proceeded to pass most repressive measures.

Moderate-minded people wanted peace and a reasonably formed Government. We tell Lloyd George that we will not have his form of bayonet control, that we will have none of it, but we must be moderate in our views, and liberal and generous to the other side. We must admit that the Sinn Féiners are just as well able to govern the country as any body of men; that they are an intelligent body; that they want a prosperous and happy Ireland; that they do not think this form of crime is satisfactory, but were dead against it. He was not desirous of sticking to the name of Dominion Home Rule or any other name, but he thought if the proposal had a name it should be that of self-government under the British Empire. Then they should say to the Sinn Féiners – "We will give you everything except a republic". Dominion Home Rule meant a republic without the name of a republic.

He wanted no partition, but they should have the whole of Ireland as one. If they got the Sinn Féiners and those calling themselves Republicans on their side, they could go to Lloyd George and say — "We will have self-government and we will have none of you here at all." When they were unanimous enough, Lloyd George might change his mind, if he was as changeable as the wind, but his military bayonets and courts would not be the least use to him. Not a single person would help him to obtain a conviction, and he was only getting into a greater mire than he was in at present. Concluding he declared, "every one of us will before long be damned republicans."

Sir Horace Plunkett, the founder of the Cooperative Movement, who received an ovation lasting some minutes, said:
The best way to deal with the dual problem before them — that was, the difficulty between England and Ireland, on the one hand, and the difficulty between the majority and minority in Ireland, on the other — was to follow exactly the same course that with proper adjustment had proved successful in solving both of those problems in many parts of the British Empire. Many of those present had been dragged into politics at present by the stern necessities of their country's condition. He thought they would agree that the present situation was largely due to the fact that the large majority of businessmen in Ireland had hitherto taken no part in politics. He was not now going to argue in favour of Dominion Home Rule. It was not the purpose of the meeting to decide on any definite solution, and no attempt should be made, he

thought, to get the meeting to adopt a cut-and-dried solution as a so called panacea.

Having referred to the destruction of some 20 creameries and the injury done to so many other societies of farmers — the establishment of which he had devoted a large part of his life to — and also to the destruction of a Carnegie Library, he continued:

> He mentioned these matters as illustrating the necessity for trying to find some way out of the present terrible impasse. He pointed out that the enormous majority of Irish people had come under a de facto-Government, which probably had done more already than any Government had ever done in this country. He would go so far as to say, however, that, while circumstances had compelled the leaders of that policy to exercise their power in that direction, they must know perfectly well that their solution in this respect was no solution to the Irish question at all. It might be quite justifiable as an emergency policy, but these people must be ready to confer with their fellow countrymen upon some compromise. He did not say what the compromise should be he thought it was pretty clear from the speeches which had been delivered that those present in the hall would give to the party now dominating Ireland nine-tenths of what they demanded.

Capt. Stephen Gwynn, former IPP MP, urged that in order to get national self-government they must have national unity.

> There was no unity in Ireland he declared, and that was one of the facts they had to face. The real obstacle to unity was Ulster. In all his years in politics he heard nothing more hopeful for a solution than the speech by Lord Shaftsbury. Let us bear it in mind. It is to us a real offer of peace. The curse of Ireland in the past has been indirect dealing. The Irish question must be settled by Irishmen amongst themselves and at home.

A Mr I Varian, Dublin commented on the fact that the Dublin business men were not largely represented at the conference. He believed if the business men of the north and the rest of Ireland came together, they would arrive at a settlement.

James Brady, also of Dublin, expressed his warm appreciation of the noble speech delivered by Lord Shaftsbury, and said the only way, in his opinion, to restore peace was to put an end to militarism. "Let them stop firing on both sides, and give the people an opportunity to breathe and understand where they were."

Dr McWalter, City High Sheriff, said: "In his opinion a better way out of the present difficulty would be repeal of the Act of Union. The meeting ought, he said, call on the Government to withdraw every soldier from Ireland as a means towards attaining the state of mind necessary to bring about a settlement. He had a document in his pocket from the Lord Lieutenant, Lord French, stating he was given charge of the City of Dublin. I am prepared to take charge of this City if every soldier is withdrawn. I am equally certain that if every soldier is withdrawn from the other parts of Ireland, the sheriffs could maintain peace, with the volunteers on each side, and the ex-soldiers. Only in that way can we come to get that atmosphere in which it is possible to bring about peace."

CHAPTER 10
THE WAR CONTINUES

(i) Creameries wrecked

The War of independence continued unabated throughout 1920. It was showing no signs of a settlement being offered from either side, as all internal and international offers of mediation had by late 1920 fallen on deaf ears. The proposed partitioning of the country was as inflammatory to nationalist Ireland as the shooting of policemen and the burning of their barracks was to Unionists. Mass counter-reprisals by the police and military particularly by the Black and Tans on the civilian population were commonplace. One of the most serious reactions by the police and military during this time was the burning down of rural creameries throughout Tipperary, Limerick and Cork. The orders to carry out such deeds had to come from a higher authority in Dublin Castle or London. These thoughtless deeds were done in all probability to hurt the Irish economy and to turn the farming community against Sinn Féin. The market for the dairy products from these fledgling processing units would be the dining tables of many English households. These rural creameries were part of the dream of Sir Horace Plunkett, the moderate Unionist and Home Rule supporter. They were established for Irish farmers to gain some form of economic independence over their own produce. The Irish co-operative movement introduced collective food production methods for rural Ireland.

Reports of such activities in the autumn of 1920 were widespread in the British newspapers and the *Daily Mail* commented:
> The wrecking and burning of creameries by police and military is on the increase. There is absolute evidence that 19 of these establishments have been so destroyed. In some cases the police tried to restrain the military; in others the military sought to dissuade the police, and again both police and military combined. The result is that farmers decline to subscribe to further cooperative undertakings after the experience of Limerick and Tipperary the scheme for large creameries which had been contemplated has been abandoned.

The report went on to name 15 creameries already damaged in such frenzied attacks.

The *Manchester Guardian* said:

British soldiers and Irish Constabulary have, in some cases, taken to the sabotage of co-operative creameries and cheese factories as the appropriate retort to the burning of barracks. Since April of this year close to £40,000 worth of damage has been done in this form of frenzied raiding, and the vendetta shows no sign of abating. This is the lowest estimate of the ruin, since it includes only those acts of violence, which the Government admits to have been perpetrated by its servants. There may be, and almost certainly are, enthusiastic Republicans among the co-operators, but, quite apart from the ethics of revenge, the menace to a valuable cause does not a jot of harm to Sinn Féin. Rather does it strengthen separatism by stimulating hatred of England, while it imperils Ireland's chief industry and increases the chance of famine this winter; and that most terrible possibility has seriously to be considered owing to the incessant and destructive rains.

The estimate of the damage does not include that caused by the burning of Loughmore, Killea and Castleiney creameries recently as reprisals, it is alleged, for the shooting dead of Mr. Wilson D.I. In Castleiney the wreckers arrived in a police motor van and carried crowbars, sledges and petrol.

Sir Horace Plunkett, President of the IAOS (Irish Agriculture Organisation Society) in a letter to the Chief Secretary, drew attention to the burning of creameries in the south, and pointed out that:

Unless drastic action is taken, the most serious consequences to the peace, order and material interest of the country (including the food supply) must result. Nor will the mischief end with the societies, which have actually suffered loss. The Society has, through all the recent troubles, been not only permitted but encouraged by general agreement to continue its non-political work for the social advancement and economic development of Ireland. If it is unable to help its member societies in their present trouble, its influence will be destroyed. We are informed that already groups of farmers, who were anxious to organise themselves under our auspices, have stated that it is no use putting their savings into buildings and plant which may be wrecked by agents of the Government. You will recognise that the evil is one for which the Government alone can provide the remedy. Obviously, the first step is to have an open inquiry into all the facts, in order that public confidence may be restored. At the same time we are entitled to ask for an authoritative assurance that, where the destruction of property is traced to servants of the Government, full compensation will be provided from the Imperial Exchequer, and not charged through the local rates, on the people whose property is so destroyed.

Sir Hamar Greenwood (Secretary of State for Ireland) replied, stating "that the Irish Government would do all in its power to put a stop to these outrages and punish those responsible. The difficulty is to obtain evidence as to the persons responsible. So far, the outstanding difficulty has been that the sufferers have been unable or unwilling to come forward with such evidence, and I am very glad to see that you undertake that the officers of the society will do all they can to aid us in this respect. If evidence is brought forward proving that any servant of the government is guilty of any such outrage, the offender will be dealt with severely. As regards compensation, no question of the charge of compensation against public funds can arise until the claims have been preferred in the ordinary way in the Courts and the Courts have adjudicated on them."

It has to be noted here that the Secretary of State did say in his reply to Sir Horace Plunkett that he would do all in his power to put a stop to these outrages, which by its tone indicated that others had the power to do so. Also, in his utterance to obtain evidence, he was putting the responsibility back on the native population to identify unknown persons in government uniforms who were perpetrating these atrocities. Co-operative employees and the local population, if they saw their creamery being burned down or looted, would have to bring this to the attention of the same authorities who were encouraging the same acts.

In May 1921, in a report on a co-operative congress held in Scarborough, the *Westminster Gazette* said:

> Already 400 cooperative societies in England, Wales and Scotland have passed resolutions against the Government's neglect to stop the destruction of the cooperative creameries in Ireland. The Central Board of the Co-operative Union submitted to the congress a strongly worded protest against the attacks on co-operative properties in Ireland and deploring the bloodshed. It called upon the government to compensate the victims of outrages and reprisals; demanding that

freedom for the pursuit of their cooperative activities be granted to co-operative societies and co-operators in all parts of Ireland, and that similar freedom be granted to all other persons in Ireland for the enjoyment of their lawful civic rights. The Congress was asked to go further and express itself in favour of a policy of conciliation in Ireland and the granting of a measure of self-government which will be acceptable to the Irish people as a whole.

What was Lloyd George's attitude to these events in Ireland? An observation by the *Anglo-Celt* reported:

People who saw the Premier during the week were surprised to find how rapidly he had aged of late says The *London Dispatch*. It is all the most ironic of all the incidents in Mr. Lloyd George's dramatic career that he who risked everything to protest against the farm-burnings, which were operations of war in South Africa, should cover with his authority the sacking and burning of towns and villages in Ireland as a means of enforcing law in what is supposed to be a time of peace, says *Public Opinion London*.

(ii) A New Force.

The *Impartial Reporter,* Enniskillen, was reporting weekly on the many atrocities throughout Ireland as committed by Sinn Féiners against the forces of the Crown — the shooting of policemen, burning of police barracks and the ambushing of military. There was little reference to the activities of the same forces in the attacks on civilians, burning and looting of property and the more recent acts of burning down creameries. An article published 16 September 1920 was questionable in its intent with the heading "The New Force for Ireland - Well Disposed Citizens To Be Armed - Volunteers to Assist the Army - Ulster's 100,000 men - Early Appeal for Recruits."
The article continued:

The official announcement regarding the enrollment of well-disposed citizens to assist the authorities foreshadows an important development in Ireland. An appeal will be made throughout Ireland for loyal citizens to come forward to assist in the maintenance of order in the country. It is not proposed to limit the number of those who respond, and it is expected that a large force (numbering many thousands) will thus be recruited. The greater number will doubtless come from Ulster, where a volunteer force estimated at about 100,000 exists. Probably most of these would volunteer for service.

Suggestions have been made to the Government tantamount to an offer of the services of the Ulster Volunteers, but this has not been accepted...

William Copeland-Trimble, the editor of the *Impartial Reporter,* may have had some insider knowledge of what was being advised to the government at Westminster by Edward Carson and James Craig. The paper could also be accused of being somehow mischievous in its utterances, stating as fact what was apparently a suggestion from within Ulster to bolster the Ulster Volunteers as upright citizens in the eyes of government. The paper showed a total lack of understanding of and objectivity towards the situation throughout Ireland with the potential of fanning flames of an already burning fire. In the following issue the paper, while welcoming the cabinet decision to appoint an additional under-secretary to deal with Ulster affairs of which it heartily approved, attacked the Dublin press for not expressing the real feelings of her citizens:

> The Nationalist Press writes violently of the Government's announcement regarding the proposed enrollment of well-disposed citizens to assist the government as a proposal to recognise and arm Sir Edward Carson's Volunteers. No such proposal has been made or foreshadowed by the Government. There is, however, room for doubts of the expediency and wisdom of that portion of the scheme which seems to contemplate enrollment of men strongly tinged with politics to handle affairs in a city where political and so-called religious feelings at the moment are not normal, but explosive. Clearly the police and military are the proper parties to keep order and preserve the peace with an impartial hand ... Events have shown that a deep gulf divides the special interests and needs of Ulster from those of the three southern provinces. Recent happenings have made that gulf both deeper and wider and common sense suggests that since that gulf cannot be bridged, the time has come when Ulster should possess administrative and executive machinery adapted to her special needs...

The *London Daily Herald*, commenting on the proposed arming of Ulster loyalists, said:

> The Government, in fact, is said to be arming one section of Irish civilians to fight another. If this is not promoting a heavy civil war, we would like to know what it is. The story is almost incredible but the Government's Irish policy has been so amazing that one can now believe

anything. And since its European and Asiatic policies have been based on the pleasant principle that another little war would do us no harm, there seems to be no reason for doubting its cheerful intention to keep the Home Rule fires burning on imported fuel.

Mischievous journalism was becoming the norm, as earlier in April 1920 the *Impartial Reporter* reported that a quantity of arms and ammunition was discovered at Liverpool docks, hidden among hogsheads of German beer and destined for Ireland. The paper implied that they were for republicans in Dublin who were organising another Easter Rising while also saying that the British navy was patrolling Irish waters in readiness for another such event. Throughout this time, the paper was reporting that there were as many as 200,000 rebels or Sinn Féiners at large throughout Ireland, a figure that was well exaggerated, for reasons best known to the editor. Given the scarcity of arms and ammunition in the hands of the IRA, and the scarcity of money to procure more, the number of active armed rebels at any one time would have been in the region of 3,000 to 4,000. These were facing at that time 41,000 heavily armed British military and 12,000 armed policemen.

According to an item reported in the *Evening News* in October 1920 the formation of the new state of Ulster was under way. Its Derry correspondent wrote:

> The organisation of the Ulster Civic Guard is now nearing completion. It is to be divided into three categories: Class A — Permanent Police, Class B — Occasional Police and Class C — Volunteer Police. There are to be 800 men in Class A and they will do service in any part of the six Ulster counties. Class B will be composed of men whose service can be called upon at any time for duty in their own town or district, and their numbers are being regulated according to the circumstances. Class C will consist of regular volunteers whose service could be requisitioned in any special emergency and their numbers unlimited. The members of the first two classes are to be paid — "A" men to get 10/s a day. "B" men will be similarly paid when doing actual service. "C" men will be voluntary and unpaid.
> An intelligence staff has been organised, with a network of secret service agents, all over the six counties, their duty to combat Sinn Féin activities...

Back in west Cavan, the *Anglo-Celt* reported that an outlying farm of some 80 acres belonging to the late Robert Hutton's estate had been bought by the

Swanlinbar Sinn Féin Club for distribution among uneconomic holders who lived alongside.

At the same time in Swanlinbar, written notices were posted concerning the boycotting of a Protestant merchant in the town. This was repudiated by the Sinn Féin Club which denied any boycott of the person or business mentioned.

Farmers in the parish of Templeport met to agree to withhold rents until a proper scheme for land purchase was put in place in their area.

Against this backdrop the committee stage of the Partition Bill was being passed at Westminster. The technical issues around this bill seemed to have little relevance to the people of west Cavan or south Fermanagh.

(iii) Bloody Sunday

The British military approach and intelligence network can best be described as totally amateurish in dealing with the situation in Ireland. The person whom the authorities most wanted, dead or alive, was Michael Collins. He was Commander-in-Chief of the IRA while at the same time openly collecting money to fund his war and, more importantly, to finance the functions of Dáil Éireann. Collins had a network of agents inside all sections of the Castle administration who kept him informed at all times. This allowed the poorly armed IRA to keep the forces of the Crown busy. The British, wanting to up their intelligence game to capture Collins, sent Colonel Ormonde Winter to Dublin in the summer of 1920. Collins organised a welcoming party for him with an ambush in Thomas St, Dublin. Winter was injured. This intensified British counter operations with the introduction of the "Cairo Gang" to Dublin.

One such counter operation by the British was the shooting dead of the unarmed John Lynch, an elderly man from Kilmallock in the Exchange Hotel, Dublin on 23 September as he lay in bed. Lynch was a Sinn Féin Loan organiser in his area and was in Dublin to hand over £23,000 to Collins. Due to poor intelligence work and much egotistical in-fighting among the British military and the RIC. Lynch was probably mistaken for Liam Lynch the IRA leader in Cork.

The military authorities refused permission to the city coroner to hold a formal inquest into the death of John Lynch. The inquiry by the authorities was private and a subsequent report was issued, stating that an attempt was made to arrest Lynch and that he fired with a revolver and fire was returned. On examination of the room where Lynch was shot, there was evidence of only one bullet being fired. The military gave notice that a public funeral would not be permitted when they disrupted the funeral Mass at Kilmallock and removed the tricolour from the coffin. Collins was not to be outwitted and his network established that the killers of John Lynch were secret-service men. As Commander-in-Chief of the IRA, Collins compiled a report on the shooting of Lynch and the British intelligence network at work in Dublin for Arthur Griffith. Later he presented it to the Dáil cabinet and the army council where he had to prove that each and every man on his list was an accredited secret-service man of the British government.*

Collins had almost 100 per cent loyalty and respect from his many political friends and full support from the IRA men around him. The time came for him to assemble "The Squad", men of the Dublin Brigade who knew Dublin and were trusted volunteers. They were to carry out the one mission that Dublin Castle or British intelligence could never have imagined – "to take out the Cairo Gang". This was organised and executed with prime precision on the morning of Sunday 21 November 1920 when 14 British army officers, ex-officers and two Auxiliary police were shot by "The Squad", and all within half an hour, at eight different city locations. The British forces retaliated with venom later that afternoon when they stormed a Gaelic football match being played between Dublin and Tipperary at Croke Park. They killed 12 people and injured over 50, all innocent civilians. Bloody Sunday was born. Bloody indeed on all sides.

After the event, the *Impartial Reporter* had the following opening paragraph:

Dublin on Sunday last was the scene of an unprecedented outbreak of crime, resulting in the murders of 14 Army officers and ex-officers associated with bringing to justice of Sinn Féin gunmen. In addition two members of the Auxiliary police were shot dead. In the cases of the officers and ex-officers the victims were killed in bed or in rooms in hotels and lodgings at which they had been residing. Four of the assassins were captured, including one who was wounded.

One of "The Squad" was arrested on that day and later escaped. The other three men who had been arrested in Dublin on the previous evening were Dick McKee and Peadar Clancy, both active IRA men and Conor Clune, an innocent civilian. All three were detained at Portobello Barracks, tortured and shot on that Sunday evening under the guise of "trying to escape".

The *Impartial Reporter's* account of the day's events continued:

Later in the day, forces of the Crown proceeded to the venue of a Gaelic football match, to effect arrests and were fired on by Sinn Féin

* *Michael Collins, Tim Pat Coogan*

"picket". The fire was returned, and 12 people were killed and over 50 wounded. After the fighting, between 30 and 50 revolvers were found by the troops and police inside the football grounds.

Historically, it was proven that there was no IRA or Sinn Féin picket or outlook in the vicinity of Croke Park, (probably ticket sellers or touts wrongly described), and one revolver was found in a garden in the Drumcondra area that evening.

The article went on to detail a full account with names and addresses of the British military agents murdered most of whom were in their beds. The report contained two sub-sections (obviously taken from a Military Press Release.) " Croke Park Affair":

> A number of gunmen came to Dublin ostensibly to attend the Gaelic football match between Dublin and Tipperary at Croke Park, but their real motive was to take part in the series of murderous outrages, which took place in Dublin on Sunday morning. In this belief it was decided to make investigations at the match itself, and for this purpose a mixed party of military, RIC and Auxiliary police were detailed. They approached the grounds at Croke Park from different directions and found that pickets had been posted at the various approaches to the field to give warning, on the arrival of the military.

> A second sub-section headed "Dublin Murderers - Strangers From Country - Girls Act as Guides", said:

> The men who attacked the officers on Sunday were strangers to the city, but they were put into the hands of guides, some of whom, it is stated, were girls who knew the private houses in which the officers were occupying apartments.

> The suspicion that the football match was needed as a cover for the men who were appointed to carry out the series of murders prompted the authorities to turn their attention to Croke Park with the result now known.

There has been much written and said about this day in Dublin. However, it seems that the *Impartial Reporter*, as a newspaper, had lost its impartiality and was, by this time, an official organ for the British military in its reporting. (It had four working days to establish independent findings)

Arms of the press were now divided, all to target their own audience, but for what purpose? Bloody Sunday in Dublin and the manner of the reprisals conducted by the military and police brought much global condemnation on the British government, particularly from within the Dominions.

In December, the President of Sinn Féin, Eamon de Valera, returned to Ireland, having spent 20 months in the USA campaigning for Ireland's national and international rights while collecting funds to finance Sinn Féin and the fledgling Dáil. His return would lead to greater divisions within Ireland.

The War of Independence was now at its peak.

(iv) Report by British Labour Commission

On 29 December 1920 a British Labour party commission presented its findings to a special conference on the Irish question. The commission visited Dublin and parts of the south and west of Ireland. The report described the Irish situation as a tragedy, whether viewed from an Irish standpoint or that of British honour and prestige. The report was supported by police reports and photographs. It found sufficient evidence to justify the strongest condemnation of the government's policy. It cited the difficulty in obtaining reliable evidence owing to eye-witnesses fearing the consequences of disclosure in the atmosphere of terror prevailing. The report confirmed that:

> A negligible proportion of the RIC to be of intemperate habits and utterly unsuited to their duties...The men who mattered in the Auxiliary division, those of ability and education, but inflamed by political passion, were apparently given a free hand in the south and west and carried out reprisals causing the maximum amount of loss... Up to then reprisals by Auxiliaries had been hushed up as far as possible and efforts made to impute the blame of their misdeeds to innocent civilians. The commission considered this force enjoys a special and powerful protection.
>
> The IRA, is formidable, because intangible. If it functioned as an army it would have to concentrate to fight, and then be defeated without difficulty. But with fighting being dispersed, it is everywhere all the time and nowhere at any given moment, and enjoys the support needed for its existence more generally and effectively today than at any previous period. So great has been the provocation of the Crown forces that 80 per cent of the Irish population now regard the shooting of policemen and lorry bombing with the same philosophic resignation that Mr. Lloyd George displays towards arson, pillage and the shooting of civilians in the presence of their wives and children. Under such

conditions it is practically impossible to bring the IRA to bay...
The policy of reprisal by destruction, if carried out to its ultimate
conclusion, would ruin Ireland outside Ulster, but would not defeat the
IRA. The operations of this army against the forces of the Crown had
increased in numbers and scale. Though the government had only
admitted very few cases of arson committed by the Crown forces,
there was ample evidence to show that buildings had been deliberately
burned, and in some cases totally destroyed by servants of the Crown.

The commission recited instances from the evidence taken on the spot and
definitely accused the Crown forces of the crime of arson. It said it was part
of the policy of the Black and Tans and Auxiliaries:

It suggested that the destruction of houses formerly tenanted by Sinn
Féiners together with Sinn Féin halls and public buildings in places
where local authorities had a Sinn Féin majority, or at least an anti-
British majority, were the result of deliberate Sinn Féin activity,
seemed unreasonable and even stupid, especially as in many cases
people had been shot and ill-treated. Such a policy against their
friends, even by the most extreme Sinn Féiners, was inconceivable.
Even if only a few of the fires which have occurred in the past months
were caused by the government agents, the case against the Crown and
Government would in the commission's judgement be amply proved...
Looting is carried on more extensively than the government would be
prepared to admit and it expresses shame that servants of the British
Government should so besmirch in Irish eyes, the honesty of the
British people.
    The commission cited the beating and flogging of men and women
with whips by the Auxiliaries, but there was much worse.
In conclusion, the commission said:
    The Crown forces are gunmen ever ready to brandish their weapons
to inspire fear or to elicit information. Unfortunately their arms have
been used for a much deadlier purpose. Members of the Crown forces
have deliberately shot men in cold blood. These crimes, as revolting as
the murder of British officers in their beds, deserve equally thorough
denunciation. Even if Irish victims were gunmen, we do not think this
in any way loosens the guilt of those who committed the murders.

(v) Partition elections

FIXING BOUNDARIES
Lisnaskea and The Partition Act.

This was a front page column headline of the *Anglo-Celt*, on 22 January 1921:
Lisnaskea Guardians met on Saturday, Mr. William Bryson presiding.
The Local Government Board wrote informing the Board that, under
the Government of Ireland Act, the County of Fermanagh will form
part of the Northern area of the country and the County of Monaghan
part of the Southern area. It became essential for administrative
purposes to alter the present boundaries of the union, and they
accordingly, stated the Board, had given instructions for the issue of an
order separating the townlands comprised of Clones No. 2 Rural
District, situated in the county of Fermanagh, from the Union of
Clones, and adding them to the Union of Lisnaskea, as and from 1st.
April next. In consequence of this alteration the Guardians will find it
requisite to alter the estimate and demand (if already made) for the
next financial year...
The republican people of Clones showed their feelings in many ways as
their natural hinterland was being cut off. A "Special" Ulster Constable was
shot dead. Multiple attacks were made on the RIC and military in the area.
Strong local leadership continued the boycott of Belfast goods.

Lloyd George was treating the German people at the Reparations
Conference in London with the same disdain as nationalist Ireland. The
Allies, asked Germany to pay £11,300,000,000 in reparation for World War 1
over 42 annual payments, plus 12 $1/2$ per cent duty on all German exports.
The German delegate asked for a postponement of five years and argued that
Germany was prepared to shoulder the burden itself, but they could not put it
on the shoulders of their children or grandchildren. Lloyd George, on behalf
of the Allies refused this proposal and the Allied forces occupied Dusseldorf,
Duisburg and Ruhort on the following morning. The USA did not cooperate
with this action.
Politically Lloyd George was on the wane. Labour won two out of three
seats in the by-elections of early 1920. It is worth noting that 8.4 million
women over 30 years of age were now voting in British elections. Was the
Labour party's success a reaction to the Irish question and Lloyd George's
policy of recrimination?

In February 1921, Sir Edward Carson resigned as leader of the Ulster Unionist party and Sir James Craig was unanimously elected to lead the party into the new Ulster Parliament. Carson meekly departed Ulster, regretting that Ireland, contrary to his original wishes, was now to be partitioned while stating that the six counties was having self-government and not Home Rule.

The War of Independence continued with the execution of Volunteers and the shooting of civilians by the military and sporadic attacks by the IRA in return throughout the country. The boycott of Belfast goods was boosted by an announcement from Dáil Éireann on 23 March of the boycott of imported agricultural equipment from Britain under the Importation of British Goods Prohibition Order No. 1. In response, some local councils in the north east voted to boycott goods from southern Ireland.

De Valera told the press that it was the intention of Dáil Éireann to put forward candidates for every constituency in the two partition parliaments. On the entente between Sinn Féin and the constitutional nationalists in "Carsonia" he preferred to make no public statement until the agreement was completed... "Our cause is just, and it will surely triumph. Let us finish the fight finally this time in order that it will not recur for our children or our children's children. The sacrifices we must make will be great, but the peace they will bring will be worth the price. Our losses as a nation in the fight will not be comparable to the losses we shall suffer by the political disturbances and uncertainty of leaving this question unsolved, by the continuing in a position ceaselessly exploited by Britain. For the hundreds we are losing now in a manly fight for freedom, as conscripts, for example in one of Britain's imperial wars we should lose hundreds of thousands — and in the ignoble business of imposing slavery on others. The loss in the present destruction of property, enormous as it is, is but slight when we compare it with the sum annually exacted from us as a subject province in direct imperial tribute. It is altogether insignificant when compared with the indirect, economic and commercial losses inflicted on us through British control."

His statement continued on the unity of the people and in particular the role of the farmer. He went on to advise the people to avoid, as far as possible, purchasing those things British, and in particular liquor and tobacco, which contributed to the British Exchequer. "We can easily save £10 million for Ireland and deprive England of it. There should be one unforgivable offence for any Irish citizen at the present moment — that of helping the enemy." On the recent number of executions, he said: "These men gave up their lives for the Republic, and the Irishmen and Irish women who live will not be of the class that lose faith with those who die."

Asked for his interpretation of a recent statement to parliament by the British Prime Minister, he said: "Lloyd George, being a political opportunist himself, measures others by his own standard; being a moral coward himself, conscious of knowing the right course and of being afraid to follow it, he thinks that we are similar cowards."

De Valera continued lambasting Lloyd George and his associates while also speaking on and rejecting Dominion Home Rule. "We sincerely desire peace. It is natural in conditions like the present that we should yearn for it from our very souls. We are conscious of nothing in our heart but a spirit of fairness and goodwill, but we are not going to make the mistake of imagining that the British Government is similarly disposed when we have definite daily proofs to the contrary..."

The big question put to de Valera by the press was "What will Dáil Éireann do with regard to the elections for a Northern and Southern Parliament?" His response was:

Dáil Éireann is concerned with one question only, whether it should give its sanction to the holding of these elections or whether it should refuse to recognise them, place a ban upon them and order the citizens to boycott them. As they can be made use of to prove once again how unalterable the heart of this country is fixed upon its independence, and how determined is the opposition of almost all sections of the Irish people to any attempt to partition their country into hostile camps, the Dáil has decided not to place a ban upon the proposed elections. The duty of the Dáil as the National Parliament and Government ends here — the rest is a matter for Sinn Féin and the other political parties... Our present intention is to put forward candidates in every constituency. I am confident that the people, who now realise to the full what is at stake, and how much world opinion in favour of Ireland will depend upon her votes, will return none but Republican candidates outside the six county area, and within the latter area that they will strive to return the greatest number possible. Negotiations with the English Government on the basis of the Partition Act are therefore altogether out of the question.

De Valera's words were a little hollow as the Dáil's acceptance of the partition elections confirmed that Ireland, as was the wishes of the British government and the Unionists, was now divided. The Ulster compact was agreed between de Valera and Joseph Devlin to field 42 Sinn Féin/Nationalist candidates in 10 of the six-county constituencies, with all candidates pledging themselves to abstain from the proposed parliament of Northern Ireland and accepting the principles of self-determination for Ireland. Ten candidates from the Republican/Nationalist viewpoint, five from Sinn Féin and five Nationalists were to be nominated to contest the constituency of Tyrone-Fermanagh. This cooperative compact was brought about by the intervention of the Catholic Primate to try to get as much nationalist representation as possible in Northern Ireland, which was projected at 14 seats in the 52-seat six-county parliament.

The day on which certain provisions of the Government of Ireland Act came into operation was fixed for 19 April 1921. The main provisions would become operative on 3 May after which date it was anticipated that the new Parliaments would be summoned. The boycotting of Belfast goods continued and many traders and manufacturers were now feeling the financial loss in the Belfast area, where a counter-boycott was in place.

Dáil Éireann announced that it had decided to recognise the popular elections under the Partition Act, so that the will of the people might once more be demonstrated. County Councils were told to take no part in the partial elections proposed for the Senate of the parliament of Southern Ireland. This was a reaction to the Imperial parliament having the right to nominate members to this senate.

The Dáil also voted not to co-operate with the proposed Census of 1921.

Sir James Craig, speaking at Banbridge, said: "if Sinn Féin was supreme in the Southern Parliament, it was for Mr. de Valera to head his quota in a Council of Ireland and meet his Northern colleagues to discuss matters for the benefit of Ireland as a whole. Instead of Ireland being divided, two families were asked to go into partnership."

In a report in the *Anglo-Celt* of 14 May, it was officially announced that Sir James Craig had been summoned to Dublin to meet the new Viceroy, had an interview the same day with the leader of Sinn Féin, at de Valera's request. According to the report, this meeting was not connected to his interview with the Viceroy. Sir James said that he undertook the meeting, while not having time to consult with his colleagues, to meet the leader of Sinn Féin as his own choice, "to assist all who desired the cessation of the campaign of crime in Ireland and what happened in no way modified Ulster's determination to go on". He called a private party conference on the following day to brief his Unionist colleagues. "My conversation with Mr. de Valera having taken place, and Ulster, by the acceptance of the provisions of the Government of Ireland Act, and by her undertaking to work them having reached the limit of concession, no further concession will be entered into. When the Parliaments have been established and the Council of Ireland has been constituted, there will be the necessary constitutional link between Northern Ireland and Southern Ireland." He requested the candidates to carry this message to the loyalist electors throughout the six counties.

The writs for the partition elections, under Proportional Representation, were announced with nominations closing on 13 May and polling on 24 May. The Northern Parliament was to open on 7 June and the Southern Parliament timed to open on 28 June. In Co. Cavan, Sinn Féin ratified Arthur Griffith and Peter Paul Galligan (both in jail) with Seán Milroy as the third candidate for the three seat constituency of Cavan, to serve in the Southern Parliament and they were elected unopposed. A total of 124 candidates were elected unopposed in 34 constituencies for the Southern Parliament.

During the election campaign for the Northern Parliament, over 50 of the most prominent Sinn Féin personnel and active IRA men in Fermanagh were rounded up. Some were later released. The majority were sent to Belfast and detained at His Majesty's pleasure. Among them was Terence Fitzpatrick, a native of Corlough who was a draper's assistant in Enniskillen at that time. On his release he joined the Free State army until 1926, when he came to the gent's department at Toomey's (Rudden's) in Ballyconnell. Terry was happy to forget the past and move on from the terrible days of conflict and the Irish Civil War. His dying request was consistent as he left strict instructions that he was not to have a military-style IRA funeral.

During the campaign for the Northern Parliament, a correspondent for *Truth* publication, London, alluded to the "certain phenomena", which one hopes is peculiar to the north-east corner of Ireland.

> Businessmen who have denounced the new Parliament as a farce, figured on the platform of the Unionist candidates, and cheered profiteers to the effect that the Parliament will be not only a success, but a model of its kind. Men and women who have protested for years,

and never more strongly than in the past few weeks, that in the temperance cause lay the only salvation for the country, have openly supported Unionist candidates connected with the licensed trade. Workers of both sexes who were never tired of denouncing certain employers as "sweaters" of the worst type were heard protesting that unless these employers were returned to Parliament, Ulster will be lost for ever.

A correspondent for the *Daily News,* London, reported from Belfast on the election to the Northern Parliament:

It would be hard to find an election fought with such ruthlessness, such corruption and such unfairness as the election for the Northern Parliament. The result was never in doubt. The Unionist majority will be ample enough to enable the new Parliament form its quorum and constitute a government and a Senate. That was all the more reason why considerations of fair play might have operated, and a party that took its stand on "liberty and freedom" and made the Union Jack its election symbol might have given its opponents the same opportunity of exercising their opinions through the ballot that is granted in most democratic countries.

Mr. Joseph Devlin said: He had never known an election more brazenly corrupt. "Not only have we lost hundreds of votes by intimidation, but the Unionists have personated our voters and thus gained two for every man and woman they kept away. Ulster Volunteers, armed, were inside every booth and at the doors. Wherever we were strong, there were military and police along with the volunteer Specials, wherever we were weak there was nobody to protect our voters, but the Unionists Specials. Personation was common and organised. A nationalist family of five voters from Mayo St., West Belfast arrived at the booth; they found they had all been personated. There were many such similar incidents in the West Belfast Constituency." When Mr. Devlin's agent interviewed the Chief of Police, he replied that he was short-handed and powerless and could not call on military assistance.

In West Belfast there was a 93.5% turnout, which should have comfortably returned two Nationalist/Sinn Féin candidates, but only Joseph Devlin succeeded, proving personation on a large scale.

Sir James Craig in a special article in the *Pall Mall and Globe* wrote:

There need be no fear that when the Ulster Parliament is established on a sound, workable and loyal basis — as I firmly believe it will be— the ideal of liberty for which the Ulster race has fought for so long will be abrogated or impaired by prejudice. Religious intolerance will find no favour in our counsels. A man's conscience is his own, and every man in the six counties will be free to worship God according to the dictates of his own heart.

In the constituency of Tyrone-Fermanagh, 11 candidates contested the eight seats for the Northern Parliament; Sinn Féin nominated 5 candidates — Arthur Griffith, Seán Milroy, John O'Mahony, Sean McEntee and Kevin O'Shiel. Arthur Griffith (in jail) polled 21,677 votes, the next highest to Sir James Craig's vote in Down. Griffith's surplus of 12,371 votes ensured the election of Milroy and O'Mahony. T.J.S. Harbison was elected for the Nationalists and Rt. Hon. E.M. Archdale MP, W. Coote, J. Cooper and W.T. Millar were elected for the Unionist Party. Tyrone-Fermanagh voted 54.4% for the Sinn Féin/Nationalist alliance and 45.6% for the Unionists. On the eve of the election, police and Ulster Specials disrupted Sinn Féin rallies at Derrylin and Kinawley. From the percentages indicated there had to be some personation of votes in Fermanagh/Tyrone.

Also elected for Sinn Féin were: Eamon de Valera (16,269 votes) in Down; Michael Collins (12,656 votes) in Armagh and Prof. Eoin MacNeill (11,866 votes) in Derry. All refused to take their seats and they forfeited their deposits.

Sir James Craig, the Unionist leader, received 29,829 votes in the eight seat constituency of Down.

Following the elections, an editorial in the *Impartial Reporter* was headed: Unionists Triumphant, — The Union Jack has swept Ulster, – – Not one Unionist candidate has been defeated, — SINN FEIN ROUTED.

After the elections to the six-county parliament, the IRA carried out what is often said to be its last major operation against the British establishment in Dublin. On 25 May 1921, at one o'clock in the afternoon an estimated 120 IRA men advanced on the Customs House, one of the main centres of British administration in Ireland, and set the building on fire. The men were poorly armed but were well supplied with petrol and flammable material to set the building ablaze. It was the wish and direction of de Valera that a major show of strength had to be shown to the British in order to bring them to negotiations. Michael Collins, as Commander-in-Chief was over-ruled as he knew that his men had very little ammunition left and wanted smaller and more effective operations carried out. Dublin-based IRA men who had guns, some with as little of three rounds of ammunition, cycled, walked or took the tram to the Customs House where they discharged their ammunition and left the scene; some it is believed threw their weapons into the Liffey. Eight civilians and Volunteers lost their lives and 111 members of the IRA were arrested. Volunteers blocked streets around the area to prevent the fire services getting to the building. One of Dublin's most prestigious and best architecturally designed building was gutted. Military operations by the IRA were to continue.

CHAPTER 11

THE KING SPEAKS

(i) Six-county parliament opens

The newly elected parliament for the six north-eastern counties of Ireland assembled in the Council Chamber, City Hall, Belfast for the first time on 7 June 1921. The elected Unionist members and their guests were present and all formalities were carried out in the presence of the Viceroy, Lord Fitzalan. Addressing the house, Lord Fitzalan announced that King George V would officially inaugurate the new parliament in person.

Meanwhile in west Cavan, in the early hours of Sunday, 12 June, the IRA carried out one of the most cowardly acts of the War of Independence when an estimated 20 Volunteers knocked on the door of Brackley House, Bawnboy, and demanded admission. The elderly Dean Finlay, a retired 79-year-old Church of Ireland clergyman, was awoken, taken from his house and murdered. His 83-year-old wife and others in the household were taken to a nearby farmhouse in their nightclothes while the house was ransacked and burned. His wife afterwards discovered Dean Finlay's body, just yards from the burning building.

Rev. John Finlay had been Dean of Leighlin in Carlow from 1895 to 1912. He retired back to his old homestead outside the village of Bawnboy, where he was born and where he wished to die. It was rumoured in the area that Crown forces were to occupy his house, as some weeks earlier, military officers were seen inspecting it. Dean Finlay was a very popular gentleman, not only within his own Church of Ireland community, but also with the Catholic Bishop of Kilmore and local Catholic clergy. These, together with their communities, rightly condemned this atrocity. This was an official and sanctioned act of the War of Independence, undertaken by the Corlough command of the IRA. From oral comments recorded in later years, "the operation went terribly wrong".

The *Impartial Reporter*, in an editorial of 16 June 1921, informed its readers of the impending visit of King George to Belfast in the following week to open the new parliament for the six counties and also on the details of the atrocity at Bawnboy. It also reported on the death toll of Crown forces in Ireland in the previous week which, according to the paper, was greater than during the Easter rebellion. Lambasting the British government, it said:

The present government are incapable of governing. Sinn Féin outwits our military commanders at every turn, the public offices are honeycombed with Sinn Féin spies, the proclamations of the military government are scoffed at, our soldiers are incapable of acting promptly when required, and in many cases they are but the tools of women who lead them to their doom... Sinn Féin is making war. The government are only pretending to make war on Sinn Féin...

Why was the *Impartial Reporter* and its editor being so critical of the Westminster government which, under the Partition Act, had just given the six counties its own elected parliament on terms which most Ulster Unionists wanted. Or, was the paper acting on the intentions of Winston Churchill, Chairman of the Cabinet Committee on Irish Affairs, who along with his "diehards" within the cabinet, were planning to unleash a new reign of terror on southern Ireland to defeat the IRA? A formal dossier was drawn up by Churchill for such a campaign in Ireland and probably in line with an interview given by Michael Collins to the *Philadelphia Public Ledger* when Collins said: "Our army is becoming stronger every day, its morale is improving, its efficiency is increasing." Collins was bluffing, as only he well knew that the IRA had nothing left to fight with.

Ten days after the Bawnboy atrocity, King George V and Queen Mary arrived in Belfast by sea and both were given an enthusiastic welcome. The carriage carrying the King and Queen was escorted through Belfast by the 10th Hussars brought from the Curragh Camp for this special occasion. The King and Queen were received with due pomp at the City Hall where King George officially inaugurated the six-county parliament. He said:

For all who love Ireland, as I do with all my heart, this is a profoundly moving occasion in Irish history. My memories of the Irish people date back to the time when I spent many happy days in Ireland as a midshipman. My affection for the Irish people has been deepened by the successive visits since that time, and I have watched with constant sympathy the course of their affairs.

I could not have allowed myself to give Ireland by deputy alone my earnest prayers and good wishes in the new era which opens with this ceremony, and I have therefore come in person, as the Head of the Empire, to inaugurate this parliament on Irish soil.

I inaugurate it with deep-felt hope, and I feel assured that you will do your utmost to make it an instrument of happiness and good government for all parts of the community which you represent.

This is a great and critical occasion in the history of the six counties, but not for the six counties alone, for everything which interests them touches Ireland, and everything which touches Ireland finds an echo in the remotest parts of the Empire.

Few things are more earnestly desired throughout the English-speaking world than a satisfactory solution of the age-long Irish problems, which for generations embarrassed our forefathers, as they now weigh heavily upon us.

Most certainly there is no wish nearer my own heart than that every man of Irish birth, whatever be his creed and wherever be his home, should work in loyal co-operation with the free communities on which the British Empire is based.

I am confident that the important matters entrusted to the control and guidance of the Northern parliament will be managed with wisdom and with moderation, with fairness and due regard to every faith and interest, and with no abatement of that patriotic devotion to the Empire which you proved so gallantly in the Great War.

Full partnership in the United Kingdom and religious freedom Ireland has long enjoyed. She now has conferred upon her the duty of dealing with all the essential tasks of domestic legislation and government; and I feel no misgiving as to the spirit in which you who stand here today will carry out the all-important functions entrusted to your care.

My hope is broader still. The eyes of the whole Empire are on Ireland today, that Empire in which so many nations and races have come together in spite of ancient feuds, and in which new nations have come to birth within the lifetime of the youngest in this hall.

I am emboldened by that thought to look beyond the sorrow and the anxiety which have clouded of late my vision of Irish affairs. I speak from a full heart when I pray that my coming to Ireland today may prove to be the first step towards an end of strife amongst her people, whatever their race or creed. In that hope, I appeal to all Irishmen to pause, to stretch out the hand of forbearance and conciliation, to forgive and to forget, and to join in making for the land which they love a new era of peace, contentment, and goodwill.

It is my earnest desire that in Southern Ireland, too, there may ere long take place a parallel to what is now passing in this hall; that there a similar occasion may present itself and a similar ceremony be performed.

For this the parliament of the United Kingdom has in the fullest measure provided the powers; for this the parliament of Ulster is pointing the way. The future lies in the hands of my Irish people themselves.

May this historic gathering be the prelude of a day in which the Irish people, north and south, under one parliament or two, as those parliaments may themselves decide, shall work together in common love for Ireland upon the sure foundations of mutual justice and respect.

This was a most conciliatory address by King George, which surprised Sir James Craig and his fellow Unionists, in expressing his personal wish that all Irish people would come together in the mutual interests of Ireland and the Empire. The King coming to Belfast to open the new parliament for the six counties did not at first have much enthusiastic political support within Westminster. King George was determined to visit Ireland to deliver his message and for southern Ireland to have an equal parliament. Normally British monarchs would have their official speeches or addresses composed by advisors in collaboration with relevant government ministers, but not on this occasion. After rejecting the official speech given to him by his government, the King's message was composed by himself with advice from the Prime Minister of the Union of South African, General Jan Christian Smuts.

In spite of such appeasing tones, the troop train returning from Belfast to the Curragh Camp, which was carrying the 10th Hussars, was derailed and ambushed near Dundalk, Co. Louth. Three Hussars were killed and 21 injured while 30 of their horses were killed. Two civilians and a guard also died. The ambush was carried out by the IRA, who earlier took the men working on the line and held them in a house nearby. The rebels then loosened sections of the line and placed mines, which were exploded by the passing train.

(ii) Anglo-Irish truce

At this time the British Premier David Lloyd George was coming under increased internal and international political pressure to address the Irish situation, while diehards within his government were quite happy to allow the war in Ireland to continue and escalate. On 24 June, and just 48 hours after the King had spoken in Belfast, the following invitation was sent by Lloyd George to Eamon de Valera, President of Sinn Féin, to attend a conference in London:

Sir,

The British Government are deeply anxious that, so far as they can assure it, the King's appeal for reconciliation in Ireland shall not have been made in vain. Rather than allow another opportunity of settlement in Ireland to be cast aside, they feel it incumbent upon them to make a final appeal in the spirit of the King's words for a conference between themselves and the representatives of Southern and Northern Ireland.

I write, therefore, to convey the following invitation to you as the chosen leader of the great majority in Southern Ireland, and to Sir James Craig, the Premier of Northern Ireland:

That you should attend a conference here in London in company with Sir James Craig, to explore to the utmost the possibility of a settlement;

That you should bring with you for the purpose, any colleagues whom you may select. The Government will, of course, give a safe conduct to all who may choose to participate in the conference.

We make this invitation with the fervent desire to end the ruinous conflict which has for centuries divided Ireland and embittered the relations of the peoples of these two islands, who ought to live in neighbourly harmony with each other and whose cooperation would mean so much not only to the Empire but to humanity.

We wish that no endeavour should be lacking on our part to realise the King's prayer, and we ask you to meet us, as we will meet you, in the spirit of conciliation for which His Majesty appealed.

A similar invitation was sent to Sir James Craig who convened a meeting of his cabinet to consider it. Accepting the invitation he responded: "In view of the appeal conveyed to us by His Majesty in his gracious message on the opening of the Northern Parliament for peace throughout Ireland, we cannot refuse to accept your invitation to a conference to discuss how best this can be accomplished..."

De Valera responded to the invitation:

... I am in consultation with such of the principal representatives of our nation as are available. [Arthur Griffith and others were in Mountjoy Jail and were released within days on instructions from the British cabinet]. We most earnestly desire to help in bringing peace and a lasting peace between the peoples of these two islands, but see no avenue by which it can be reached if you deny Ireland's essential unity and set aside the principles of national self-determination ... I am seeking a conference with certain representatives of the political minority in this country...

To discuss the political situation and how it would affect the minority in Ireland, de Valera invited Sir James Craig and the southern Unionists, the Earl of Middleton, Sir M. E. Dockrell, Sir R. H. Woods and Mr A. Jameson, to meet him at the Mansion House, Dublin, on the following Monday. Sir James Craig refused, indicating that he had already accepted the Prime Minister's invitation to the London conference. De Valera believed it was courteous and valuable to meet with the southern Unionists prior to the London conference because he felt it would strengthen his hand in negotiations.

Meanwhile discussions were also under way between the British authorities in Ireland and Sinn Féin on a military truce.

De Valera's meeting with the invited southern Unionists took place with Arthur Griffith and senior Sinn Féin personnel present. General Macready representing the British forces joined them for their views on the proposed military truce. Political developments between Dublin and London were moving rapidly and the terms of a military truce were published on 9 July in a special issue of the *Irish Bulletin* from Óglaigh na hÉireann GHQ Dublin and signed "By General Order":

To Officers Commanding all Units -
In view of the conversations now being entered into by our Government with the Government of Great Britain, and in pursuance of mutual understandings to suspend hostilities during these conversations, active operations by our troops will be suspended, as and from noon, Monday, July Eleventh.

Signed: Risteard Ua Maolghatha (Mulcahy), Chief of Staff

The terms of the truce were finally agreed on that same day as negotiated by General Macready, Col. J. Brind, and A. W. Cope, Assistant Under-

Secretary acting for the British forces and Comdt. R. J. Barton TD and Comdt. E. J. Duggan TD, acting for the "Army of the Republic". The truce was warmly welcomed by the people. Its main term was to confine the British military in Ireland to barracks, while the IRA agreed to cease all hostilities while the London conference was taking place.

On 12 July, Eamon de Valera, Arthur Griffith, Austin Stack and Robert Barton travelled to the conference in London. The Irish delegation held a preliminary meeting with their British counterparts on 14 July to form the basis for the conference.

Commenting on the rapidly changing military atmosphere in Ireland and the prospects for the London conference now under way, the *Anglo-Celt* in an editorial said:

> … The Truce which has been agreed upon is being honourably observed on both sides and life for the ordinary citizen has once more become bearable. To judge from the press opinions of other lands, there is a widespread feeling of pleasure at the likelihood of peace coming to this country and an optimism as to the effect this would bring to many considerations of worldwide importance. That the anticipation of the Irish people themselves may be realised and the old feud ended is the wish of all who desire the future welfare and happiness of the country.

All British newspapers were forecasting that the conference would go on for many months.

In the 28 July issue of the *Impartial Reporter*, an article headlined "The King's Part in Irish Truce" was most revealing. It quoted Lord Northcliffe in an interview with the *New York Times* and other American newspapers, as published on the previous Monday, on the King's responsibilities in bringing about an Irish armistice. The main context of the interview came when Lord Northcliffe told the papers:

> The King informed Lloyd George: "I cannot have my people killed in this manner". It is not generally known, said Lord Northcliffe, that in our constitutional form of government, the King has still a good deal of power when he chooses to use it. In this case he has done so to good effect. At the last meeting he had with Mr Lloyd George before leaving for Ireland, the King asked him: "Are you going to shoot all the people in Ireland?" "No, your Majesty", the Premier replied. "Well then," said the King, "You must come to some agreement with them.

This thing cannot go on. I cannot have my people killed in this manner." [Also editorial comment in the *Anglo-Celt* 3 August]

Lord Northcliffe confirmed that the famous speech delivered by the King at the opening of the Northern parliament was of his own inspiration. He got under the skin of the Irish people by his generosity and that is what gave them confidence in the peace overtures which they would not have felt in the Lloyd George cabinet without his backing. It was the King who saw General Smuts and got him interested in the Irish question. I know that he [Smuts] had a great deal to do with winning over the Sinn Féin leaders to the idea of a conference. When Lloyd George and the Cabinet had realised the feelings of the King and the people on the question of peace with Ireland, the invitation to Mr de Valera from London followed in 48 hours.

When King George sailed for Ireland, continued Lord Northcliffe, the cabinet tried to spike his efforts by making speeches in the Lords and Commons three hours afterwards, which were intended to irritate the Irish people. This annoyed the English people very much. When the King returned from Belfast, he had the biggest reception outside Buckingham Palace that he had ever received since the war began.

Lord Northcliffe added that he had noticed that the Crown had not been mentioned in the terms that purported to have been offered to de Valera for the Irish people. Northcliffe thought this might mean that the "oath of allegiance" to King George might not have to be taken by members of parliament when it met in Dublin, as that had always been a stumbling block years ago. The King, said Northcliffe, probably said to the cabinet: "I trust them".

King George V (1910-36) was a moderniser and an active monarch as demonstrated by him during the Great War. At the beginning of his reign, he promised Herbert Asquith, the then Liberal Premier, that he would create sufficient peers to overcome the Tory majority in the House of Lords to facilitate the passing of the Parliament Act. The Lords passed the act in 1911 without the King having to create the vast number of peers required. (There was a "whiff" of some irregularities surrounding Lloyd George on the issue of creating Peers at that time) This was critical in creating stable government in Britain with the support of the IPP, leading to the introduction of the Third Home Rule Bill. King George was the first British sovereign of the Empire to use modern means of communications when he addressed the Empire on radio at Christmas 1932.

Perhaps it was the Irish question and the use of Lord Northcliffe's interview to the American press that was the first occasion for a British monarch to indirectly use the media to make his point known. Lord Northcliffe's interview was timely in that it was perhaps used to quell the anti-British bias that was growing in America on the Irish question and to encourage the treaty negotiations that were under way in London to continue to a successful conclusion.

The peace overtures continued during the summer of 1921 and the military truce was holding. Discussions between Lloyd George and de Valera continued in private and did not appear to produce much by way of agreement. Dáil Éireann, under the terms of the Partition Act 1920, was obliged to meet in late June but did not reassemble formally until mid-August to discuss political developments with London. De Valera addressed the house on his political deliberations and recommended rejection of the British Premier's proposals. De Valera confirmed this rejection to Lloyd George. The British Premier replied that they could not acknowledge Ireland's right to secede from its allegiance to the King.

Lloyd George's difficulties getting anywhere in negotiations with de Valera were confirmed some months later when he said that "arguing with de Valera is like trying to catch a man on a merry-go-round, or picking up mercury with a fork". On hearing this comment, de Valera replied: "Why doesn't he try a spoon?"*

Prior to the British parliament adjourning for its summer holidays, Lloyd George, in regard to Ireland, said:

> They had put forward everything that they could concede to purchase peace and the goodwill of the Irish people. If the proposals were rejected by Sinn Féin, it [parliament] would be summoned again... Nothing could be said at this stage, he feared, that could possibly be helpful... The Irish atmosphere at best was always full of suspicion and suspicion distorted the facts ...Britain must accept its full share of responsibility for the condition of the Irish atmosphere...

Correspondence between Dublin and London continued in the interest of maintaining the truce. The terms of the truce were periodically broken,

* (Conor O'Cleary - Ireland in Quotes)

particularly in Belfast, and with some incidents in the south as a new generation joined the IRA. Sir James Craig withdrew from the London conference at an early date, saying he would return when the government and de Valera had agreed peace terms.

At that time, a correspondent from the French publication, *Liberté*, interviewed de Valera who said:

> During the war, Irishmen wanted to fight for France, not to fight for England. My only mandate is to obtain independence for our country. My work will then be ended … The powerful minority in Ulster consists of elements foreign to the country and my government will make every possible concession to Ulstermen who recognise their Irish nationality. We will give Dominion Home Rule to those opting for Ireland and will fully compensate those opting for England and wanting to leave Ireland to establish themselves elsewhere...”

(iii) Anglo-Irish Treaty

On 6 October 1921, Lloyd George sent a fresh invitation to de Valera and his chosen delegates to a conference in London on 11 October. The conference would meet, the invitation said, “with a view to ascertaining how the association of Ireland with the community of nations known as the British Empire may best be reconciled with Irish national aspirations”. De Valera’s response said: “... Our respective positions have been stated and are understood, and we agree that conference, not correspondence, is the most practical and hopeful way to an understanding. We accept your invitation…”

De Valera was adamant that he would not return to London and he assembled his plenipotentiaries to be led by Arthur Griffith and a very reluctant Michael Collins. The other members of the team were Robert Barton, Eamon J. Duggan and George Gavan Duffy. Erskine Childers, an English convert to Irish republicanism, travelled as one of the secretaries to the delegation. On accepting de Valera’s request to lead the plenipotentiaries, Griffith said: “But I know, and you know, I can’t bring back a republic.” The people of Ireland were somewhat surprised and disappointed that de Valera did not return to London to lead in the fresh negotiations at Downing Street. His reasons are still debated.

As the Treaty negotiations got under way in London, both sides dealt with procedural matters and issues prior to the serious questions being addressed. As the talks were continuing the truce was coming under threat, when

Unionist fears were raised that republican arms and ammunition were being moved northwards under the veil of the truce. This IRA action was in response to sectarian attacks against Catholics in the Belfast area.

The Sinn Féin members of Fermanagh County Council continued to wobble between their allegiance to Dáil Éireann and the British Local Government Board. "They recognise the latter when it suits their purpose – that is, when they are seeking grants or the sanctioning of newly appointed officials. For window-dressing purposes, they profess allegiance to Sinn Féin when the business is innocuous and of no value." This was the *Impartial Reporter* view of the situation in November 1921

Real political friction was evident in Fermanagh when at a meeting of the Lisnaskea Board of Guardians, a circular was read about the transfer of powers and duties to the parliament of Northern Ireland. The chairman Louis McElgunn asked: "Gentlemen, are you going to accept this document and send our business to Belfast, or, to put it briefly, to send it to an 'Orange Lodge', which it simply means? There is no such thing as a Northern parliament; it is only a farce and is bankrupt already." He proposed the following resolution: "That we, the Guardians of Lisnaskea Union, do hereby change our allegiance to Dail Éireann Local Government Board for the future and that the above resolution applies to all our officers in future." Omagh Urban District Council likewise voted to transfer its allegiance to Dáil Éireann.

Sean T. O'Kelly TD, who was the Envoy of the Irish Republic to Paris, in an interview in *Excelsior*, said:

Dáil Éireann is desirous of the success of the negotiations, which alone can offer a solution to the Irish question. The general feeling in Ireland is favourable to peace but Ireland will not have peace at any price obtained by the denial of her inalienable right ... The Irish policy with regard to Ulster is very clear. The Irish government has no intention of dominating Ulster, which it views with fraternal sympathy, and there is no idea of coercion or reprisals. Ulster will enjoy in the bosom of the Irish Federation the largest measure of autonomy compatible with national sovereignty, in which it will participate without restrictions or reservations

As the serious matters of the Anglo-Irish negotiations got under way at Downing St, Arthur Griffith attempted to row back the Government of Ireland Act 1920. He cited Grattan's Parliament of 1772 as a template for a new all-Ireland parliament in Dublin as opposed to the two parliaments proposed. Griffith's argument was somewhat futile, as the six-county parliament was already mandated from the elections of May 1921 and Ireland was in every respect partitioned. Lloyd George, through political connivance and perhaps with some respect for Griffith, asked Sir James Craig: "Would the parliament of the six counties be subjected to the authority of a Dublin parliament?" Sir James replied with an emphatic Ulster "no" and "not an inch".

However, this point was inserted into the formal agreement, which the six-county parliament had to accept or reject within 30 days. The answer was obvious and "Ulstershire", the fear of the Fermanagh writer, Shan F. Bullock, was formally ratified. This decision would remain an issue of importance for the nationalist people in the north east and a political hot potato for the new Irish Free State.

By late November, the London talks were reaching a stalemate and according to an announcement from the Press Association: "The deadlock had been averted and a totally different phase had been entered upon, as a result of the bringing forward of an entirely new set of proposals." The Boundary Commission idea became Article 12 of the Treaty, "to determine the wishes of inhabitants" in border areas and to be "compatible with local economic and geographic conditions". The oath to the King to be sworn by members of the Dáil was diluted to suit the Irish situation. It firstly was an oath of allegiance to the Irish Free State, and secondly a promise of fidelity to the King as head of the Commonwealth to which Ireland belonged. This second element was agreed in recognition of the King's role in advancing the military truce and the Anglo-Irish Treaty. Britain was to retain control of a number of Irish ports.

As the negotiations were reaching a conclusion in London, de Valera was in Limerick with Mrs Tom Clarke where they received the freedom of the city. De Valera, who in the opinion of the majority of the people should have been in London, was on a tour of the west, reviewing the IRA volunteers and undertook a personal campaign by encouraging many more young men to join the ranks.

Griffith and Collins were finally negotiating full "fiscal control" for the Irish Free State. The new state would have full liberty to control its own finances and to generate its own taxes. It was on this point that Griffith and Collins were finally convinced to accept what was negotiated. Lloyd George, with the threat of war, gave the Irish negotiating team a deadline of one and a half hours to accept and sign or reject. The plenipotentiaries deliberated for over four hours until 2.30 a.m. on 6 December 1921, when they decided to sign. They were very tired men. In their wisdom, Griffith and Collins accepted the political option and signed, knowing that the Irish people were tired of war. They had nothing left to fight another war against the might of the Empire. E. J. Duggan signed and then the reluctant Robert Barton and George Gavan Duffy signed. The latter two, having deep reservations, could not shoulder the responsibility of another war in Ireland.

The Treaty was received with great jubilation by the majority of the people in Ireland and congratulations were sent from Pope Benedict XV to de Valera and King George. But de Valera and the hardline republican members of Dáil Éireann were not so approving and after a cabinet meeting on 8 December, de Valera issued this statement:

> The terms of this agreement are in violent conflict with the wishes of the majority of this nation as expressed freely in successive elections during the past three years. I feel it is my duty to inform you immediately that I cannot recommend the acceptance of this Treaty, either to Dáil Éireann or the country...

Much has been said and written about the Dáil debates over the Anglo-Irish Treaty and the many acrimonious clashes on the issues, which would split the Sinn Féin movement and result in Ireland's Civil War. It was during these debates that Michael Collins, in putting forward his convictions as to why he signed the Treaty, most famously said:

> In my opinion it gives us freedom; not the ultimate freedom that all nations desire and develop to, but the freedom to achieve it.

The historic words expressed by Collins then can be compared with the words of Nelson Mandela, on his release from prison in 1989:

> When I walked out of prison, that was my mission: to liberate the oppressed and the oppressor both. Some say this has now been achieved. But I know that is not the case. The truth is that we are not yet free; we have merely achieved the freedom to be free, the right not to be oppressed.

Lloyd George's Dream

There's a yarn going round in old Ireland today,
From Queenstown's fair harbour to famous Lough Neagh.
It tells of Lloyd George's most wonderful dream.
To some of our people quite strange it may seem.
It happened one night as George tossed in his bed,
To add to his troubles, he dreamt he was dead.

He fancied he heard a wild curdling cry:
"Your time has come, David Lloyd George, you must die."
It was all Gaelic leaders surrounding his coffin,
With lots of Sinn Féiners all smoking and laughing.
There were no friends amongst them to mourn his sad fate,
So he made straight to Heaven and knocked on the gate.

St Peter called out, that the whole World might hear:
"You little Welsh twister, you can't get in here.
You'd better be off for Saint Patrick and Colum
Don't give one straw for the Defence of the Realm.
And maybe perhaps in much less than a jiffy,
You'll be somewhere in Erin quite close to the Liffey.
Amongst those whose loved ones were slain by your horde,
Because they loved Erin next to the Lord."

"For all sakes, Peter," says George, "do be civil;
A better reception I'd have from the devil."
Then he started on Ireland and her place in the war,
When a roar from St Patrick tumbled a star.
"Don't believe him," he cried, "he was always a liar.
You had better dispatch him right off to the fire."
One thought up to then David's mind had not crossed:
That an English Prime Minister's soul could be lost.

One last look at Heaven and off he did go
In a great submarine to the regions below.
But when he got there he was filled with dismay
As he landed in time to hear Satan say:
"Look here, boys, I want to give you a tip.

I'm expecting Lloyd George in a new style of ship.
He must not get in here; he has for too much cheek.
He'd be head gaffer here in much less than a week.
Then he'd send for McPherson and Mr French too,
And that, my dear friend, would be our Waterloo."

Just then he eyed David, his ear cocked outside.
"You've been listening, you rascal," he loudly cried.
"I've heard of your mean dirty tricks before,
But I'm hanged if I thought that you'd spy at my door."
"Don't chase me," said George, "I've got lots of gold.
Lucifer, Jewel, I'm shivering with cold.
Let me into a corner, that least wee bit hot."
"Oh no," said the old fellow, "certainly not.
We cannot admit men for riches alone.
Here's brimstone, be off, make a hell of your own."

Then Pitt wired John Bull: "Oh what a sin.
Our boss wouldn't let your Prime Minister in."
And Oliver Cromwell and Lord Castlereagh,
Their heads bowed in sorrow, led David away.
And Milner and Churchill appeared in the smoke,
And then, with a start, the Welsh Wizard awoke.

"That's a dream," he said, "I will never forget.
But maybe I'll be even with these fellows yet.
"There's one de Valera, the MP for Clare,
I'll have him locked up in a dungeon I swear.
T'was he who made me dream I thought Ireland was free
And if he is leader, free she must be.

"But the Castle will continue to fix up each little plot,
And old Johnny French will make things nice and hot.
But, those darn Rebels will know what they are at,
and for King George and the Realm, that will be that.
For I won't go to heaven, I know very well,
But it will be very humbling to be kicked out of hell."

Author or Authors unknown

CHAPTER 12

THE GREAT DIVIDE

(i) Debating the Treaty

The first edition of the *Anglo-Celt* for 1922 reported on many aspects of the new Ireland that was developing on foot of the Anglo-Irish Treaty. Local authorities and organisations such as farming societies and trade unions expressed their support for the treaty.

"A View from Abroad" was a headline given to the following letter received from New York and published on the *Celt*'s front page:

As a former Cavan boy, son of a well-known clergyman, and for 40 years an American citizen, I wish to tell my Irish friends and relatives in Ireland that liberal American opinion endorses the Treaty between the Free State of Ireland and the British Empire. Since manhood, in sympathy with my deceased father, I have been a constant Home Ruler. Today is Ireland's grandest opportunity. Her best friends in America endorse the Treaty. To refuse it would be suicide. As an Irish-born American Protestant, who has no bigotry in his blood, I say: stand by Collins and Griffith, without any prejudice to my honest and brave friend de Valera. Let us deal with realities and not be carried away by impracticable sentimentalities.

Signed: William John Guard

Other front-page articles included: "Republican View – Why the Treaty is Opposed", taken from the first issue of *Poblacht na hÉireann*, edited by Liam Mellows TD;

"A New Year's Peace Message" from Sir James Craig was published while a report from a meeting of Cavan Co. Council supported the Treaty by a majority vote of 17 to two.

The ratification of the Anglo-Irish Treaty on 7 January 1922 by a majority of seven votes (64-57) in Dáil Éireann was welcomed throughout the county with the tricolour being displayed. The Rev. P. O'Connell, PP , Cootehill, sent a telegram to Dublin: "Cavan unanimously congratulates Griffith and Milroy." In Swanlinbar, the local creamery announced the ratification of the treaty with two hours of siren blowing on the following Sunday morning. It could be distinctly heard over Slieve Rushen at Ballyconnell .

Eoin O'Duffy, TD for Monaghan in one of the many acrimonious Treaty debates in Dáil Éireann, said:

He was not very enthusiastic about the Ulster clauses in the Treaty. But no one suggested that Ulster should be coerced. They were unanimous about that ... He held that it was the business of a Deputy who had lived in Ulster to come forward with a suggestion. He knew the businessmen of Ulster did not want separation but would demand of the so-called Northern parliament to come to terms with the rest of Ireland, and if they refused, they would kick them out. During the war between Ireland and England, Belfast lost thousands of pounds in business. They had since made a desperate effort to bring back their customers and he was satisfied that they would not cut themselves off from a prosperous Ireland. The businessmen of the North would want to join up under the Treaty, but the Orange assassins were against them. Personally he would prefer – and leading Catholics agreed with him – that it would be better, perhaps, that Ulster should not come in at the present, that they should stay out just for a trial, as later on they would find they would have to come in and they would be easier spoken to.

Whatever tones of understanding shown and expressed by O'Duffy up to this point were soon dissipated when speaking about the abandoned Unionists in Monaghan, Cavan and Donegal when he said:

They were no fools but knew the treatment they would get if they joined up with their enemies. He continued by referring to "using the lead" against those who had committed many atrocities, some of which he described in gruesome detail, against people in Newry, Belfast and Cookstown. He concluded by asking the Dáil to consider what would happen if the Treaty was rejected: "There would be callous cold-blooded murders. For all of the atrocities committed in the country by the Black and Tans – and these were many – there was nothing to equal the atrocities committed on the Catholic people in Ulster by the Specials. The Ulster Deputies who voted against the Treaty should understand that they had a grave and solemn responsibility before them when they did so...

John O'Mahony, TD for Fermanagh/Tyrone, and Seán McEntee, O'Duffy's fellow TD for Monaghan, voted against the Treaty. The three Cavan TDs, Arthur Griffith, Seán Milroy and Peter Paul Galligan, voted for the Treaty.

After the Treaty was accepted, de Valera resigned his position as President of Dáil Éireann. Three days later, the Dáil reassembled and de Valera was proposed as President, which was defeated by two votes. He and his anti-Treaty supporters walked out of Dáil Éireann, and so a new government had to be formed. Arthur Griffith replaced de Valera as President and he appointed a new cabinet, comprising Michael Collins, George Gavan Duffy, Eamonn J. Duggan, W.T. Cosgrove, Kevin O'Higgins and Richard Mulcahy.

(ii) Collins-Craig pact

On 14 January 1922, the pro-Treaty Dáil deputies and the four Trinity College Unionists met in the Mansion House Dublin and formed a Provisional Government with Michael Collins as its Chairman. Eoin MacNeill, Fionán Lynch, P.J. Hogan and Joe McGrath were also added to the cabinet. This Provisional Government, under the terms of the Treaty, took control of the 26 counties from the British at Dublin Castle on 16 January, a very symbolic occasion. Major cracks were developing within the Sinn Féin party and the IRA – internal matters which Collins and his cabinet would have to deal with as they undertook the bread-and-butter issues of government.

Michael Collins took on the leadership of the Provisional Government with renewed energy to activate the conditions of the Anglo-Irish Treaty while holding the position of Minister for Finance. Up to the time of the Treaty, Collins was better known as a soldier but he was now to show all the prowess of a statesman in the early days of the Free State as he also set up a Constitutional Committee to draft a new Constitution for the Free State.

On that same January day, a Monaghan County Gaelic football team travelled to Derry, ostensibly to play Tyrone in a football match, with a mission to spring three republican prisoners from Derry Jail who were under sentence of death. The Monaghan men were all arrested and detained without charge by the B Specials at Dromore, Co. Tyrone. This action, in association with on-going attacks by the Specials on pockets of the Catholic population in the six counties left Dublin with no option but to retaliate. The Provisional Government and the pro-Treaty forces had to rapidly organise military actions within the six counties while Collins was negotiating with Sir James Craig and London to implement the conditions of the Treaty. The campaign to be carried out by the IRA within the six counties was to kidnap as many prominent Unionists or Orangemen as possible and to hold them hostage for the release of all republicans held. This action had a more important internal political motive to bring the anti-Treaty forces in line with the pro-Treaty forces to fight the partition issue. Michael Collins wanted to heal the divisions within the Sinn Féin family while also wanting to make partition unworkable. The IRA activities in the six counties would encourage Sir James Craig to the table, to talks with Collins, so he could be seen to be acting from a Unionist perspective in bringing these IRA actions to an end. Collins would still be in control.

The *Impartial Reporter*, in an editorial of 23 January 1922, commenting on the Collins-Craig pact and headed "The Understanding," said:

Sir James Craig and Mr Michael Collins justified their meeting by its results. It was a bold stroke by the Ulster Premier to meet Mr Collins, and better still, to meet without a third party, for if those two could not come to an amicable arrangement, the Englishman could not help them. On no account would we trust any representative of Mr Lloyd George or Mr Austen Chamberlain on such an occasion. Those two themselves have been faithless and would expect faithless service.

The Ulster Boycott is declared off – not as great a bargain as some people might consider, as the retaliatory measures of Belfast were already causing dismay in the opposite camp. But it will enable the man of business to deal as he likes and how he likes with Belfast or out of it, without tyranny of those boycotters who in their ignorance think they can divert trade from its legitimate channels by coercion. It may succeed for a little time but only for a time.

The facilities for the return of Sinn Féin workers to the shipyards may be smoothed. These men did not suffer so much because they were Catholics as because they were Sinn Féin members of a bloodthirsty organisation, and later religious bigotry did develop to an abnormal degree. It is hoped that this bigotry is at an end.
[Note the misunderstood profile given to Sinn Féin].

As to the Boundary Commission, we are glad that the English element is eliminated, as the average Englishman is dense as regards Ireland and because any representative of the Lloyd George government could not be trusted. It would be much better that the two governments – of Northern and Southern Ireland – should arrange this matter themselves without recourse to the services of a third party.

Finally, it is much better that North and South should begin their respective spheres of government by mutual respect and understanding, without friction, and dominated by a desire to benefit both. In that spirit we welcome the regulations, but it would be a great mistake for anyone to conclude therefore that Ulster is not as staunch as ever in regard to pursuing her own way as part of the British Empire.

From that course there will be no deviation, no matter what the Irish Free State may say or offer by way of inducement to depart from.

The historical importance and potential impact of the Craig-Collins pact of January 1922 has been somehow, and unfortunately, lost in the "muddle" of Irish history. The important points agreed and later countersigned by Dublin, Belfast and London, if enacted, would have made Northern Ireland and border areas of the south much happier places for all. The principal points of agreement of the Collins-Craig pact were in essence the following:

> Peace declared between the two parts of Ireland and all IRA activities to cease in Northern Ireland, with both governments undertaking to cooperate in every way to restore peace.
>
> Police to be reorganised in mixed districts [Catholic and Protestant] and Specials withdrawn and arms handed in. All police to be numbered and arms strictly controlled.
>
> An independent committee to be set up in Belfast to investigate complaints of intimidation etc. and such committee to have direct access to heads of government.
>
> A plebiscite in five counties to ascertain the views of the people to set the border and eliminate the necessity of the Boundary Commission.
>
> A sum of £500,000 to be contributed by the British parliament to Ministry of Labour Northern Ireland to be expended proportionally for relief work in the Belfast area.
>
> The two governments appealed to all concerned to refrain from inflammatory speeches...

Sir James Craig, speaking at the annual general meeting of the Ulster Unionist Council in relation to his negotiations with Michael Collins, said: "He wanted Ulster to be a free part of Ireland, not a part of Ireland at war."

At the same time, Arthur Griffith, president of Dáil Éireann, in a press interview, said:

> ... We want not only peace but brotherhood with our, at present, dissident countrymen. We seek for our nationalist people in the north east nothing but the quality of Irish citizenship, and we offer frankly and sincerely to our fellow Unionist countrymen in the north east the same equality. We are at the beginning of an epoch – the rebirth of a nation – and we desire to sink the old distinctions of Unionist and Nationalist in the common name of Irishmen, whether the Irishmen be of Dublin, Cork or Belfast.

(iii) Attack on Enniskillen

In the early hours of 8 February 1922, the pro-Treaty IRA launched a concerted attack on Enniskillen and its neighbourhood with the objective of capturing prominent Unionists and holding them hostage for the release of republican prisoners held in Belfast and Derry. As a result of this poorly planned attack, the police and Specials detained 15 IRA Volunteers, most of whom were from Fermanagh. Prominent among the prisoners was the O/C Leitrim Brigade IRA and a James Reilly from Arva, Co. Cavan.

The IRA first struck the home of James Cooper MP but their action failed as Mr Cooper was well armed and able to repel the attack on himself and his home. Nearby the IRA attacked the home of George Elliott, a member of Enniskillen Urban Council and again the attack was repelled by Elliott. Ivan Carson, who had just stepped down as High-Sheriff of Fermanagh, was attacked and wounded in his home and kidnapped by the IRA. Two car loads of armed IRA men were arrested by Special Constabulary on patrol as the rebels were seeking the home of C.F. Falls, a leading Orangeman in Fermanagh. According to the *Impartial Reporter*, the rebels attacking Enniskillen came from the Irvinstown Road/Belcoo/Derrygonnelly area and from the Swanlinbar/Sligo Roads. The Provisional Government still believed that the majority in Fermanagh and Tyrone did not want to be partitioned from the Free State. The IRA took only three prisoners in the Enniskillen area.

On the same day as the Enniskillen raid, two Crossley cars full of Special Constabulary were ambushed at Newtownbutler, with five Specials wounded and one car seized along with arms and ammunition. The remainder of the Specials were detained by the IRA.

The raid on Enniskillen in the early hours of 8 February had its origins, in part, in 29 Main St, Ballyconnell. A few days before the event, Emmet Dalton, Gen. Seán Mac Eoin and Gen. Tony Lawlor, with orders from Michael Collins, came to Ballyconnell to organise the attack on Enniskillen. Dalton, Mac Eoin and Lalor arrived in Drum's and gathered prominent local people to plan "the Attack of Enniskillen". At the initial planning meeting, Ellie Drum heard her father John Drum ask Dalton if he had a map of Enniskillen. When told no, he further asked if Dalton knew that Enniskillen was a garrison town and that there was only one way in from this end (west) and if he did get in, had he a plan on how to get out.

Sixty years later in a conversation with Capt. Seán Sheridan (old IRA Ballinagh/Crossdoney) he confirmed that there was in the region of 100 IRA men gathered in Ballyconnell who were ordered to proceed, on foot, over Slieve Rushen to attack Enniskillen. Motor transport was scarce and depended on vehicles being hijacked in the locality. These men depended on local knowledge as they did not have a map or compass. According to Capt. Sheridan, their total ammunition consisted of 26 rifles, 350 rounds of ammunition, eight hand grenades and the rest were armed with pikes and pitchforks. Off they went over the hills to take Enniskillen. Capt. Sheridan did not indicate that there were other IRA commands taking part in a broader campaign of action.

The IRA men who undertook this operation were from the Corlough Brigade, South Leitrim, Crosdoney/Ballinagh and the Mountain Road. After two days, the men returned to Ballyconnell. They had got lost, and were cold and hungry. It was said that they unloaded their meagre supply of ammunition at Florencourt Police Station. They returned over the hills to Ballyconnell. All turned up in small groups over days, bar one, Gen. Tony Lalor who got separated from the rest and was feared dead. He "trundled" into Drum's yard two days after the rest.

This IRA campaign was intense over a short period in the border area from Louth/Armagh to south Donegal. Some 36 prominent Unionists or Orangemen or police Specials were kidnapped and detained for the release of republican prisoners. The centre of operations was Clones under Eoin O'Duffy. It was at Clones Railway station that four B Specials and Commandant Matt Fitzpatrick IRA were killed in a gun battle on 11 February in the Clones affray. The main Belfast to Enniskillen train, which was conveying extra B Specials to Enniskillen, had to pass through Clones, now part of the Free State. The local IRA command on hearing that 'Specials' were at the station mounted the attack. There were multiple civilian injuries; among them was Patrick Crumley, ex-IPP MP for Fermanagh/Tyrone. In late February there were exchanges of prisoners and the impasse ended.

The split in Sinn Féin and the IRA was not healing in spite of attempts at holding a Volunteer convention to address differences. The Provisional Government, in agreement with the anti-Treaty members of Sinn Féin, called a general election for the 26 counties in June 1922, as a further plebiscite on the Treaty. The Sinn Féin party managed to have pro and anti-Treaty candidates stand under Sinn Féin as before, but now using "Coalition of pro and anti-Treaty Labels". In Co. Cavan, Arthur Griffith, Seán Milroy and W. L. Cole were elected. P.F. Baxter, a prominent Sinn Féin party member, was the unsuccessful Farmers' Union candidate.

This election further deepened the split in the Sinn Féin ranks. Many independent and new small socio-economic party candidates stood, representing farming and trade-union interests. A number of sitting Sinn Féin TDs stood down, Peter Paul Galligan included, preferring to enter civilian life. From the 620,283 people who voted in the general election, pro-Treaty Sinn Féiners and other small party candidates, who were also considered pro-Treaty, received 78 per cent of the votes. The vote received by the anti-Treaty candidates, at 22 per cent, showed a decline in their support. Within days, Ireland was to enter a terrible but short-lived civil war.

(iv) The Civil War

As splits were appearing all over the country during this time, the one piece of machinery which still played its part in holding law and order together was the Dáil Courts and the degree of structures in place with the local Irish Republican Police. In Ballyconnell, the court and the Republican Police appeared to be at one, as reported in the *Anglo-Celt* on 3 June 1922:

> On the previous Sunday, before John Drum and Patrick McGinn at Ballyconnell Barracks, Vice-Commandant Joseph Robinson charged three young men named Con Donohoe, Scotstown and Belfast, John Donohoe jnr, Scotstown and Pat McGovern, Scotstown, a six-county refugee, with the alleged intimidation of Robert Crawford, coachman to J. A. Benison, Slieve Russell at 11 p. m. on the night of 27 May. Brigade Adjutant Woods deposed that a complaint was made to him concerning three men and he sent Vice-Brigadier Robinson to see them. They were asked to sign a guarantee that they would not interfere with this man's place. Con Donohoe consented but subsequently by alleged influence, he went back on this. Had these men signed the guarantee there would have been no trouble and no arrests. He requested the court to deal firmly with these men, as cases of this kind were spreading. He asked if a citizen of the Free State was to be molested and ordered out of his house, the same as was being done in Belfast and the six counties. That would not be allowed. Con Donohoe was asked to give an undertaking on the lines asked and he replied that he would but reserved his rights. He signed a written undertaking and was put under a rule of bail for six months. The cases against his brother and Pat McGovern were dismissed. An order was made against Ed Donohoe, a brother, to appear at the next Court on 10 June.

> The Donohoe household at Gortawee was about half a mile from Crawford's home at Rathkeelan.

When the motion was put before the Ballyconnell Sinn Féin Club meeting in November 1917 to re-establish a corps of the Volunteers, which was deferred, it was a case like this that the local Sinn Féin executive members were afraid would happen. Members of the local Volunteers could not be made aware of the role Annie Crawford and her father Robert would and did play during the War of Independence. Crawford's house was a target for the Volunteers looking for arms. This was for no other reason than they were members of the Church of Ireland community.

On 28 June 1922, the Provisional Government ordered the Four Courts, Dublin to be attacked to drive out the anti-Treaty forces occupying it since the previous April. Formal hostilities in the Civil War had begun. The first gun to fire on the Four Courts was manned by a young Pt. Michael McCaffrey, Swanlinbar.

Within two months, the fledgling government of the Irish Free State was to endure a double political bereavement with the sudden death of its President and TD for Cavan, Arthur Griffith, on 12 August and 10 days later the shooting dead of its Chairman, Michael Collins, in his native west Cork. Ireland's Civil War would intensify.

On the evening of 8 November 1922, Annie Crawford, now the postmistress at Ballyconnell, was threatened as she returned to her father's residence at Rathkeelan. She was followed into her home by two masked men carrying revolvers. In the house, one of them took out a watch and, placing it on the table, gave her three minutes to sign a document, which they stated was an order to clear out of the post office by noon the next day. A revolver was held to her head. Both men were total strangers to her.

Annie Crawford complied and both men signed their names, in Irish, after hers. She was advised "that the position was wanted by a soldier who had fought for his country". She left the area the next morning to stay with friends. It transpired later that a notice had been pushed under the post office door on the previous Sunday night ordering her to clear out by noon on Monday or the place would be burned down. In the interim, the district postmaster at Clones appointed Miss Crawford's sister as acting postmistress until Annie returned, intimating that if there was any further interference with the Crawfords, the office would be closed.

This action was contrary to the principles of good order and republicanism in the fledgling Free State. Annie Crawford who, a few years earlier had done so much to protect the citizens of Ballyconnell from the ravages of the forces of the Crown, became a victim of the Civil War without justification. On the retirement of Ms Montgomery from the post office, Annie Crawford was appointed postmistress with the total support of her community, Protestant and Catholic. At the time of her appointment, there was only one other applicant for the position, who was also a Protestant.

As rumours were being circulated in the district to connect a political organisation with the affair, a public meeting was called in the Town Hall (Market House) to discuss the matter. The following resolution was adopted unanimously:

> That we condemn in the strongest manner possible the action by some irresponsible individuals whom we believe do not belong to the district, in interfering by threats or otherwise with the postmistress at Ballyconnell, and we hereby request her to resume duty at once, as we are sure she has the good wishes of all the people in the district. Signed: John Drum, Chairman; Francis Dolphin, Secretary.
> According to the *Anglo-Celt*:
> Since the incident, the place has been guarded by Free State soldiers and Ms Crawford has been visited by a Catholic clergyman who advised her to return, and it is expected she will do so in a short time.

Annie Crawford did return to her post office where she remained a gracious and loyal postmistress to the people of Ballyconnell until her death in December 1968.

(v) The Sack of Ballyconnell

In the early weeks of 1923, Ballyconnell was to witness the blackest days in the history of the town. A report issued in August 1922 indicated that there were an estimated 80-100 anti-Treaty forces in west Cavan, equipped with a dozen rifles and about 20 handguns. These anti-Treaty forces were undisciplined and untrained and so little or no military action took place, due to the fact that the majority of the people were hostile to them. According to Peter Paul Galligan: "What actions there were in Co. Cavan tended to be raids from anti-Treaty columns based in the Arigna mountains in Leitrim/Roscommon." This gang was known as 'the Irregulars' and their leader was Michael Cull, an anti-Treaty volunteer, but the gang or group he led has been historically referred to as 'lawless bandits'. On 13 November 1922, it was believed that this gang shot dead James Martin, a civilian, at his home at Drumcar, Cavan and on 10 December there was a large-scale raid on

Blacklion, Co. Cavan by some 60 of these same guerrillas, where they looted shops and kidnapped Dr Hamilton."

On Saturday 6 January 1923, two cars with these Irregulars entered Ballyconnell from Ballinamore and proceeded to raid the post office and "Foster's" Hardware Store. One car pulled up outside the post office and two men entered while the second car pulled up lower down the street and two men entered "Foster's" Hardware Store to raid the tills. At the post office they dismantled the telephone system and enquired where the cash was kept. The assistant said that she would get the postmistress but the men continued to raid for cash, inquiring about government money. Annie Crawford, on hearing the commotion, went out the back way and alerted two members of the Free State army, in civilian clothes, who then confronted the raiders, shouting "hands up".

The raiders made their way to the street and shooting started. Meanwhile the leader of the gang in Fosters, ran out and was fatally wounded by gunfire. The rest of the gang escaped towards Ballinamore pursued by the military. Knowing that their leader was killed, one of the gang was heard to say when making their escape: "We'll be back for the 'months mind'." The leader of these Irregulars was Michael Cull and Ellie Drum remembered seeing his body being brought up the street on the pork market handcart to the Market House.

Here is a report of the inquest held in Belturbet Military Barracks on the following Tuesday, Miss A. Crawford, Ballyconnell P.O. said "that at approx. 1.30 p. m. two armed men entered the office and demanded all the cash. They took £10. They searched for letters for the military and disconnected the telephone. She never saw either man before."

John Reid, an employee of Foster's, said: " Two men, one of whom carried a revolver, raided the shop and took money from the till. He believed the deceased was one of the men".

John Richardson, part owner of the shop, said "the men took about £33".

William Ovens, also part owner of the shop, testified "to seeing the two men in the shop. He went out and down the entry. He then heard firing from the street and saw a motor moving away and one of the raiders running to get into it, which went towards Ballinamore. Deceased made in the opposite direction and the raiders appeared to get confused. The raider on the footboard of the motor fired at the shop wall and at this time there were six or seven shots fired, and deceased fell in the middle of the street to the right of the shop."

Capt. McGovern, National Army, Longford identified the remains as that of Michael Cull from Arigna. He knew the deceased personally.

Dr W. O'Rourke, Ballyconnell, said: "He heard a shot and saw the deceased stumble forward and fall on his face. He went to him and saw him bleeding profusely from the mouth. Witness turned him on his back and saw a Mills bomb underneath him and gave instructions to have it handed to the military. The man died within seconds."

Dr Stuart, Belturbet, said, "a bullet entered the left shoulder and the exit was on the right shoulder."

The Legal Staff Officer "said that the production of the officers of the National Army, who were in Ballyconnell, in evidence, could throw no light on the case as firing was going on, on both sides, and they could not say if it was their bullet killed the deceased..."

One month later, a lorry was commandeered in Ballinamore, Co. Leitrim and was used to convey the Irregulars from Arigna to Ballyconnell to return for "the month's mind" of their deceased leader Michael Cull. Shortly after 8 a.m. on 6 February, the train from Belturbet to Ballinamore was halted about two miles from Ballyconnell and was made to return to Ballyconnell station. The gang, which numbered around 50, travelled by lorry and two motors, were well armed having two or three machine guns.

They attacked Ballyconnell with open gunfire, looting and burning many premises. In Foster's Hardware Shop one of the assistants, William Ryan, was taken onto the street and shot. He stumbled across the street and collapsed into McMullen's front door where he died. Willie Ovens, who was one of the joint owners of the premises, was brought out onto the street, questioned and shot in the face and knees. He survived after treatment at the Royal Victoria Hospital, Belfast but suffered the consequences of his injuries for the rest of his life. Foster's shop was set alight but brought under control.

The Irregulars methodically moved up Main St, bombing Thomas Dolphin's shop and burning the hotel owned by Mrs Dolphin. The windows of the Ulster Bank were broken and about £200 was taken. All shops were looted. Most of the town's business premises were damaged by fire or the breaking of glass and doors. Continuous rifle shots terrified the people. All approaches to the town including the railway station were covered and threats were made of further reprisals.

The attack on the town continued to Drum's, which was raided. Mrs Drum (Annie Malanaphy) was in the shop with her daughter Emily who was forced by a young man with a rifle out into the kitchen where her father, grandfather and youngest sister were. The young Irregular cocked his rifle at the four in the kitchen. As the raid on the town was going on, Seán McGrath, a lodger in Drum's, was in the stables at the back of the premises with the yard hand, James McCabe (Snugborough). On hearing the shooting, they both hid under the hay in front of the horses. When the shooting had died down, McGrath, against McCabe's advice, decided to go down to the house to see what was happening. He entered by the back door and the gunman in the kitchen opened fire and fatally shot him in the abdomen.

According to Una Drum, who as an eight year old sitting on her father's knee: "If Seán McGrath had not come in at that time, in all probability her father, grandfather and herself would have been shot". She said that the young man who carried out the deed was no more than 14 or 15 years of age. The raid on Ballyconnell lasted for the best part of an hour. Emily Drum, then a 15 year old, cradled Seán McGrath in her arms for many hours as he lay dying. He died at 4.20 that afternoon. He was a 21-year-old native Irish speaker from Milltown, Co. Galway and was teaching Irish in west Cavan. Emily Drum, later Mrs Emily Clarke, Wicklow, spoke very little to her family afterwards of her ordeal and trauma experienced in her home on that day.

An inquest was held at Ballyconnell on the morning of 8 February, where the jury found that Seán McGrath and William Ryan died from gunshot wounds and were wilfully murdered. Emily Drum gave evidence on the death of Seán McGrath. Maggie Thompson testified that on opening McMullen's door, William Ryan crawled in and died. Dr O'Rourke gave medical evidence.

Immediately after the inquest, an order was made for burial. The remains of Seán McGrath left Drum's, carried by his students. The cortege was led by Fr Magee PP and Fr Brady CC, and the chief mourners were the deceased's brother and sister. On Main St, outside "Fosters" Hardware Shop, the funeral was joined by that of William Ryan, headed by Rev. D. Martin, Killeshandra and many Protestant clergymen from surrounding parishes.

Ryan's father and three brothers led the cortege and the coffin was carried by his fellow employees. The united cortege moved towards the Diamond and stopped for a moment when Ryan's remains moved onwards to Killeshandra and McGrath's remains were brought on to the Ballinamore Road and then to Tuam, Co. Galway. The people of Ballyconnell were united in grief, suffered at the hands of fellow Irishmen. It was said locally that Ryan and McGrath were the last civilians (non-combatants) to die in Ireland's terrible Civil War.

In the Dáil on the day of the removals, General Mulcahy addressed the Ballyconnell incident, indicating that press reports were correct. He said: "Occurrences such as those in Ballyconnell disclosed a type of madness that could not be coped with by an army of 35,000 men ... and those opposing the government would not deflect the army from its course."

Seán Milroy TD said he was satisfied with the speech of the Commander-in-Chief, who said that he had taken steps to see that what had happened in Ballyconnell was not likely to happen in that area again. "Society and the Irish nation were of much more importance than the predilections or the disposition of those who menaced Ireland today." In the Dáil on the previous day, Seán Milroy, referring to the Ballyconnell tragedy, urged the safety of the civilian population. "What had happened reminded him of the Black and Tans" and he added "that if incidents such as these would not cease, the government must come to their aid, and must have at their disposal all the resources that the nation can provide."

President W.T. Cosgrave promised a full investigation.

Thomas Johnson (Labour) asked for a full and frank statement of the position, military and political, and the reason why the Ballyconnell incident was possible.

Kevin O'Higgins said "that it was not a natural thing to expect that a body of Irishmen would descend upon a little town and proceed to murder their fellow citizens. The only way to deal with anarchy was by the way of force."

The government reacted and several thousand Free State troops from Sligo and Finner Camp Donegal mounted an extensive sweep of the Arigna area, in search of the Irregulars. They finally tracked down and arrested their new leader, Ned Boffin, and three others in a farmhouse, all heavily armed, at Riverstown Co. Sligo on 25 March.

There are questions remaining concerning the second raid on Ballyconnell. Why was the army not present to challenge it? Notice was given that they would be back for "the month's mind". There were army people there on the first day, in mufti, as credited in reports and at the first inquest. Why was William Ryan singled out and shot? It was said in Ballyconnell that when Michael Cull was raiding the tills in Foster's, he put his loaded revolver down on the shop counter and on hearing the commotion on the street he ran out and left his gun behind. At that point, Ryan picked up the loaded gun and followed Cull out and he fired what is believed may have been the fatal shot, killing Cull with his own gun.

Did any members of the raiding gang see this or was there "a mole" in the town? The answer seems to be that the Irregulars, wanting to avenge the shooting of Cull, sent a number of men, at least one of whom was dressed up as an old lady, to Ballyconnell on the following fair day (third Tuesday) to "suss out" the place and to get as much information as possible. This they obviously got. Tom Dolphin's shop and car showroom were totally destroyed. This was probably retaliation for his son, Paddy, who was a member of the Free State army, and was present on the first day and firing at the Irregulars. Paddy Dolphin would have been known to them as he had been a member of the South Leitrim Volunteers in Ballinamore.

If the Irregulars were anti-Treaty, there was no reason for them to carry out the raid, and murder Seán McGrath, in Drum's, as John Drum was quietly anti-Treaty. He was anti-partitionist, logically due to the fact that his native hinterland of Fermanagh was now politically cut off. The modus operandi of the Irregulars seemed to be based on criminality under the guise of military operations.

In September 1923, John Drum died from progressive heart failure, or as his family always said: "He died from a broken heart." He saw the terrible deeds carried out by Irishmen on fellow Irishmen during the Civil War, actions much worse than anything carried out in the area by the RIC, the Auxiliaries or the Black and Tans. The Free State government was represented at his funeral by Major-Gen. Seán Mac Eoin, Col. Cooney and Commandant Woods, Custume Barracks, Athlone.
Annie Malanphy died in 1934.

Historically, civil war is often a consequence of a country attaining independence from its colonisers, an almost inevitable and horrific step to establish political beliefs and new governance. It can go on for years as the innocent suffer. In Ireland, the Civil War was short lived, lasting 11 months and was, an event, which the majority wanted to forget. It still left Ireland with its array of social, political and economic consequences. Political stability was established in the Free State by men of no political experience. They cannot be accused of anything, other than that they did their best. The greatest hangover from this time in Ireland was the known mistreatment and execution of republican prisoners by their former comrades on the Free State side in many parts of the country. These deeds sowed the seeds of personal and political mistrust of democratic politics, which regretfully, pushed many to extremes in the name of misunderstood republicanism.

Ireland's Civil War was a further stake driven to compound and to seal partition.

CHAPTER 13

20 YEARS ON SEÁN MILROY REFLECTS

"Here, in Seán Milroy's own words, are his reflections on the first 20 years of Irish independence. He wrote the following in the early 1940s."

I remember well that morning, 20 years ago, when the Treaty was signed. Going into the headquarters of the Irish delegation in Hans Place, London, I met Arthur Griffith. He was coming slowly downstairs, one hand resting heavily on the stair rail. The picture of him, as I saw him then, and as he asked me in a tone of infinite weariness if I had heard what had been done, will always remain in my memory. He looked like a man utterly exhausted, like one who had wrestled with giants through the night, had overcome them, but in doing so had expended the last ounce of his vitality. It was not until some time later that I learned all the odds he had to contend with in his efforts to wring a settlement out of the negotiations.

When the Irish delegation signed the Articles of Agreement for the Treaty on 6 December 1921, they set their seal to the wisest act of statesmanship that had ever marked the relations between this country and England. "It is the first Treaty," said Griffith, when recommending the agreement for acceptance to Dáil Éireann, "between the representatives of the Irish Government and the representatives of the English Government since 1172, signed on an equal footing."

We can appraise that statement through the perspective of 20 eventful years, and the process of development in that period bears evidence that Griffith did not overstate his case; he faced his critics and defended the results of the negotiations.

Such a review of events must also lead to the conclusion that a refusal of the Irish delegation to sign the Treaty, or a subsequent rejection of it by the Dáil, would have been an act of calamitous folly from which nothing would have emerged save disaster, chaos, suffering and the extinction for generations of any hope of national liberation.

It is true that the first years after the inauguration of the Saorstát (Free State) were darkened by internal strife, tragedy and disillusionment in many aspects of national outlook, but something stronger and more enduring than transient emotional idealism was born out of that period of agonising ordeal, namely, the beginnings here of a sense of political and civic responsibility and a growing realisation both in Ireland and Britain that issues not finally determined by the Treaty could eventually be resolved by reason and negotiation rather than by violence and repression.

Statute of Westminster

Outstanding among the achievements which marked the new Irish State under the Premiership of Mr Cosgrave was the Statute of Westminster, an enactment which affected in a profound and far-reaching degree the status and growth in political enlargement of all self-governed states of the Commonwealth, and which established beyond question the right of the people of the Saorstát to determine their own mode of life and their relations with other states.

It also made crystal clear, what was enshrined in the Treaty and which Sir Robert Horne admitted at a gathering in Washington in 1925, that this State could itself decide its attitude and policy it would pursue in the event of Britain or any other state of the Commonwealth being involved in war. Here then lies the constitutional grounds and authority which have enabled the present Government to proclaim and maintain a policy of neutrality in the present war.

Neutrality under Document No. 2

It is indeed a moot point if we would now be in as fine a position as we are to exercise neutrality had Mr de Valera's Document No. 2 been accepted in 1922 as an alternative to the Treaty. Paragraph 2 of the document states: "That for the purposes of common concern, Ireland shall be associated with the States of the British Commonwealth viz: the Kingdom of Great Britain, the Dominion of Canada, the Commonwealth of Australia, the Dominion of New Zealand and the Union of South Africa."
Paragraph 4 of the document determines that "matters of common concern" on which there shall be "concerted action based on consultation between Ireland and the states of the Commonwealth" shall include "defence, peace and war".

There appears to be little doubt, therefore, that the freedom of action in regard to defence, peace and war, and of course neutrality, which we secured by virtue of the Treaty and the Statute of Westminster, is definitely greater and less liable to external influence or pressure than would have been the case under the provisions of Document No. 2.

*Document No. 2 was an alternative to the Treaty that de Valera put to the Dáil during the debates on the Anglo-Irish Treaty.

There is no warrant whatever for the belief that had the opponents of the Treaty overthrown the Saorstát in 1922-23, and had war been then resumed by Britain, that this country could have emerged victorious or in a position to secure again the rights and power which would have gone with the Treaty. It is safe to say that such could not have happened. Inevitably British authority would have resumed control and today we would have neither Republic, Treaty, Statute of Westminster nor neutrality. The most fanatical 1922 opponent of the Saorstát who has lived through the period, and who has had the wit to profit by experience, must be conscious of the truth that the worst thing that could have happened to Ireland then would have been the success of his group. He will probably realise now, whether admitting it or not, that their defeat was the only possible basis upon which tangible hope for the nation's future could be preserved.

The First 10 Years

The first 10 years were the most vital part of the period, the years when the structure of the new State took shape and direction. It is only when we look back through the records of that decade that we can appreciate the formidable character of the task which awaited the men who undertook the guidance of the country.

The death of Griffith deprived them of the wise counsel and inspiration of the man whose work for over a quarter of a century had been the main political driving force behind the movement which led up to, and won, the Treaty, and the death of Collins robbed them of one whose tireless energy had brought that movement to consummation. On the death of Collins, W.T. Cosgrove was appointed head of the government and remained in power until 1932.

A mere recital of some of the chief tasks, which they carried through in those 10 years, will indicate how onerous and exacting was their situation;

The drafting and enactment of a Constitution for the new State;
The revision and, in some cases, the entire remodelling of the machinery of administration;
The creation of a new army and a new police force;
The recasting of the judicial system;
The creation of the Saorstát's own instruments of international intercourse through the medium of diplomatic representatives to foreign nations and through membership of the League of Nations;
The devising and development of the State's economic policy;
The restoration of order and the enforcement of the authority of the people's government;

The establishment of normal business and economic relations with Britain;

In short, the construction on modern lines of the framework of ordered and progressive life within which the new State could function.

Notable too was the legislation of 1925 by which two new factors were introduced into the country's economic life viz: the harnessing of the River Shannon for the production of light, heat and power for the country and the creation of the beet sugar industry in Carlow. Both of these far-seeing undertakings are now making important contributions to the efforts to cope with the present "war conditions" emergency.

Thick and fast grew the difficulties of our first Irish Government as the assaults of the anti-Treaty forces proceeded, but these eventually gave way before the resolute policy of the government, backed as it was by the judgement of the electorate repeatedly declared. When in 1923 the defeated elements sounded their "ceasefire" order, they left behind them a trail of havoc and destruction which in costs to the community ran to some £30 million, and had infected the social and political atmosphere with poisonous, blasting passions and hatreds which have not yet been entirely eradicated.

One important, though perhaps lesser, disturbing aspect of that sorry episode was the difficulty which it created in regard to a full and exhaustive overhauling, at the commencement of the Saorstát, of the system of local government. A real beginning of this very desirable revision had to be deferred, and though certain substantial changes were made, and others are now impending, there still survive in the procedure and organisation of local government, and in the department responsible for it, much dead wood and many remnants of the obsolete regime, the removal of which will necessitate further drastic reforms if the machinery of this department is to work intelligently and efficiently.

The Ulster Problem

The partition problem is still with us. How and when it will be solved remains a cause of distressing perplexity to all who desire the ultimate reunion of the nation. When the Treaty was signed, there were many, myself among the number, who confidently believed that the provisions in the Articles of Agreement relating to the six counties would effect a solution. Subsequent events regarding the matter might be construed as showing such confidence was not well founded. That particular point of view is, however, largely a speculative one and can never now be brought to any conclusive test. In my opinion, the trend of events in the 26 counties immediately after the ratification of the Treaty by the Dáil had an enormous influence in negating the operations of the provisions. The following is interesting in this connection.

I was attached to the Irish delegation during the negotiations for the purpose of preparing and supplying data and maps bearing on various aspects of the six-county question. One of my chief sources of information in this respect was George Russell, who had many intimate contacts with the North, especially Belfast. He told me later that when the Treaty was signed, the businessmen of Belfast were organising to bring pressure to bear on the six-county government not to opt out of the Free State, but when the civil war was started down here, these efforts were abandoned. The adverse reaction on the Ulster question of the events of 1922-3 has not yet, it is to be feared, been extinguished.

O'Higgins and Hogan

Two forceful realists of those 10 years were Kevin O'Higgins and Paddy Hogan. They both left a deep impress on the work of founding the State. O'Higgins by his fearless assertion of the government's authority grounded on the people's declared will, his masterly piloting of the constitution through the Oireachtas, and his work at the Imperial Conference, 1926, which later fructified in the Statute of Westminster, earned him a reputation for high administrative capacity and maturing statesmanship which the country could ill afford to lose.

Hogan's clarity of outlook in regard to the basis and position of the Saorstát was no less acute than that of his friend and colleague, O'Higgins. The legislation which he sponsored, as Minister for Agriculture, for the improvements of Irish agricultural produce and livestock, opened up the prospect of a new and brighter era for the farmers and went far to increase and stabilise their position in the British market during the Cosgrave administration.

The Second 10 Years

The years of the Cosgrave Administration had been years of exacting, tenacious, constructive effort. They were directed towards economic reconstruction, building up credit stability, initiating administrative reform and generally evolving an order of things which, given time and opportunity to develop normally, should have produced general social betterment and national progress.

It was fortunate that this policy of conserving and increasing the strength of the State had at least a decade to operate, for in the next few years it was to be subjected to a continuing series of ebullient shocks and political adventurings which strained its economic and financial endurance severely.

The year 1932 saw the advent to office of the Fianna Fáil party and though the administration of Mr de Valera's Government has been eventful, it has been so in rather a different sense from that which characterised its predecessor. The policy on which Fianna Fáil based its appeal to the electorate made it inevitable that if that party secured power, the community must be prepared to brace itself for new social experiments and renewed controversies with Britain. Outstanding among the headlines of this policy were the retention of the land annuities, reduction of taxation by a couple of million pounds a year and a solution of the unemployment problem. The fact that the promises to the last two mentioned items have not yet been redeemed does not alter the fact that they helped to make Fianna Fáil's election programme an attractive one to the electors.

Principal Events of the 10 Years

The chief features of the Fianna Fáil period in office may be indicated as follows:

The land-annuities dispute and the economic war: This dispute lasted close on six years and according to an expert calculation cost the Saorstát over £56 million. It is doubtful if any substantial section of the farming community has yet recovered from the withering effects which the dispute had upon their sources of livelihood. However, the country was too relieved by the announcement that the economic war was finished to dwell with close scrutiny upon the hardships which it had imposed.

The Ottawa Conference: This conference accentuated the violent disruption of our economic relations with Britain, which the land-annuities dispute began. This disruption and the consequent failure of the Saortsát's representative at Ottawa to conclude any trade agreement with Britain, meant a loss to the Saorstát of its preferential position in the British market, a loss which has not since been recovered, and the recovery of which at present appears impossible.

Abolition of the Senate: The Senate was abolished in May 1936 and a new second chamber established under the new Constitution. That the new Senate is definitely inferior, both in usefulness and composition, to the one it replaced is undoubted. The machinery by which the majority of its members are elected is also a matter of serious concern, being open to obvious abuse which has frequently been commented upon.

The New Constitution: The most ardent admirers of the new Constitution can hardly claim that it has produced the internal political tranquillity which its sponsors predicted. It is difficult to see in what respect it has brought any addition of freedom, power or status, nationally or internationally. I know of nothing of material importance which the people of this State are now doing, or likely to do in the future, under our second Constitution which they could not have done with equal freedom under the first.

The 1938 Settlement: This settlement with the British government was comprised of three agreements. The first dealing with matters of defence, brought about the transfer of the ports of Cobh, Berehaven and Lough Swilly to the government of Éire. The second was a financial agreement, which in effect meant that the land annuities and certain other periodical payments were compounded for the sum of £10 million which the Éire Government agreed to pay to Britain. The third was a comprehensive trade agreement which terminated the penal tariffs imposed during the economic war. The settlement, though it left the question of partition untouched, was generally heartily welcomed by the country, and was no doubt materially helpful in securing the return to power once more of Fianna Fáil at the general election in June 1938.

Shortly after the general election, the Banking Commission Report was published and the conclusions embodied in the majority report proved severely critical of much of Fianna Fáil's economic policy. What consequences may yet flow from this report is still a matter of critical speculation.

In September of that year, Mr de Valera was elected President of the League of Nations Assembly, a distinction which was a direct outcome of the work of the Cosgrave Government at the league. The Munich crisis arose about the same time and there and then began the trend of events, which a year later, were to create problems and situations of extraordinary complexity and abnormal character.

These are matters that hardly come within the scope of this review, which is only intended to survey in brief outline the progress of the State from its beginnings up to the advent of the present emergency conditions. In that period we have seen and, let us hope, learned much as regards our possibilities from the blunders committed in the name of the State. This should prove an important asset for the future if we are disposed to profit by that experience.

Looking back on 6 December 1921, we can now see clearly that Griffith and Collins then seized the first real opportunity that had been presented to this country for centuries to recover control of its own destinies, and that because of their courage to seize and hold that opportunity, the people of Éire today can exercise the rights and powers which every independent nation claims.

Cost to Irish State of Economic War

The following calculation is from a special article published in the *Irish Independent*, 28/04/1938, on the settlement and what the economic war cost the Irish State, the gross losses, actual and consequential, and the burdens endured by the farmers, taxpayers and consumers under the abnormal and dislocating conditions of the previous six years.

Payments to Britain	£26,066,222
Land annuities paid to Irish Government	£17,087,081
Loss on decreased volume of Agr. exports	£26,391,544
Export bounties and subsidies	£16,150,878
Loss on non-agr. exports	£ 3,000,000
TOTAL	£88,695,725

By the halving of the land annuities, farmers obtained relief of	£9,834,851
The Exchequer was relieved of liability for payments withheld, other than land annuities	£11,024,435
Received, proceeds of land annuities in dispute	£11,100,000
TOTAL	£31,959,286

The net loss to Ireland of the six-year economic war with Britain was	£56,736,439

The Land Annuities and the Economic War

The matters involved in the land-annuities dispute were settled by agreement reached in 1938 with the Chamberlain Government. As to what the land annuities were may be enlightening to those who are not familiar with the subject. By the Land Acts, under which Irish tenant farmers were enabled to purchase their holdings, a Land Purchase Fund or account was set up and the yearly payments of the purchase price of their holdings by the farmers were paid by the Land Commission into this fund, and out of it were paid the dividends and sinking fund in respect of land stock. By the Land Act of 1923, it was enacted that the transference of these annuities to the Land Purchase fund would be exercised by the Minister for Finance instead of the Land Commission.

The management of the Land Purchase Fund was under the direction of the National Debt Commission in London, and after the Treaty this method was continued, largely, it may be assumed, to avoid the expense and administrative difficulties which would be involved in setting up in the new State a separate department or service to deal with the matter.

This procedure continued without dispute until Mr de Valera and his party adopted the view that there was no statutory authority, which made it obligatory on the Irish Government to transfer the annuities to the National Debt Commissioners. The Cosgrave Government resisted this contention and so the matter rested until the advent to power of Mr de Valera's party after the general election of 1932. Immediately after assuming office, the new Government discontinued the transfer of annuities and certain other monies to London.

With this action of the de Valera Government there began what was known as "the Economic War", in the course of which penal tariffs were imposed by both countries. The preferential position for its produce which the Irish Free State held in the British market was in consequence lost and at the Imperial Conference in Ottawa in 1932, no trade agreement was concluded between the representatives of the British and the Irish Free State.

In negotiation initiated by the Irish Government in regard to the disputed monies with the Chamberlain Government in 1938, agreements were made which terminated the matter of the annuities and other monies involved. These were in fact compounded for a sum of £10 million, which the Irish Government agreed to pay to Britain. The ports of Berehaven, Cobh and Lough Swilly were transferred to the Irish Government and certain trading facilities arranged of mutual advantage to both countries. The preferential position, however, which the Irish State had held in the British market was gone and has not yet been recovered.

Seán Milroy (1877-1946) wrote the above in c.1941-42. He was a native of Maryport, Cumbria from where he came in his youth to Co. Cork. He befriended Arthur Griffith and joined Sinn Féin, serving (1909-1912) as a member of its executive. He was arrested in 1915 in Dublin and sentenced to three months' hard labour for delivering an "inflammatory speech". He joined the Volunteers and served in the GPO during the Easter Rising and was imprisoned afterwards in England. He was re-elected to the Sinn Féin standing committee in 1917 and contested two unsuccessful by-elections in Tyrone and became the party's Director of Organisation. He came to Co. Cavan in 1917 to structure Sinn Féin in readiness for Arthur Griffith to contest the East Cavan by-election in 1918.

He was arrested in 1918 under the "German Plot" and imprisoned in Lincoln Jail. It is there that he played his part in the now famous prison breakout when he, Eamon de Valera and Seán McGarry escaped. Michael Collins, Harry Boland and Fintan Murphy used a key made from a drawing sent by Milroy to Ireland on a 1918 Christmas card. After his escape, he helped establish the Irish Self-Determination League in Britain. He was elected TD for Cavan in 1921 and 1922, and MP for Fermanagh/Tyrone in 1921. He was a member of the Dáil sub-committee which drew up the first Constitution of the Free State. He was a member of Seanad Éireann 1928-36.

He remained single and had one sister who was a nun in Reading, England.

Other famous Englishmen who played their part in Ireland's fight for independence are Roger Casement and Erskine Childers. Seán Milroy's political contribution ranks with the best.

* Sourced in Sean Milroy's personal papers at National Archives, Dublin.

CHAPTER 14

LIVING WITH PARTITION

(i) Getting on with life

Did partition make a difference to the people who lived on both sides of the imposed Irish border? The answer would have to be yes, but not a lot. Communities accepted political change but adapted to changing situations and still maintained all contacts on both sides. The boundary between north and south was made and, like most things in Irish life, there had to be emergency and ecclesiastical exceptions – which in time allowed the exceptions to become the norm. Ballyconnell had two church parishes, with both traversing the border, and people were allowed to drive freely on the unapproved road to church on Sundays and for cross-border funerals, without having to endure the humility of Customs etc. Doctors, nurses, veterinary surgeons and emergency services were likewise allowed to cross the border. Many farmers on the northern side had lands in the south and were happy to keep it that way and away from officialdom. Partition did not lead generally to a blocking off of unapproved roads and if and when that happened, the people could and would always go by the fields and laneways.

The people of west Cavan and south Fermanagh were not partitioned or partition minded and were little influenced by the political impositions from Belfast or London. Westminster and the Belfast Unionists were remote from the common people of south Ulster – "a people apart" – who in essence were indifferent to change. It was the "B Specials" on the northern side who maintained the boundary in those early years with their paid nightly presence on border routes. On the southern side it was maintained by Customs officials, not really knowing what their function was. The Sunday-observance laws and restricted weekday pub-opening hours in the six counties were a benefit to the southern border area. Fermanagh people came south to celebrate special occasions and to have "the craic" as alcohol was always that bit cheaper.

The economy of Ireland in the 1920s was poor and in keeping with the international situation. The "economic war" from 1932, or as it was more commonly referred to locally as "Dev's Comical War", between the Irish Free State and Britain, was the first occasion for those living along the border to make commercial advantage, particularly on the northern side. Bonhams or young pigs could be purchased in fairs in Co. Cavan for as little as one shilling and six pence (1/6d) each and smuggled into Northern Ireland while avoiding British tariffs. If they were brought legally into Northern Ireland, the Free State government paid an export subsidy to try to counteract the British tariffs. Pig litters in Northern Ireland dramatically increased from an average of seven or eight piglets to as high as 12. Northern Ireland cows started to register twin calves born, especially in the south Fermanagh and south Armagh areas. Animal geneticists in Britain observed that these unaccountable local phenomena were "interesting". The commercial advantages to be gained from smuggling, on both sides of the border, were necessary to survive in hungry times.

The Irish Taoiseach, Eamon de Valera, speaking at a fair day in Arva, Co. Cavan, during the economic war, said, "The British market is gone and gone forever" and the crowd cheered and flung their hats in the air – while there was nobody to offer them a shilling for a beast. The situation became so critical that de Valera's government gave farmers a subsidy of half-a-crown per head, to slaughter calves at birth. Northern farmers and the economy of Northern Ireland gained from this situation and the better prices in the British market.

At the outbreak of the Second World War, it was necessary for citizens of the Irish Free State to apply to the Royal Ulster Constabulary (RUC) for a permit of identity to allow them to travel within Northern Ireland. Were the southern Irish a wartime threat to Belfast, even though they were still part of the King's Dominions? The six counties were being maintained on fear and suspicion and plenty of government jobs were created. The Northern Irish could travel freely within the Free State. Travel via approved routes, both ways, was controlled by Customs stations, to inspect and stamp vehicle passes within daytime hours. For after hours, a special request to pass had to be applied for.

(ii) World War II and a new economy

"It's an ill wind that doesn't blow some good" as the Japanese attack on Pearl Harbour in December 1941 brought unforeseen advantages to south Ulster. America, which up until then was supportive of the Allies in Europe, was now forced into the war, both in the Pacific and in Europe. The US forces needed a landing stage in northern Europe and Britain needed the North Atlantic patrolled to counter the German U-boats, which were endangering much-needed supplies vital to the war effort. Northern Ireland became the initial US landing base in Europe – and an immediate boost to the economy of Northern Ireland with an overflow into the border counties of the south. It may sound ironic but the war situation in Europe was both liberating and opportunistic for the people of the region.

Ireland with its neutral status stayed out of the European conflict but did not baulk at the American presence in Ireland. Fermanagh was saturated with thousands of American military personnel who came laden with dollars, cigarettes, coffee, chewing gum and nylon stockings. The Irish government allowed the Americans shelter at Killybegs and a free flight passage over south Donegal to facilitate "the flying boats" from Lower Lough Erne to patrol the Atlantic. The American military, while awaiting their postings to Europe, certainly made the best of life and they could have drunk Lough Erne dry, as they drank whiskey by the bottle in pubs throughout Fermanagh and with many freely taken excursions to Ballyconnell, Belturbet and Swanlinbar to drink and dance as they spent their very welcomed dollars.

Jack Cashin, a Dublin man, was the resident Customs officer at Ballyconnell during those early war years and he aptly described, against himself, an early incursion by American personnel into the Free State while he was on duty on the Ballyconnell-Derrylin Road. Wearing his official uniform, which consisted of a Customs officer's peaked cap, he stood in the middle of the road and put his hand up to halt the approaching vehicles coming from Fermanagh. The vehicles slowed down and on seeing Cashin was alone, a cheeky Yank said to him, "Out of the way, postman!" and they proceeded with speed to Ballyconnell. Nobody cared if the "Yanks" were in uniform or mufti; they were coming to spend their dollars like there was no tomorrow and in all probability the resident Customs official was very soon the recipient of Yankee hospitality. The Free State's stance on neutrality was not under threat and certainly the local dispensation to Ireland's neutrality was welcomed and Dublin was known to shut its eyes to the situation.

The economy of the border counties was now booming, with requests coming from many parts of the country for scarce goods, which the Yanks had or could get in abundance. A consignment of green coffee beans, obviously bartered for, was stored at 29 Main Street, which in all probability made its way to the capital for roasting and grinding. Agricultural produce moved towards the border and inevitably on to a better market as the war effort was paying a premium. The Free State had sugar, sweets and alcohol in abundance. There was even a good trade for poultry as a young pullet or a laying hen was worth at least £3. The women of the south had a sudden craving for nylon stockings.

The American presence and in particular the needs of their airforce were another commercial opportunity as St Angelo Airport, Enniskillen, had to be constructed with great urgency. Gravel was the gold and every small farmer in Fermanagh with a hill of gravel started to dig with pick and shovel with the aim of getting rich. The Mountain Road was always renowned for its quality gravel, which resulted in unemployed men from south of the border being wanted "to dig". Ten-ton lorries were filled by men with shovels from morning till night while there was always someone on the lookout to observe for officialdom coming to check out the status of the casual workers. St. Angelo Airport was now getting gravel to build its runways from everywhere and of course there were some who took advantage, such as Joe "Fat" who was contracted to supply. He sent one lorry of gravel each day. It drove in and out of the site without unloading, had its number plates changed and went back in again with the same load to record many loads delivered for payment!

Ireland's neutrality was a bonus to the British war effort. As British men, and indeed many Irishmen, enlisted to fight Nazi Germany, the unemployed Irish women availed of the opportunities and travelled in their thousands to Britain to take up work in the munitions factories and other industries vital to the British war effort. Upwards of 5,000 Irishmen deserted the Irish army to fight on the Allied side in the war and more young Irishmen travelled north to join the US forces. The Irish needed the work and the British needed the Irish. Nearer home many women from the southern border area went to Belfast and other towns in Northern Ireland to work in the textile and linen industries, manufacturing clothing and parachute material.

Friendships made in Belfast during the war years, irrespective of politics or religion, still endure with the next generation. While the Free State was militarily neutral, the majority of Irish citizens were supportive of the Allies and Britain. The Irish were neutral on the British side and they also had to endure wartime rationing of vital food supplies well into the 1950s. In retrospect, a neutral Ireland at England's back was more strategically advantageous to her during those war years, and more than may have been appreciated at the time and afterwards. Winston Churchill did not show his appreciation of what the Irish did with his venomous address to de Valera and Ireland after the war. This was triggered by the Taoiseach's visit to the German Legation in Dublin to offer his condolences to Germany on the death of Hitler.

(iii) An important weather forecast

A vital strategic service, which Ireland gave the Allies during World War II, was that from the fledgling Irish Meteorological Service. Accurate scientific-based weather forecasting was needed then by the proposed development of the trans-Atlantic aviation services between Foynes (Co. Limerick) and North America, international shipping, industry (including agriculture) and the public. Ireland and its location on the eastern Atlantic was pivotal in creating accurate weather information to bridge the 1,850 miles of water between north-western Europe and Newfoundland, information which was to be crucial to the future development of trans-Atlantic air travel. The Valentia Observatory and its network of eight coastal stations had been supplying weather forecasting to naval and commercial shipping around the British Isles from 1868.

A request from the Netherlands for Irish climatological data was refused in February 1940 by the Department of Industry and Commerce, Dublin, on the grounds that the policy adopted was based primarily on the necessity of avoiding prejudicing the especially close collaboration between the Irish Meteorological Service and the British and Canadian services. This was essential to the Irish service, not only for trans-Atlantic purposes but also for the protection of Irish civil and military aircraft. During the war years, no meteorological data was to be published, except that which was exchanged with Britain and Canada prior to a 15-day rule. References in the press as to the activities of the Irish Met Service were not allowed.*

Ireland's important position within the now international reciprocal weather-forecasting service was crucial to the success of the D-Day landings in Normandy in June 1944. A weather forecast, from the Irish Met Service at Blacksod, Co. Mayo, predicting inclement weather, caused the landings to be deferred for one day and contributed to the beginning of the end of the war in Europe.

Ironically, during those war years, southern citizens, although still members of the King's dominions had to apply to the RUC for a "Document of Identity" to travel within the six-counties.

As the economy of the border region was growing, the mood of the people wanted more from life. The growth in new entertainment outlets such as cinema, ballroom dancing, variety shows and the availability of newspapers met this demand. A travelling company, (the Carrickfords) that came to

* *Establishment of the Meteorlogical Service in Ireland: The Foynes Years 1936-45. Tom Keane.*

213

Ballyconnell during the war years. It came to the town for a week to stage a variety show and play nightly in the Market House. It was this troupe which brought Joseph McLaughlin, a young Derry-born tenor, who sang to packed houses in Ballyconnell. After the war, he shot to fame in Britain under the stage name Joseph Locke. Ned McKiernan's travelling cinema was ever popular from the days of the silent movies and now "the talkies", went from town to town every night, but not across the border, with the local driver and projectionist, Joe Gormley.

'The Humours of Ballyconnell', a popular traditional Irish tune reflects "the jigs and reels" of the many characters of Ballyconnell of that time.

The family of Curley Wee and Gussie Goose, as published in the *Irish Independent*, was to be a new source of fun among the town natives, when many characters from the fictional family of furry and feathered friends gave their names to some of the natives, such as The Ram, Mrs Sheep, Gussy Goose, The Fox, The Ass, The Goat and The Rat. Mischief or fun making was a norm among people who were becoming more carefree. There are many stories told and one concerned Pe McKiernan who had a pub on Main St, which was a popular and recognised "early house" or "Lourdes". Pe was up early one morning awaiting clients for "the hair of the dog" when he observed that there were two mice caught in an old-style wooden block mousetrap. To generate some fun and confusion, he removed the mice and put them back into the mousetrap, in reverse. When the expected clients duly arrived, he drew their attention to how stupid mice were as they were now reversing into mousetraps. The clients thought otherwise – were they "in the rats"?

(iv) After the war was over

When European hostilities ceased, activity in the border region stalled and the people had to resort to living at a much slower pace. The first majority Labour government in Britain was elected and Winston Churchill, their war hero, was rejected by the people. Britain was to be politically reformed with the nationalisation of strategic industries, the introduction of the welfare state, National Health Service and food supports for the people in a new industrial Britain. The Irish government declared the Free State a republic and left the King's Dominions. For some in the six counties, the southern people were now "aliens". To drive within Northern Ireland southern people still had to apply for a Northern Ireland driving licence under Acts of 1926 and 1937. Was this contrary to the provisions of the Ireland Act 1949, which declared that Irish citizens were not foreigners in the United Kingdom?

As there was now little work or part-time work in the border region, the emigrant boat beckoned for a better life in England or Scotland, from where some travelled on to Australia for a "tenner". This mass emigration led to the depletion of the southern Irish population throughout the 1950s.

Britain introduced the Agricultural Deficiency Payment System in the 1950s, which gave a new lease of life to smuggling activities. Ballyconnell became a resting station for cattle and pigs moving northwards as the new market conditions dictated. For cattle to qualify for payments or subsidies, heifers and steers were ear punched with a sharpened half-inch copper pipe to make them bona-fide northern animals, and left to heal for a time. They would then move on "in the night" across the border to Telfords, Wilsons, or Fosters to be sold in their names at Enniskillen fat-stock market and sometimes to Belfast via others. Large Fermanagh farms were now building modern pig-fattening units and bonhams were bought in the fairs of Co. Cavan for onward movement via Ballyconnell to Fermanagh. These young pigs were a little problematic as many small litters had to be mixed and settled before movement. When mixed, they were sprinkled with a dilution of Jeyes fluid to give them a common scent, to stop them fighting. It seldom worked. Young hogs had to be castrated, to prove their Northern Ireland citizenship. This operation was carried out with surgical precision. A quick lift of a young hog by a hind leg, followed by holding the head steady between the knees, which allowed the young hog to be relieved of his "credentials" with a blessing of dettol. Batches of upwards of 60 bonhams were counted out from the rear of 29 Main Street to walk the cross-border mountain path guided by silent men under the light of the moon.

The mutual trust and goodwill between all persons involved in smuggling was sacred. The free service, which many families and householders gave to so many people moving goods, both ways, had to be experienced and now acknowledged. It was a place where everyone's venture, however big or small, was respected and safe. Beating the system was always a bonus.

In the culture of smuggling, silence was golden. When certain individuals turned up, you knew that there was some movement taking place – learned or caught perceptions. Smuggling could only be successful through silence and if you happened to witness a smuggling operation, you opened a gate or blocked a gap without a word being spoken. You never knew when you might need a turn yourself. It was not all cattle or pigs, as cheap northern butter was commonly available during the 1950s. New Zealand butter was available in Fermanagh for as little as 1/3d (7c) per pound, when our own Killeshandra butter was retailing at 3/6d (20c) per pound in Ballyconnell. A saving of 2/3d (13c) per pound of butter meant a lot to a family. From the late 1950s, items that were not available in a depressed Irish Republic were easily purchased and brought south as sterling was the common currency. Enniskillen was always the principal town for west Cavan people to shop.

Trusting friendships ignored religious borders. Victor Telford, who was pivotal to much of the cattle and pigs' movement north via Ballyconnell, died in July 1957. Attending Victor's funeral, Dan McMonagle, contrary to Catholic teaching at the time, entered the Church of Ireland at Derrylin to pay his final respects. Being "his own man", his Christian acknowledgment of the mutual trust and friendship between them is a template for many to live by. Thankfully the election of Pope John XXIII in 1958 reversed archaic teachings and opened all Christian church doors and windows. Pope John was often spoken of, on all sides, and affectionately referred to as "the Protestant Pope".

(v) More fun and games

Gaelic football was ever popular and in the golden age of Cavan football, the county team did their two weeks' training in Ballyconnell, prior to the All-Ireland meeting with neighbouring Meath in 1952. The first game was drawn and Cavan won the replay. Dr Sam McQuade and his young assistant Dr Ned Farrelly travelled to that final, both being from Virginia, and they came back to Derrylin with the "bragging rights" . Sam McQuade did not take a drink but Ned Farrelly certainly made up for it. On the following morning, surgery was due to commence at the dispensary at 9.00 a.m. but there was no sign of Dr Farrelly. The dispensary waiting room was full of patients awaiting attention when Dr McQuade asked them to help him get Dr Farrelly "up out of bed". Those who had and could play musical instruments were sent home to bring their fiddles, melodeons, tin whistles etc. back to arouse the young doctor. This they did in the pouring rain. By midday there was a fine "session" in the dispensary, when the county medical inspector called from Enniskillen as Dr McQuade was playing his own tin whistle among them. The official was not amused and duly sent a report to Belfast. Some days afterwards, Dr McQuade had a telephone call informing him of the complaint. The conversation ended that "laughter is the best medicine".
Ballroom dancing was now the rage and dance halls were built in every

parish to meet the post-war craze for the music of Glenn Miller and Bill Hayley. The Star Ballroom and Cinema, Ballyconnell, was opened in 1949 to become a regional mecca with dances held on Thursday nights to the music of the local Red Sunbeam or Derrylin Starlight Bands and on more special occasions Dave Dixon and his Band from Clones. This was escapism for all on both sides of the border in depressed times. Later, dance bands came from far and wide led by Johnny Flynn, Tuam; the Skyrockets, Enniskillen and Jimmy Johnstone, Belfast. The Star Ballroom hosted a new Enniskillen based dance band in the late sixties "Gene and The Gents", which had a young blonde lead guitarist called Henry McCullough. The stage in Ballyconnell was too small for Henry as he went on to be Ireland's only playing representative at Woodstock. Later he joined Paul McCartney and Wings to achieve international fame.

Summer carnivals of dancing, in the south, extended the craze, when a marquee with maple flooring was set up for two or three weeks in many places. Dancing and dance bands would appear to be the only thriving industry in rural Ireland as many individuals headed for the mail boat to work in post-war Britain. The northern people loved to come south to dance, if it was only to annoy the "B Men" on the way home.

Poverty was common on the marginal lands of the area where proud people tried to live while having to pay rates to the local authority. Part-time employment opportunities were scarce and the evidence of mass emigration was seen on Monday mornings on the Enniskillen-Cavan bus as it picked up men and women with little baggage along the roadside making their way to Dún Laoghaire and England. Everything they had was gone. They were just another Irish social and economic problem for Britain to "hoover up".

Thankfully many of our emigrants returned in August and at Christmas each year to try to keep the old homesteads alive and to spend their crisp "fivers". Many, on returning home, upheld their honour and paid off the few pounds they owed to shops or friends from the past. When emigrants returned, the change in their accents was very noticeable, even after only a few months away. One great story told by Joe Baxter was of a "Young Judy" coming into his butcher's shop late on Christmas Eve and asking him in her best cockney accent: "Have you got any Cantebury Lamb Mr Baxter." There was no time for a geography lesson and Joe gave her all the "Cantebury" lamb she wanted as he "copped on" that she was in London for only four months. After a few years, homecomings became fewer as the small farms they had were sold to the government for as little as £1-10s an acre, paid for with worthless land bonds. These lands are now producing their second crop of evergreen trees since they were planted in the 1960s.

Cinema was an outlet for young and old and Ballyconnell had "the pictures" on Sunday, Monday, Wednesday and Friday nights with a Sunday matinee for the children. Joe Gormley was the projectionist and Molly Curran took in the shillings. People travelled from all parts of the region to see such great epic movies as *Casablanca* and *Gone With the Wind* and of course "*The Cowboys*". A monthly cinema programme was displayed in every business in the town. Joe Gormley delivered these and on calling to 29 Main Street, he decided to have a bottle of stout. The customers started to ask Joe about the programme and he being a great wit and psychologist went through the programme, putting "in the bed' after each title. It was not long before he had the place in stitches.

May to October was the season for cock fighting. This old, anti-establishment, cruel activity was associated with illicit drinking and gambling and organised by a few. Farmyards in Fermanagh had fowl aplenty with sounds to match – a breeding ground for young "fighting cocks", bred by crossing a bantam hen with a cock pheasant. A bantam hen, with a reputation for being "wicked", would rear them until it was time to confine the semi-wild birds. Cock fights were held from anywhere on the border to as far south as Mullingar. One common date for cock fighting in the border area was on the Saturday night or early hours of Sunday prior to an Ulster football team playing in an All-Ireland football semi-final at Croke Park. The gardaí and the people would be focused on the match, so movements to a cock fight would not be so obvious. One popular local venue was the Castle Saunderson Estate on the Cavan-Fermanagh border, the former home of Col. Saunderson, MP for Armagh and the first leader of the Ulster Unionist Party. This bleak, sodden and isolated spot was ideal as it gave a choice of escape. If the gardaí or RUC came on the scene, the protagonists could move either way to avoid arrest. If both police forces came on the scene, it was always preferable to move south. This so-called sport had an official handicapper.

From the mid-fifties the communications revolution commenced when Ballyconnell got many telephones and Ballyconnell 31 at 29 Main Street was to become a busy contact point for all kinds of messaging from home and abroad. In 1957 the communications revolution advanced when BBC Television could now be received in border counties. The first major event seen on TV and not very clearly was the FIFA World Cup final from Sweden. The children were allowed out of the Catholic school early to see the funeral of Pope Pius XII on television in the autumn of 1958. Many assembled in the workshop of Leo O'Grady to view the funeral. Those who stayed away had more sense, as from the reception, if one did not know any better, it appeared to snow a lot in Rome that day?

The influence of British television and its presenters was immense and it was enhanced with commercial television coming later from Ulster Television (UTV). American programmes such as *I Love Lucy* and *Sergeant Bilko* were popular, while the first commercials were as entertaining as the programmes. The outside world was changing and the people lapped it up. Free television and no licence to pay for a few years was certainly another plus from partition.

(vi) An influx of gardaí

Ballyconnell Garda Station was a quiet place until late 1956 when an influx of gardaí came to the town to do border duty in connection with the IRA campaign. The IRA attacked Derrylin, Lisnaskea and Roslea RUC Barracks in mid-December and it was at Derrylin that the first RUC constable was shot dead in that campaign. This was followed on New Year's Eve with a major IRA attack on the RUC barracks at Brookeborough by 14 Volunteers, where Fergal O'Hanlon from Monaghan and Sean South from Garryowen lost their lives. The leader, Seán Garland, suffered serious leg injuries but made his way back across the border to Monaghan for treatment.

This campaign made it much easier to smuggle cattle and pigs; as one local man said: "It's not animals they are looking for, it's guns." In the spring of 1957, a number of IRA men were arrested near Ballyconnell and charged with "failing to give an account of their movements". Among them were Ruairí Ó Brádaigh, John Joe McGirl and Patrick Duffy, all leading men in the West Cavan/Leitrim/Fermanagh Brigade of the IRA. Attacks on RUC stations at Kinawley, Florencecourt and elsewhere were to follow. James Crossan from Templeport was shot dead at Mullan (Swanlinbar) on the night of 23/24 August 1958. The Ballyconnell to Derrylin unapproved road had been blown up and later spiked to prevent cross-border incursions as the B Specials were on duty nightly to defend "Ulstershire". This act by the northern authorities inconvenienced many like the local veterinary surgeon, Greg McGovern, who had much of his practice in Fermanagh. He bought a car in Northern Ireland and built a garage on Murray's land "on the other northern side of the spikes". This was living and coping with partition. While travelling to a night call in Fermanagh, he was stopped by B Specials on patrol who asked him his name and to account for himself. This was embarrassing, as the questions came from Bertie Bennett, Gortmullan, his client. It was the same Bertie Bennett's father who had built Drum's premises in Ballyconnell. Real partition was now evident.

This IRA campaign was in the planning from 1953 and was not due to start for some time, to allow time for recruitment and training. However, it was a breakaway group in Monaghan (Saor Uladh) who went ahead in 1955 and the campaign started a year later to maintain unity. This campaign was totally focused on attacking British military and police targets. From the summer of 1957, the Irish government interred hundreds of IRA and Sinn Féin members in the Curragh Camp; they were detained for over three years. Many were also detained in Northern Irish jails. The then Archbishop of Dublin, John Charles McQuaid, undertook under his own "papacy" to excommunicate all the men detained at the Curragh, until they renounced their membership of the IRA. This was later overturned after a Mons. Cunningham visited the prison and with authority acted against the archbishop's decree. Of those detained, a minority were active volunteers, the balance being genuine Sinn Féin political activists and many who talked themselves in.

The IRA border campaign continued with small isolated incidents. Not all reported incidents were carried out by the IRA as B Specials in their localities carried out small explosions and reported suspicious movements to sustain their nightly paid duties. The most common quote in news reports from the BBC during that time was "the police saw men speeding towards the border in a small green van". One of the last acts of this campaign happened in 1961 when a small bridge was blown up near Teemore Chapel. Evidence as to who did it was told a few years later when a young Protestant man from the area told of how his father was forced to join the B Specials and the antics they got up to to sustain their paid duties. Many of them were small farmers or tradesmen who were not rich by any means. Their duties were reviewed every two or three months and if there was no incident in their area, they would in all likelihood be stood down. This bridge was chosen as it was going to inconvenience many Catholics going to Sunday Mass. Being perceptive, the local Catholics always suspected this as the IRA by that time had gone away. The local people filled in the hole on the main Derrylin-Ballyconnell Road and a wide pass was made to allow a car by-pass the spikes. Later, the spikes were removed.

A child could not avoid becoming politically aware during the 1959 Presidential election when the then Taoiseach, Eamon de Valera, and Seán Mac Eoin, two patriots from the War of Independence, were seeking the office. This was the last Civil War election, which de Valera won handsomely with the machinery of his Fianna Fáil party behind him.

Shortly afterwards, when Seán Lemass was elected leader of Fianna Fáil and Taoiseach, a common comment heard was, "he should have got that job after the war". Could this be taken to mean that the people elected de Valera President as a means of promoting him sideways so he could do less harm in the "Park" and Lemass would now be able to do something? The same comment was heard from Protestant or Unionist people, as they had a social drink, expressing the same thought about their own aging and not very popular Premier, Sir Basil Brooke.

Political awareness within Ballyconnell was generated by Francy McCabe, who was a die-hard "Blueshirt" with a list of political hates headed by de Valera and followed by Fianna Fáil and its representatives, the *Irish Press* and anyone reading it [The *Irish Press* was founded by De Valera in the 1930s] and drink going up in the budget. He always referred to Dev as "the snake charmer" and when in a more acerbic mood, "the anti-Christ". Francy was always a subject for a throwaway political comment to extract a political outburst – an opportunity he never shied away from and his audiences were always entertained.

The most apt comment on Francy was made, some years later at his funeral, when a Fine Gael local representative said: "Nobody called me to tell me Francy was dead and I wouldn't have known had I not read it in the *Irish Press*.
God knows, I think it will kill him".

(vii) Employment

West Cavan was typical of rural areas in the 1950s in that employment was in services and casual work. In Balyconnell a lucky few had jobs with A.W. Ennis Milling and Saw Mills, which at its peak employed up to 30 people. The narrow-gauge railway line employed a few until its closure in 1957. Jobs faded from McGee's Egg and Poultry Merchants and casual farm work was scarce. Garda Pat McHugh found it difficult to field a junior football team, West Cavan Gaels, from the bulk of four parishes.

Ballyconnell did not lie down and a community Development Committee was established to create some form of local industrial employment to stop emigration. Angling tourism from England was growing and the town welcomed fishermen, who loved the abundance of water, fish and hospitality. The town entertained coach loads of boys and teenagers from the east midlands of England to fish the local waters.

A monthly céili was held in the market house to gather funds which resulted in £500 being collected and was believed given to an agent in America to try to get an industry to come to the town. This was at the same time that Fr Michael Kelly, the then parish curate, went to America to gather funds to build a new chapel at Kildallon. The Irish-American community were very receptive and Fr Kelly made a strong friendship with Tom "Barney" McGovern in New York, a native of Corlough, who was then working with a company called Marvick in Brooklyn, manufacturing internal plastic parts for cars. Tom and his wife were anxious to come back to Ireland to raise and educate their family and Tom also saw the success which his brother Ben had made in returning to west Cavan where he built the successful Wonderland Ballroom at Bawnboy.

With the encouragement of Fr Kelly, Tom and his wife returned to Ireland and Ballyconnell. In February 1961, Star Plastics Ltd commenced, with two teenage employees in the old creamery building. Local businessmen A. W. Ennis and R. M. Richardson, who owned the building, became directors. It was to grow and continues as Boxmore Plastics, a member of the Chesapeak Corporation today. It is now based in a modern purpose-built unit, employing 180 people and supplying blow-moulded containers in all shapes and sizes to the food and pharmaceutical sectors.

Starting up a modern plastics-moulding enterprise in an old building was not without its problems. Tom McGovern had a vision and knew what he wanted to do. Special moulding machinery was imported from Germany but did not come with installation instructions in English. Local innovation and common good interest overcame the absence of a German speaker or the availability of an industrial engineer to install the machinery. Local man Davy Breiden worked long nights after he closed his own garage to help Tom McGovern set up plastic moulding in the old creamery. In those early days, like any new venture, it had its teething problems, which were overcome.

Tom observed Darcy's Service Station where motor engine oil was sold in traditional heavy-duty glass bottles. The need for change to lighter and more cost-effective plastic containers was obvious. Castrol was the first oil company to go with the new plastic oil containers and the patent to manufacture was granted to Tom McGovern. Star Plastics could only grow and employment opportunities for young men and small farmers were available. In those early days, the moulds to shape these new style oil bottle and other plastic containers were manufactured by Basta Enterprises at Tubbercurry, Co. Sligo. All was going well at Star Plastics when in 1966 the Irish bank officials went on strike, a situation that was going to be difficult for paying the growing wages bill in cash. Tom acted on his social responsibilities and approached an American bank in Dublin, which accommodated the fledgling industry in Ballyconnell. Cash was collected every Friday morning for six months to pay the employees. This was crucial to the workers and the local economy. The people of the area are appreciative of the creative outlook and social conscience which Tom McGovern and his co-directors brought to the area and stemmed the flow of emigration. Star Plastics was later sold to the Guinness Group which, within a few years, was taken over by the Boxmore Group plc.

In the early sixties the First Ulsters Gaelic Football Club was revived in Ballyconnell under the direction and influence of Eugene O'Reilly who showed his Cornafaen passion for Gaelic games. Eugene "the Chemist' was more native than the natives themselves through his openess, sense of fun and community. He was facinated by the Fermanagh dialect. Stories about and around Eugene's chemist shop abound and here is one of them.

It was in the late 1960s when a Dublin commercial traveller called to his shop with a great offer on the recently invented packs of "twin toilet rolls". Eugene gave the traveller a break and order a consignment which was delivered in the double. They duly arrived and were stacked in the shop for all to see and purchase. Some months later the same salesman called with a great offer on toothpaste and the 'twin packs' were still on display. Eugene was busy and the sales banter soon irked, when the salesman was told in no uncertain terms: "You can see for yourself - if the people around here aren't going to wipe their backsides, they are hardly going to wash their teeth."

(viii) Hands across the border

In February 1962, the republican movement held a conference in Dublin which officially called off the IRA's cross-border campaign but where the seeds of potential further revolution were sewn. In 1963 Sir Basil Brooke stood down as Northern Premier and was replaced by Sir Terence O'Neill. Seán Lemass, as Irish Prime Minister, started Ireland's campaign for entry into the European Economic Community (EEC) in 1962, an ideal which could only be made possible along with a British application. Anglo-Irish relations were put on a new footing after Harold Wilson came to power in October 1964. The Labour Premier wanted more equality and social justice in Northern Ireland. It was during that election in Northern Ireland that a tricolour in a West Belfast candidate's window caused some rioting, stirred by Ian Paisley, a little-known militant preacher. Britain looked upon Lemass as a pragmatist and a leader with the qualities of an excellent chairman and chief executive.

In January 1965 Seán Lemass travelled to Belfast to meet with Terence O'Neill which was to open a new chapter in north-south relations; The importance of the occasion was also associated with Ireland's and Britain's future application for membership of the EEC. There were some within Unionism who were entrenched but the young liberals within Stormont were happy as this would help to improve trade between north and south. One of the "welcoming parties" to Belfast for Lemass was led by the militant preacher just mentioned, throwing snowballs at his car from a street corner.

Life along the border was quiet and smuggling as we knew it was fading from the radar. People travelled freely as more cross-border roads were approved for motorists and commercial traffic. The openness of the 1960s questioned the validity of partition, and the existence of the Orange Order. When 12 July came around, local Orangemen would attend demonstrations in Fermanagh, "just to be seen". After doing their duty, they would return early across the border to enjoy their day in their own local hostelry, expressing their frustrations and questioning the order for not moving on.

The Belturbet to Enniskillen Road was approved but the Ballyconnell-Derrylin was not. There were continuous cat-and-mouse games played daily as commercial traffic was always avoiding the Irish Customs. The northern customs were seldom seen. At Ballyconnell, some seizures were made, which irked many people and which was exasperated when Customs men would not allow any traffic whatsoever coming from Fermanagh to Ballyconnell and diverting them to approved routes. The people of Fermanagh were, as was traditional, coming south to spend money, shopping for groceries, drink, tobacco and petrol – mostly excise-collecting items to keep the same Customs men in their jobs. The actions of the Irish Customs brought the ire of the community on them when they stopped people going to church on a Sunday morning, ordering the same people to travel to Ballyconnell via Swanlinbar or Aghalane.

A cross-border community committee was established to take some action. Representations were made to John Brooke, then a junior minister at

Stormont and to the Duke of Hamilton, the MP for Fermanagh/South Tyrone, to bring some pressure on Dublin. They were most supportive and sympathetic. From these meetings, the untapped potential of the Woodford Canal was discussed and recorded for action. When meeting with John Brooke at the Ortine Hotel, Lisnaskea, he openly admitted: " I was proud to represent Ireland under the tricolour in junior equestrian events, but of course this could only be done under an assumed name."

The same committee members met with Paddy Smith, Fianna Fáil TD for Cavan, to make a formal complaint about the Irish Customs and all that can be said of his reception is that it was a total embarrassment when compared to the welcome received from the Fermanagh representatives. Did this humble committee interfere in some way with Fianna Fáil's only foreign policy at that time?

(ix) Offer of a pension

After the golden jubilee celebrations of the Easter Rising, a call went out from Dublin, seeking former members of the old IRA and Cumann na mBan to offer them military pensions. On the Whit weekend of June 1967, Paddy Dolphin called to 29 Main Street. In conversation with Ellie Drum they recalled Seán Milroy, Gen Seán MacEoin and the sack of Ballyconnell when Seán McGrath was fatally wounded in the very kitchen where they sat. When he offered her documents to sign for a Cumann na mBan pension she refused, as the same offer was not being made to Annie Crawford.

In a small town one was aware that there were genuine local people who refused such pensions, preferring to uphold their independence and to move on. Among them were those who took up the "cause" and left their families impoverished for decades having given their time and spirit to attain freedom while getting nothing in return. Of course there were others who got pensions and their merit was dubious. Ellie Drum, in a lighter moment spoke of one local woman who was in receipt of a Cumann na mBan pension, and about whom she said: "I'll put it to you like this, she volunteered to look after the volunteers".

In the course of a conversation that evening Paddy Dolphin said he was an IRB man first, then a Volunteer and a Sinn Féiner. He was most critical of the Catholic Heirarchy as "they could never be trusted" saying that they always "sold out" on republicans when offered a little by the British. On being asked who blew up Nelson's Pillar in O'Connell St, Dublin in February '66, he replied: "We did and how could you expect Dev and the old comrades to salute the men of 1916 with that one-eyed so and so of British imperialism looking down on us?" It was always believed that it was "the old guard and Dev" who employed a French expert to send Nelson skywards on that February night. The circumstantial evidence was strong, as Cleary's store had the shutters down that night, the first time in years. Also, the dance in the Metropole Ballroom was ended early, as the clock was put forward.

Paddy Dolphin was an active member of the Volunteers in Ballyconnell and spent time at His Majesty's pleasure in prison. After a short spell in the Free State army, he emigrated, like many of his comrades, to Britain to seek employment. How ironic? He returned to England after his visit to 29 Main Street and died suddenly three months later.

(x) "The Troubles"

A local authority in Tyrone allocated a house to a single Protestant woman in the village of Caledon, in preference to a deserving Catholic family. This act of discrimination was one of the catalysts that led to the formation of the Northern Ireland Civil Rights Movement in 1967. This concerned citizens and trade union-led movement held open meetings and demonstrations throughout the six-counties which became a new fear within the extreme sections of Unionism. To them it appeared as a threat and was misinterpreted as being a new republican movement rather than a movement seeking social and civil equality. Militant loyalist gangs reformed in Belfast at the same time, which helped to feed Unionist fears and innocent Catholics were murdered. Social and civil unrest grew with new fears and many Belfast nationalists having to flee their homes and seek sanctuary elsewhere.

On 15 August 1969, the "Troubles" began in earnest with the death of a youth in Belfast. The mass civil rights march in Derry on the last Sunday of January 1972 was to become known as "Bloody Sunday" when the British military, contrary to police advice, stormed the Bogside area and 14 civilians were shot dead. This was a dark day for Britain as the world reacted. The heated reaction within the Republic of Ireland resulted in the burning down of the British Embassy in Dublin, an event the Irish authorities had to allow; otherwise the consequences may have been greater. In protest against the Derry massacre, Lord Kilbracken, the Labour peer living in Leitrim and Dr Ned McQuade, Virginia, returned their war medals to the British Ambassador in Ireland as a consequence of the paratroopers' actions in Derry. Dr McQuade had served as a paratrooper in Italy during World War II. Real partition had arrived for all, on both islands. Lord Kilbracken applied for Irish citizenship.

Had the British authorities not learned from their past mistakes by still deploying military methods to address civil and political unrest? They had failed in Ireland previously and in the interim they had not learned from their political and military failures throughout a retracting empire. The British army was sent to Belfast in 1969 to protect the Catholic population from the loyalist mobs burning down their homes and intimidating them. How that simple policy soon turned. Internment without trial was introduced in 1971, an action which created a new breed of republicanism.

While ignoring the political demands for social change, the British military and politicians were working in tandem with Protestant loyalist gangs throughout Northern Ireland. The intent was to do the dirty work for the British army in combating republican activities. In those early years, republican movements were practically non-existent bar those of the Irish National Liberation Army, an IRA splinter group.

In the summer of 1972, Enniskillen witnessed its first Republican car bombing. The car used was stolen earlier that day at Carrigallen market. British military/loyalist collusion in the border area was suspected on 15 December 1972 when Louis Leonard was brutally slain in his recently opened butcher shop at Derrylin. In that year a loyalist campaign crossed the border when Swanlinbar Chapel was bombed and in late December Belturbet was hit with a car bomb which killed two teenagers. The Provisional IRA and Loyalist organisations were growing, carrying out bombings and shootings throughout Northern Ireland. Master Saunderson was brutally shot dead on 10 April 1974, at Teemore school during morning break. The IRA unit of four men cheered loudly as they drove past Ballyconnell Garda Station after their deed. Their Longford-registered car was later found abandoned in the Ballinamore area. Eleven days later, Jim Murphy, Derrylin, who had been a civil-rights activist and a former internee was murdered, allegedly by British military/loyalist action.

West Cavan and south Fermanagh were partitioned as never before. New fears and suspicions and fixed military border posts all reinforced this. The people of the six-counties had little reason to travel south as the cost of living, including alcohol, was higher in the south. Northern Ireland became ungovernable and the Stormont Government was replaced by direct civil and military rule from Westminster.

The island of Ireland was to suffer the consequences of civil unrest and its resultant mayhem. A solution could not be found for almost three decades.

For society to move on from this bloody and recent past, its members must question their own beliefs and standing. Irrespective of the church they attend or where their political allegiances may be, an exercise for all would be to ask the value of their traditions and where they have brought them and where they are going.

Understanding and accepting difference is the act of moving on to eliminate partition of the mind. Sustained peace will follow.

(xi) A Sense of the ridiculous

During those early years of conflict in Northern Ireland, while driving one wet spring morning on the Ballyconnell to Derrylin unapproved road, I was stopped by a British army patrol. They had all the appearance of being new to the area.

Formal identification was requested and I was asked "open the car boot. Where are you coming from and where are you going"?

The officer in charge then asked: "Have you got a pass to use this unapproved road"
"No"

He continued: "Do you know that you cannot use this road unless you have a special pass."

To which the reply was: "I have always used this road when necessary and will continue to do so"

The officer stated: "Her Majesty's government says that you cannot use this road unless you have a special pass"

And the reply was:

"If Her Majesty's government is so worried and concerned about this road, tell them when you go back home, that they should consider taking it away altogether."

At this the officer laughed and referred to "good perverse Irish humour."
"Carry on sir"

APPENDIX 1

LLOYD GEORGE'S SPEECH AT CAERNARVON, 9 OCTOBER 1920

Before I sit down, I take advantage of this opportunity to refer to two or three public questions, which there is a general expectancy that I should allude to, and I think there might be some disappointment if I did not dwell upon them. Wherever you go in Wales, you have a feeling of a well-governed country and a peaceful and contented people. I do not mean a people without wrongs to redress. I do not mean people without grievances to set right. I do not mean a people who are not seeking some improvement in their conditions. I should think nothing of them if they did not. There is such a thing as what is known as Divine content. There is a content which is not divine, and, therefore, I am not talking about the peaceable, contented character of the population as a proof that everybody is satisfied with all the conditions of life; but generally it is a happy and contented and a well-governed country, and that is the aspect it presents to you.

Go down to the end of this country, as I did last year. You can go up to the hill there and look across the water, and you can see another country, part of the same Kingdom, part of the same Realm, under the same Crown, associated for hundreds of years with us in common partnership, and none of these adjectives or epithets which I have applied to Caernarvonshire would in the least apply to that country. That is a grave misfortune. I am not for a moment going to examine the reasons. All I can say is this: if we are to clear our consciences we must own that the responsibility rests largely with the past record of government in that country for which we, as an island, are mainly responsible. That must be, and whenever you examine the deplorable conditions of that island, whenever there are things which irritate and exasperate you, things which appear to be indefensible upon the facts at the moment, you must look back and examine the records of ages and find certain germs of discontent, of dissatisfaction, of wrongdoing which were sown by our ancestors in that unfortunate island.

But nothing that has been done in the past can justify altogether the conditions of the present. They may explain it, but they cannot justify it. During the past 30 or 40 years more has been done to redress the evils of the past in Ireland than in any country in the world. That also has to be taken into account. The United Kingdom has put forth a greater effort to restore the conditions of Ireland than in any part or other part of the King's dominions during the past 40 years. What is the position? You have read in the papers, notably during the last few days, of attacks which were delivered against the police and the military administration for something which is called reprisals. Policemen and soldiers do not go burning houses and shooting men down wantonly without provocation, and therefore you must, if you are going to examine reprisals, try to find out how they arise. Let me give you one or two facts. During, I think, the last year, 283 policemen have been shot in Ireland and 109 of them shot dead. Something like 100 soldiers have been shot, and many more have been fired at. Of courthouses like this, I think 67 have been burned. There have been attacks upon police barracks. The police endured this patiently, enduring it in a way, which is the highest testimony to their discipline and self-restraint, for two or three years. There is no doubt that at last their patience has given way, and there has been some severe hitting back. But take the conditions – while these murders were going on, I never read or head a word from Sinn Féiners in Ireland, not a single syllable. Mr Arthur Griffith, a very able and very distinguished Irishman, communicated to the United States' and the English press an interview the other day, in which he showed great concern at the prospect of an attack on his own life. I do not believe it in the least. I do not believe that any attack has been concerted against Mr Arthur Griffith's life, but I never saw a word from Mr Arthur Griffith displaying any indignation at the killing of 109 policemen in Ireland – not one word.

The defence that is put forward for these murders is that there is a state of war. They say that the police are the garrison of a foreign country, and they are entitled to shoot them. If it is war, it is war on both sides. You cannot have one set of men standing up to be shot at and never firing back, and if the men who are shot at shoot back, no soldier ever complains. That is what he expects when he joins the army and enters into a fight. That is not all. In war there are men in uniform. Why? There may be reasons of discipline, but the main reason is that you want to distinguish between the combatant and the non-combatant. If you do not put them in uniform, an army invading a country would see an able-bodied man and could not distinguish between a soldier and a civilian, and would have shot both. Therefore, by all the rules of war, you put a man in uniform so that you know who the combatant is, and the civilian is passed by without any injury being done to him. What is the case here? A harmless looking civilian passes a policeman in the street. There is nothing to indicate that he has any murderous weapon on him. There is nothing to arouse any suspicion in the mind of the policeman that he has any murderous intent. He passes that policeman and when he has done so, he pulls out a revolver and shoots the policeman in the back. Scores of policemen have been killed in that way. That is not war – it is murder.

If it is war, give the soldier and the policeman a fair chance, and they will give a good account of themselves, but if every civilian who passes them in the street may turn out the moment they are passed to be a murderer, what is the policeman to do? Are the police in Ireland to stand to be shot down like dogs in the street without any attempt at defending themselves? It is something more than human nature can tolerate and under those conditions, the police are reserving to themselves the right to find out if a man is armed or not where they have a suspicion and they call upon him to put up his hands. If the man is a harmless man, why should he not do it? Let us be fair to these gallant men who are doing their duty in Ireland. Here you stand by your police and you protect them against any unfairness, and you are right. It is all very well for people who are sitting comfortably at home here, secure from assassins and depredators through the protection of the police, to turn round and pompously criticise them about outrages and discipline when they are defending themselves. Take another point about this. These murders take place and there is a system of demoralisation there that makes it impossible to find any evidence to convict the murderers. If a policeman was shot down here in the streets of Caernarvon, every decent citizen who witnessed the outrage would deem it to be his duty at once to give evidence. That is not the case in Ireland.

It is not the case in my judgement because Ireland would like to see these assassins caught – it is because they dare not There have been many murders there of people who have been suspected of giving information. When men are suspected of murder and they escape, it is often impossible afterwards to arrest them because of the conspiracy in a population organised and enforced by intimidation and terror. Now when men attempt to escape and they refuse to stop, then undoubtedly the police now fire upon them. Can you complain of it? Why should that be characterised as murder? It is the only way in which these men can defend themselves.

I will give you one case. Five policemen driving along a road in Ireland were suddenly fired at by civilians. If a policeman had seen the assassins 10 minutes before, he would have thought they were harmless farmers looking after their flocks and crops. They used soft-nosed explosive bullets. A second car with police comes up in two minutes. It is what the assassins had not reckoned with. Finding these men not merely killed but mutilated almost beyond description – torn – I could not give you the horrible details of what happened – the second car came up. The men saw their comrades not merely murdered but mutilated. They found the men who undoubtedly were the assassins and they shot them. Are you surprised? That is called reprisals and that is called murder when the police do it, and I never saw this anxiety to denounce murder when 109 policemen were shot down when they were trying to do their duty. It is no use talking about this being war and about reprisals when these things have been done with impunity in Ireland. No one gives any evidence about the assassins, and the police naturally feel that the time has come for them to defend themselves, and that is what is called reprisals in Ireland. There are certain cases – in fact, all these cases – which are being carefully investigated, and I am not going to express a final opinion upon them until the facts have been brought out by a careful inquiry, but inasmuch as there are people who are prejudging these cases without hearing evidence of the police, and without hearing their defence, I am just putting the facts.

There are on the other side – and I am asking the country to reserve its judgement about men who in great difficulties have shown infinite restraint, and not to think they are mere murderers wandering about Ireland shooting innocent citizens – but there is another aspect to this question to which I am bound to refer. How are you going to improve upon this condition and put things right in Ireland?

Undoubtedly you must restore order there by methods very stern. You cannot permit the country to be debased into a condition of complete anarchy where a small body of assassins – a real murder gang – is dominating the country and terrorising it, and making it impossible for reasonable men to come together to consider the best way of governing their country. They are intimidating, not Unionists, nor Protestants, but men of their own race, men of their own faith, who would be only too anxious to discuss the sanest and the best method of restoring order and good government to their country if they are left alone. Therefore, it is essential in the interests of Ireland that the gang should be broken up. Unless I am mistaken, we shall do it.

Side by side with that we must proceed with measures for conferring self-government upon Ireland. What kind of measures? I have been a Home Ruler all my life, but there are people now who want something far beyond anything which would ever have been regarded as possible within the category of Home Rule. Mr Gladstone went to what he considered the safe limit of his concessions to Ireland. There were many who thought he went too far. He went as far as he could, consistent with the security of United Kingdom, of the Empire, and consistent with supremacy in Ireland. The same applied to Mr Asquith in 1912, but there are men, and responsible men, who would go far and beyond anything Mr Gladstone ever thought safe and far beyond what Mr Asquith himself thought in 1912, and I have to deal with these appeals which have been made. Why is it done? Why are we asked to go further? I protest against the doctrine that you should go further and give more, not because Ireland needs it, not because it is fair to the United Kingdom, but because crime has been more successful. It is a fatal doctrine for any government in any land. Give it because it is right, give it because it is just, give it because it is good for Ireland and good for the United Kingdom, give it because it brings peace and goodwill, but do not give it because you are bullied by assassins.

Why are you asked to go further than Mr Gladstone was prepared to go? They say because Mr Gladstone's measure satisfied Ireland then and it does not now. There is a question I would like to ask. Is satisfying Ireland in an angry mood, which I think will pass; is satisfying Ireland in a phase of its temper, which I think is an effervescent one; is satisfying Ireland when it has got that sulky disposition, which we all have; is satisfying Ireland in that temper an essential condition of the appeal? If so, there is nothing in view but an independent republic for Ireland. There are men who would say give it Dominion Home Rule. I have asked repeatedly in the House of Commons, on the platform, of deputations of Labour, of deputations from Ireland – I have asked them to name a single Irishman who has got the authority to speak for his countrymen who would say he would accept Dominion Home Rule.

Whether we like it or not, there is not one of them who will tell you they will accept Dominion Home Rule. So if satisfying the present opinion of Ireland is an essential condition of settlement, there is only one thing you can do – cut Ireland adrift. Cut the painter. Let them set up an independent republic, an absolutely independent nation and that won't satisfy them. They will want Ulster. Ulster will have something to say to that and when we are trying to restore peace to the world, we do not want to negotiate a civil war at our own doors. Not quite. Ulster will not have an independent Irish republic You could not have an independent Irish republic if the whole of Ireland agreed and demanded it, no more than you could have an independent republic in Wales if we were quite unanimous. There is a limit, as Abraham Lincoln discovered, to the disruptive rights of a minority. The southern states of America had just as good a right to set up an independent republic as Ireland, Scotland or Wales. They were a distinct community and Gladstone thought that they ought to have been allowed to do it at that time. History now shows that Abraham Lincoln was absolutely right in saying that there is a limit to the right, which even a separate community has, to tear up a large combination that has been working together for common ends. That is the limit in Ireland.

But let us examine the proposition of Dominion Home Rule. There is Lord Grey's letter. There are parts of this letter I like, and there are parts I do not like. But, at any rate, Lord Grey is opposed to full Dominion Home Rule because, he says and says rightly, that you cannot give to Ireland the right to organise a separate army and navy. I should have thought that was common sense, but the proposal which he put forward, and which goes very far, Mr de Valera has repudiated with indignation – I might almost say with insult. He will not look at it. Dominion Home Rule means they can organise their own army and navy. As Lord Grey points out, they can organise their submarine bases. They have got full command of all the ports of Ireland, and Lord Grey says he could not consent to that.

But as Mr Asquith agrees to that, I put it to him in the House of Commons. I said: "You are talking about Dominion Home Rule. The Dominions have got armies and navies of their own, their ports are entirely in their control, they can shut their ports against British ships, and we know perfectly well we could not interfere." I asked: "Would you give the same rights to Ireland? If not, there is no use in talking about Dominion Home Rule." Mr Asquith was not prepared to answer, but what he refused to tell the House of Commons he has communicated with his old friend Lord Northcliffe. Mr Asquith has written a letter to *The Times*. I am amazed. What has the poor old *Daily News* done that it should be snubbed publicly in this way? But *The Times* is Mr Asquith's official organ, and he tells us that he proposes complete and full Dominion Home Rule. Well just see what that means. You can have conscription in Ireland under Dominion Home Rule. We have done without it here but if there is Dominion Home Rule in Ireland, there will be conscription here too.

You cannot have an army of five or six hundred thousand men in Ireland commanded by Mr Arthur Griffith and Mr Michael Collins, who vowed the destruction of this country, and only an army of 100,000 here. It certainly means conscription here. A navy Mr Griffith? Why not? They won't be so foolish as to spend money on a navy. You do not need to spend much on submarines. They are vicious little craft. They are dangerous and perilous, but they are not expensive. I am not sure that they cost as much as a respectable yacht. And mines you can have, and these are cheap. And these under full and complete Home Rule, the Irish republic can have. Why should not we have a Welsh navy?

Do you know that Ireland was our worry during the war? We did not tell you much about it. It was no use; it would only have encouraged the enemy. We might have told you what were our troubles and our anxieties and our worries and our fears for this old country we were doing our best to defend. But what was the good in doing it? It would have been reproduced in every paper in Germany. They would have said: "Ah, we have got them." Ireland was a real peril. They were in touch with German submarines. There it stands at the gateway of Britain. You cannot turn to the right, you cannot turn to the left, except by either the right or left gate of Ireland; and I saw a map the other day that was captured – a German map – a map circulated to show how Britain was having her fleet destroyed, and the coast of Ireland was black with British ships that were sunk in the Atlantic, the Irish Sea, in the St George's Channel. It is girdled with British wrecks. Yes, and the British seamen are there too. And are we to hand over Ireland to be made a base of the submarine fleet, and are we to trust to luck in the next war? Was there ever such lunacy proposed by anyone?

We got through this time – a nearer thing than I care to think about, and I think about it with reverence and thankfulness to the great Providence that guided our destinies. But I take no such risks for the future. This is a great country – a great country; it has done more for human freedom than any other country, but do not risk its destiny and its future through any folly or through any fear of any gang in Ireland. We saw this great country through at gigantic cost. We are not going to quail before a combination of a handful of assassins in any part of the British Empire. Hand our ports over to Ireland, that gateway to Great Britain! They might starve us. No, if they had accepted Dominion Home Rule, then, at any rate, you would have had the safeguard of the national honour of Ireland, and national word of honour of Ireland, and I do not despise that. I do not despise the word of a nation, but you have not got even that. Conditions change, and it will be a risk even then. There might arise conditions where they would feel themselves absolved from that obligation of honour, but you have not got even that. And then there would be the danger that in England's trouble they might achieve independence and satisfy an old feeling of vengeance of past wrongs.

In 1914 we entered the war with the unanimous approval of every representative. There were English representatives who disapproved, and I think there were Scottish representatives who disapproved, but there were no Irish representatives who were not breast-high in entering the war.

In 1916 they were shooting down, in the streets of Dublin, British soldiers, many of them not recovered from wounds received in the war. In 1917 and 1918 they were conspiring with German submarines, and we discovered documents in the pockets of men who were arrested in 1918 that they were prepared within two months of a German offensive that they knew of to raise a huge force in Ireland to stab Britain in the back when it was engaged in a life and death struggle for the freedom of the world. What a change. You are asked to trust the destinies of Britain and the Empire to people who are apt to get fits of passion that sweep away all reason, and make them swing violently from one extreme to the other in the middle of a great conflict. You must not ignore these great facts. Why did they do it? They have grievances, but so have we all. No, it is too uncertain a factor – the Irish temperament – under trying conditions for us to risk the whole life of Britain upon the chance that they will always act rationally, that they will never lose their temper at the wrong moment, and that you can depend on them, whatever the temptation, always to resist it, and to stand by Britain and her interests. You cannot do it.

This is a great country and it is vital for the freedom of the world that its strength and its majesty, which saved the world in the Great War, should still be preserved. Well, let Irishmen manage their own domestic affairs in their own way. Nobody wishes to manage their domestic affairs, but dangerous weapons, weapons like armies and navies, I think we had better not trust to them. They had better not have an army. Armies are expensive; navies are expensive too, and you do not want to condemn people into keeping an establishment which is beyond their means. And not only that; they are not only very expensive and costly, they are extremely dangerous and may blow off. So, on the whole, I think the army and navy should be under the control of the Imperial Parliament, as far as I am concerned and I speak on behalf of the government. We shall certainly resist out and out any attempt for an army and navy being set up in Ireland at our doors to menace the existence of the United Kingdom.

I will tell you another thing that Dominion Home Rule means. It means that they have control over their own finances from top to bottom and do not pay any share of our debts. But they are not our debts. The war debt is not entirely ours. We voted for the war and so did the Irish members, and you cannot have a war that you will not pay for it afterwards. There is such a thing as justice. I want to get justice for Ireland but I want justice for Great Britain. Justice means justice all round. It is a sham and a fraud all this agitation. I know what course we are pursuing. I think it is the course of peace for the world, of restoration for this country, of prosperity and contentment for its people, but it is not an easy course. I go back fortified by your kindness, strengthened by your trust to pursue and face the most difficult tasks that were ever cast upon the shoulders of a statesman in the land.

APPENDIX 2

SINN FÉIN COURT CASE OVER 1919 LOCAL ELECTIONS

As by regulations of the Local Government Board, local elections were due in June 1919 and Sinn Féin in Cavan were ready to contest every seat in every electoral division. Cavan Co. Council appointed the then Co. Secretary, William Finlay, as returning officer for the elections, which were fixed to take place on 4 June. Thomas O'Reilly was the sitting councillor for the District of Ballyconnell and he was duly proposed by John Drum and seconded by Thomas Dolphin to contest the seat by his nomination being handed in on 6 May. As this would appear to have been the last day for nominations and as there were no other candidates nominated for the District of Ballyconnell, Thomas O'Reilly, like 13 other unopposed candidates in the county, was in a position to be declared elected on 4 June.

Two days after receiving these nominations, Cavan Co. Council passed a motion to nullify or cancel the local elections as called. The *Anglo-Celt* published the list of nominated candidates for the said council elections on 10 May. This led to a court application before the Master of the Rolls, Chancery Division, Dublin on 23 May, a test case that very obviously had to be taken by Sinn Féin to extend its campaign of civil disobedience while showing up the establishment in the courts which Sinn Féin, by its own courts' system, was attempting to destroy.

This legal and political case was in all probability undertaken and financed by Sinn Féin, with affidavits from the plaintiffs lodged as a test case and an attempt to discredit local government in Ireland, which in the view of Arthur Griffith was rife with political cronyism and nepotism. Local government, as we know it today, was still very much in its infancy in Ireland in 1919.

The following is a detailed report of the case from the *Anglo-Celt* on 31 May 1919.

Mr Aidan McCabe, solr, Cavan, instructed Mr T. M. Healy KC and Mr J. McLoone KC, and Mr J. C. R. Lardner BL, who on behalf of the plaintiffs, Thomas O'Reilly, John Drum and Thomas Dolphin, applied for an interlocutory injunction, claiming:
1. A declaration that the resolution of Cavan Co. Council, passed at a meeting on 8 May 1919, whereby it was resolved that no further steps be taken in the conduct of the local elections is invalid and of no effect and not binding on

the Returning Officer appointed by said Council at a meeting on 6 February 1919 and that the said Returning Officer is not precluded thereby from proceeding with the election of County Councillors in accordance with the requirements of the statues;

2. For an injunction restraining the defendant from acting on the resolution of 8 May and for an order that he be directed to proceed with the election already entered on by him; and for a declaration that the plaintiff, Thomas O'Reilly, is entitled to be declared elected on 4 June 1919 as County Councillor for the said Ballyconnell electoral division.

Mr L. C. P. Smith Solr, Cavan, instructed Messrs E. S. Murphy KC and Mr T. A. Finlay, appearing on behalf of the defendant Mr Finlay. Mr W. E. Wylie KC watched the proceedings on behalf of the Local Government Board.

At the opening of the case, Mr Rylands, Junior Council on behalf of the Attorney General said:

He had been instructed by the Attorney General to inform his Lordship that there was at present a Bill before Parliament dealing with local government in Ireland, which it was expected would pass into law within a short period, and it was the intention of the government to insert in the Bill a clause setting aside elections that were held or might be held prior to the passing of the Proportional Representations Act.

Mr Healy: This is contempt of Court my Lord.

His Lordship: How can I take into consideration anything that may be pending in the way of legislation in Parliament? I must administer the law as I find it.

Mr Healy: I must protest against the course that is being taken by my friend the Attorney General who is not party to the suit and has no right to obtrude himself here.

His Lordship: He comes in simply as "amiens curiae".

Mr Healy: That may save his contempt.

Mr Rylands left the Court.

Mr Healy said his clients asked for an order to restrain the defendant from acting upon an admittedly illegal resolution of his Council. The facts were common and not disputed and the law was so clear that a child should have acted upon it. There was no dispute to either law or facts and the question was simply as to the application of the law.

Mr Murphy: I hope you will not ask me to admit all that.

Mr Healy: In December 1918, the Local Government Board sent out a scheme and directed that certain elections be held. Cavan Co. Council met and appointed as Returning Officer their Secretary, Mr Finlay, a most admirable official, able and intelligent and competent in every way. A date was fixed for receiving nominations and 4 June as day of election, when suddenly a faction of the Co. Council without notice to anybody, against the law and against the rules of the Local Government Board and against their own standing orders, violently arrested that decision and ordered Mr Finlay to hold no elections. Mr O'Reilly had in the meantime been nominated. There was no opposition and therefore he was entitled to be declared elected unopposed for Cavan Co. Council on 4 June next. Mr Finlay found himself, as he conceived, in a difficult position, and I wish it to be understood that we are not attaching any blame to him as he is a man of great distinction, of great probity and rectitude; but he was in a contradictory position and as Secretary of Cavan Co. Council he conceived that he was bound to obey their orders, although as Returning Officer he was as independent as a Sheriff and not bound to obey their orders. However, he obeyed the order and issued an advertisement withdrawing the whole proceedings after the candidates had been nominated, and 14 unopposed. We ask for an interlocutory injunction to restrain him from acting on an illegal resolution of the Co. Council and for an order requiring him to proceed with the election of 4 June in a normal and legal manner.

Mr Murphy said: he was instructed to treat the present proceedings as a trial of the action.

Mr Healy said that notices of the elections on 4 June were issued by the Returning Officer and sent broadcast throughout Co. Cavan. Thomas O'Reilly was duly nominated for Ballyconnell county division and the only person nominated.

His Lordship: If there is only one person nominated, does he become de facto elected?

Mr Healy: That is my submission. Of course there would be no declaration until the day fixed for the poll.

His Lordship: There would be no person competent to oppose him?

Mr Healy, proceeding, said that the resolution holding up the elections was proposed by Mr Francis McCormack, the same gentleman who was sworn to have seconded the motion appointing Mr Finlay as Returning Officer, seconded by Mr Thomas Patrick McKenna and adopted – two members dissenting – in opposition to the opinion of the County Solicitor and Mr Finlay himself, as he admitted in his affidavit.

It was done without notice of motion as required by Article 36 of the Applications of Enactments Order and in defiance of the Standing Orders of the Co. Council, so that the Co. Council broke not only the general law of the nation but the law of their own body adopted by themselves. That action was taken as stated "owing to the advice of the Local Government Board" in view of some scheme of Proportional Representation, which a party of gentlemen from the north east, headed by Sir Edward Carson, were opposing – and Sir Edward Carson generally has his way – but the plaintiff (Mr O'Reilly) did not see why his fate should be decided by the intrigues in the lobby of the House of Commons between Sir Edward Carson and the Attorney General.

Mr Murphy: Sir Edward Carson is not a defendant.

Mr Healy: Subsequent to the meeting of the Co. Council on 8 May, the Returning Officer issued a notice that resulting from the adoption of the resolution dropping the elections that "in no case will a poll be taken on 4 June", but he does not say anything about the candidates nominated and unopposed; he does not say that he will suspend action in their regard.

Counsel then referred to Mr Thomas O'Reilly being head clerk of the County Cavan Pensions Committee at £45 per annum and said that in the Local Government Board's circular in reference to the elections it was set out:

"No power is vested either in the Returning Officer or his deputies to decide upon the qualifications or disqualifications of any candidate properly nominated and if the nomination paper was properly filled up and signed by two Local Government electors and was not invalid under Rule 4 (5) or Rule 6 of the Board's General Election order, it must be accepted even though the person nominated seemed obviously disqualified. The question of a candidate's qualification could not be raised until after the election, and only by an Election petition."

The Returning Officer was liable to certain penalties if he failed to carry out his duties, and in the case of Mr Finlay the penalties might run to £5,000 as he was Returning Officer not alone for the Co. Council but for the Rural District Council as well. If the plaintiff were disqualified 40 times over, he must be declared elected as his nomination paper was accepted by the Returning Officer and he was the only candidate proposed for that particular electoral division.

His Lordship: I take it that the question of the candidate's qualification would not affect the nomination paper at all – that it would be a matter for adjudication after the election.

Mr Healy: It would suffice if we get an order enjoining the defendant not to act upon an illegal resolution of the Co. Council, and if he is seized of that fact that an illegality has been committed which cannot be tolerated. Mr Finlay, on learning that the procedure adopted was illegal will, I assume, take the proper steps in the matter. It is greatly to his credit that he entered an appearance forthwith on being served with the writ instead of attempting any arrangement for delay.

His Lordship: I suppose Mr Finlay wants to have the legal point decided at the earliest possible moment.

Mr Healy: It is greatly to his credit. In his correspondence with the Local Government Board he puts the situation in a very excellent manner to them and asks for definite instructions as to whether the elections should be proceeded with, but in a shuffling reply the board said: "We have no further information in regard to the matter." Mr Finlay has acted throughout with bona fides and absolute integrity and I will make no criticisms of his actions. He was in a state of great puzzlement and finally appealed, I was going to say, "from Philip drunk to Philip sober", and in his case from the Local Government Board to Dublin Castle. He wrote to the Under-Secretary and there was no reply and he then sent a second letter with a prepaid telegram form and in reply he was again referred to the Local Government Board.

His Lordship: Why did he write to the Castle? What had the Castle to do with it?

Mr Healy: I suppose he thought that the law officers would advise him. The Local Government Board wrote on 29 April, referring him to his circular letter of 16 April, in which they stated that they had no further information than that contained in their circular letter of 2 April, that having regard to the information obtained from the Irish Office, they "had no doubt that the elections would be postponed to a later date, fixed by the Local Government (Ireland) Amending Bill".

His Lordship remarked that they did not seem to address themselves to the great difficulty in which a public officer was placed – whether he would be entitled to disregard the existing law. Mr Finlay wanted advice on that point.

Mr Healy: The Attorney General in his extraordinary message to the court today – the likes of which has not been heard since the days of Charles I – says he "hopes" the Bill before Parliament will pass.

His Lordship: I cannot pay any attention whatever to that. I must administer the law as I find it.

Mr Healy: The notices of election in Co. Cavan having being published, the Local Government Board pulled themselves together after three weeks, and writing on 5 May stated that they "had deferred consideration of the proposed new scale of expenses and of the proposal to take the poll for certain district electoral divisions outside such divisions pending the decision of Parliament on the Local Government (Ireland) Amending Bill. It is expected that the Bill will be through the Committee stage the following day, 6 May, and would obtain the Royal Assent before the end of the present month and in these circumstances the Co. Council would no doubt consider it advisable to incur no other avoidable expense in connection with the rates."

His Lordship: Has the Bill passed the House of Commons?

Mr Healy: Not at all. The elections are being proceeded with in Tyrone and Antrim and the rest of the administered life of the rest of the country is being periled.

Mr Finlay states in his affidavit:

"As to my knowledge, statements had been made by some members of the Co. Council that an amount of unnecessary expense would be incurred by the holding of the elections in June. I desired to obtain a ruling from the Co. Council as to the holding of the said elections and at the quarterly meeting of the Co. Council on 8 May the matter was discussed and the circular letter from the Local Government Board considered. I pointed out the difficulties that might arise and expressed it as my opinion that if the Council did not hold the election according to the letter of the Local Government Board of 21 December 1918, their administrative life ends on 7 June 1919, as the Local Government (Ireland) Amending Bill contained noclause prolonging the life of the Council and that, accordingly, after 7 June 1919, it would be open to any ratepayer to challenge the right of the Council to either collect or administer rates. With this expression of opinion, Mr McBreen, County Solicitor, agreed. I was then asked by some members of the Council as to the practice adopted in counties other than Cavan. Other counties in which notices of election, to my knowledge, had been given were Tyrone and Antrim and in the remaining counties no steps had been taken with a view to the election of councillors. The following resolutionwas proposed by Mr Francis McCormack, seconded by Mr Thomas Patrick McKenna, and carried, two members dissenting: 'That no further steps be taken in the conduct of the election owing to the advice of the Local Government Board.' I felt myself bound by this resolution and it was not open to me to question its validity, and I respectfully submit to this honourable Court that in view of the relief claimed in this action, the Co. Council should have been named as defendants and that it is oppressive to institute this action against me, an officer of the Co. Council, to defend this action on their behalf."

Counsel said: The defendant was in error in the last paragraph of his affidavit, as it was not as an officer of the Co. Council he was being sued but as Returning Officer, in which position he was as independent as a Sheriff and a public trustee.

His Lordship: The office of Returning Officer is an absolutely independent office with certain duties.

Mr Healy: I was most anxious not to implead an official of the standing and repute of Mr Finlay, if the action could be brought against the Co. Council. I considered the matter very carefully as I would be most anxious to implead some members of the Co. Council, especially Mr McCormack, and make him bear the costs. I say the Returning Officer was not bound by the resolution of the Co. Council who were interested parties anxious to prolong their own lives. As Returning Officer he acts for the ratepayers and   electors as a body and not for the Co. Council. The existing Co. Council will be dissolved on 7 June. The elections might have been fixed for 8 June so that Mr Finlay would be acting as Returning Officer at a time when the Co. Council had disappeared.

His Lordship: What you are asking for is a mandatory injunction, in substance a peremptory mandamus.

Mr Healy: If Your Lordship simply warn him that the resolution adopted by the Co. Council on 8 May was an illegal resolution, I am sure that Mr Finlay, on getting that little "tap of the baton" from the Court will do what is proper, having regard to the great importance of the matter for the whole of Ireland as well as Co. Cavan, that the whole administrative life of the country will crumble into ruin on 7 June, that rates may be refused and denied and all sorts of complications arise from a local government gamble in the House of Lords or the House of Commons.

Master of the Rolls: Is the Local Government Board represented?
Mr Healy: Mr Wylie is in court.
Master of the Rolls: I cannot understand the actions of the Local Government Board or the action of the Attorney General. It really seems to me that it was his public duty to proceed himself to compel the Returning Officer to act according to law. His action is absolutely unintelligible.
Mr Healy: Here we have a Government that say the Sinn Féin party must obey law and order. They are all for "law and order", but the moment it conveniences themselves, they are the very first to deride the law. The Attorney General, by his action in coming here to tell His Lordship of a Bill pending in Parliament, I respectfully say has demeaned his office.
Mr Murphy: Apparently it is sought to crush the defendant between the nether and the upper millstone. At one moment Mr Healy attacks the Local Government Board and while I'm not here to defend them, as they can defend themselves, I submit that their letters in the matter show that they acted in a way that any board, considering the present position of affairs, would have acted. At another moment the Attorney General for Ireland is attacked.
His Lordship: Let the Attorney General look after himself.

Mr Murphy, proceeding, said he would deal with the position in which the defendant found himself with an action launched against him and relief of the most extreme character and costs claimed. Counsel challenged the statement that the defendant, a Returning Officer, was in an independent position like a Sheriff, for the Sheriff was appointed the day of an election and fixed the scale of fees, while in this case the Returning Officer was appointed by the Co. Council and bound hand and foot. The day for the poll was fixed by the Co. Council and what was still more important, the scale of expenses for the carrying out of the election had to be settled by the Co. Council and submitted to the Local Government Board for approval. The Co. Council did submit a scale of expenses to the Local Government Board, who stated they had deferred consideration of the proposed new scale of expenses and of the proposal to take the poll for certain district electoral divisions outside such divisions pending the decision of Parliament on the Local Government (Ireland) Bill. There was the position of the Returning Officer. The scale of expenses that must be approved of by the Local Government Board had not been approved and the mode of conducting the elections had not been decided, yet Mr Healy claimed a declaration that the resolution postponing the election was invalid and for an injunction restraining the defendant from acting on that resolution, for a declaration that his client is entitled to be elected on 4 June and for an order that the defendant be directed to proceed with the election. But the Returning Officer was without any means of proceeding when the very method adopted was actually not approved by the Local Government Board. In these circumstances, how could he proceed?

His Lordship: I am very much struck with what you say, but it does not follow that because the scale of expenses has to be fixed by the Co. Council, that the Returning Officer is not an independent officer.
Mr Murphy: The expenses are the foundation of election work and the scale as settled by the Co. Council does not come into operation until approval by the Local Government Board. My friend says the election must be held on 4 June but it is physically impossible to do so. The Local government Board have not approved of the scale of fees or of the taking of poll for certain divisions outside of those divisions and on the state of facts the Court is asked by interlocutory application to make amandatory order against the defendant.
   His Lordship said he did not think that the Act of Parliament contemplated that a Returning Officer should make the excuse that he could not perform his duties by reason of financial difficulties placed in his way as he was empowered to call upon the Co. Council to advance him the sum of £10 for every thousand electors.
Mr Murphy: This would not provide for an election of this kind.
His Lordship: It does not give the Returning Officer an opportunity of saying "my expenses were not provided".
Mr Murphy: If that be so, it is a remarkable fact that a scale of expenses has to be adopted by the Co. Council and submitted for the approval of the Local Government Board. Counsel submitted that as the validity of a resolution of the Co. Council challenged the plaintiff, he, assuming he had a right of action, should have proceeded against

the Co. Council, the parties most interested in upholding the resolution, joining the Returning Officer as a defendant if they wished to make him a party to the suit.The resolution in question was passed, not by a "faction", as stated by Mr Healy, but by the entire Co. Council, two members dissenting, on information given them by the Local Government Board. They merely postponed the day of election, and could have taken more reasonable action in face of the advice of the Local Government Board.

His Lordship said that to disobey the existing law because, possibly, it might be amended was an illegal thing to do.

Mr Murphy: I must frankly confess that I have not heard anything that would coerce Your Lordship at this stage to hold that the Co. Council had no power to hold the election.

His Lordship: You don't seem to contemplate that with any change in the date of the election the whole thing would break down.

Mr Murphy: There is no suggestion of malafides. In this matter, the Co. Council and Mr Finlay acted perfectly bona fide, and if the plaintiff was validly nominated on 6 May, doubtless that will stand good on the subsequent day of election, so he is not prejudiced in any way by the postponement.

His Lordship: It occurs to me that if every Co. Council acted in this way, then unless the Amending Bill went through the country would be chaos.

Mr Healy: The whole thing is a political gamble.

His Lordship: Can a Court of Justice do anything but administer the existing law?

Mr Murphy: It is suggested that if the elections are not held chaos would result, but that is speculation unless we assume that the Local Government Board and the Attorney General speak without any knowledge in making this statement.

His Lordship: The whole thing was done with the best of intentions, but was it done legally?

Mr Murphy: Presumably the responsible authorities will see that chaos does not result.

His Lordship: I would like to know if the Local Government Board wish to argue the case.

Mr W. E. Wylie: I would be perfectly willing to argue it if a properly constituted suit was brought and the Co. Council made defendants. I cannot intervene now although I would like to very much.

His Lordship: Is it your position that legally constituted bodies must suspend operations on account of pending legislation?

Mr Wylie: I understand there is no absolute mandate to have the election on a particular day. The Co. Council, if they pass a valid resolution, have perfect power to suspend the holding of election to a subsequent date.

His Lordship: It would be a lot to pass a valid resolution now because notice of election must be 35 clear days before the day of election which must be about 1 June.

Mr Wylie: Surely notice of election having been published, the actual date can be postponed? The Local Government Board do not look on this from a strictly legal sense but from a common sense point of view.

Mr Healy: Oh, I see.

Mr Wylie: There is a Bill before Parliament, which will contain a retrospective clause prolonging the life of the existing Councils.

Mr Healy: To the Irish Republic, I suppose. (Laughter.)

Mr Wylie: I am quite willing to argue the case if Your Lordship give me the opportunity.

His Lordship: Is it not possible that some member of the House of Commons may object to this retrospective clause?

Mr Wylie: The Bill has passed through the House with this clause in it.

His Lordship: Any ratepayer would have an interest in having the question decided whether the Returning Officer is bound to act on the first resolution of the Co. Council – as every ratepayer has an interest in the administration of the entire county. What is going to happen the Co. Council if the Bill before Parliament does not go through?

Mr Wylie: We must leave that to the Local Government Board.

His Lordship: I have to consider it.

Mr Healy: Mr Finlay told the Co. Council what will happen.

His Lordship: If there is not a new Council on 7 June, there is no Council at all. On the existing law, the county will be left without a Council.

Mr Murphy: Has chaos resulted anywhere?

Mr Healy: What about Sligo?

Mr Wylie: Proportional Representation cured that.

On the following Tuesday 23 May, in the Chancery Division, before the Master of The Rolls, arguments were concluded and judgment given.

Mr Murphy, in the course of his argument, said that at present a Bill was before Parliament to which His Lordship interjected: "I won't listen to that at all."

Mr Murphy: But suppose an Act is passed stopping elections under the old system, has the Co. Council no power to postpone an election which has to take place?

His Lordship: I must act according to the law.

Mr Murphy: I quite agree. But should you be compelled to hold that there is no power to postpone an election – apart from this Bill, circumstances may arise before 4 June?

His Lordship: Why if that was possible, a jury might be asked to return a verdict of innocent in the case of a man being prosecuted for bigamy because in the meantime an Act might be passed saying that a man might have two wives. (Laughter.)

Mr Murphy: And there was the Deceased Wife's Sister Bill.

(Laughter.)

His Lordship: It is the first time I ever heard of a Court of Justice practically asked to hold up the hand of the administration of the law in the interests of a political party. That was the suggestion of the Attorney General's counsel.

Mr Healy argued that the Returning Officer would be liable to a penalty of £100 for each such offence, so that the order they were asking the Court to make would save him a great deal of money. His Lordship had heard what had happened. Was the Court of Chancery to be required to follow the miry footsteps of politics? Were His Majesty's subjects not to be heard or allowed to open their mouths? Was the learned Attorney General to be allowed to come in and, with the weight of his authority, bludgeon justice? There had been a great deal in history about James I and Lord Coke 300 years ago but, at all events, they had stuck to their words. They did not say, "We did not do it", when they were held up to obloquy. A gross illegality was in course of being perpetrated here and counsel did not see why those responsible for it should not be punished for an attempt to stop the process of the law. Other people, like cattle drivers, who might be animated by the noble idea of improving congested districts were punished. Many noble people had perished on the scaffold – they had not the backing of Attorney Generals. (Laughter.) Corruption was often talked about, but what about the corruption of political intrigue? He hoped that His Lordship's decision would revive memories of those ancient days when judges declared the sovereignty of the law.

The Master of the Rolls, in delivering judgement, said:
This action has been brought by Thomas O'Reilly, and his nominators John Drum and Thomas Dolphin, against William Finlay, the Returning Officer for the county of Cavan, to obtain a mandamus compelling him to proceed with the Local Government election for the county of Cavan. At present I am concerned with the interlocutory injunction as set out in paragraph 2. The defendant is secretary of the Co. Council of Cavan, and it is quite evident that he is a man of ability and very efficient, and it is not his fault that he now finds himself in an embarrassing position. His only desire is to do his duty. I think the most that can be said against the defendant is that he rather weakly submitted to the Council's instructions. The short facts of the case are these: Under the Local Government Act, the ordinary day of elections to the Co. Council is 1 June or such day, not more than seven days earlier or later than that date, as might have been fixed by each Co. Council for the purpose of holding the election of the Co. Council for that county. The Cavan Co. Council appointed the defendant its Returning Officer and fixed 4 June as the date of the election, and I have got no hesitation in stating that once the defendant was appointed Returning Officer, he held an absolutely independent official position – a position which is independent insofar as interference from the Co. Council or any other body is concerned. He was only bound to obey the law of the land.

Now in pursuance of this, the defendant as Returning Officer, and in obedience of the order made under the Local Government Act, gave public notice of the election on the day appointed and also of the day on which nominations should be sent to him. In response to that notice, the plaintiff, Thomas O'Reilly, was nominated by the plaintiffs John Drum and Thomas Dolphin, who are, I understand, both local government electors for the electoral division of Ballyconnell in the county of Cavan, and no other candidate having been nominated, it then became the duty of the Returning Officer to give public notice that the plaintiff was duly elected and that no poll would be taken for that division, and that he would be subsequently declared duly elected. The object of that notice is, of course, to save the electors from any further trouble in case of a division where there was no contest. Now, up to this point the Returning Officer did what was his obvious duty – that is, up to the point where he should have set out the notice that Thomas O'Reilly was the only candidate. But then the Co. Council took an extraordinary and, I should say, a wholly unprecedented course. On 8 May, a meeting of the Council was held and the following resolution was passed: "That no further steps be taken in the conduct of the elections, owing to the recent advice of the Local Government Board.

I will deal first with the course taken by the Co. Council. When the resolution referred to was proposed, the defendant who, in addition to being the Returning Officer is also Secretary of the Co. Council – as he was in duty bound to do – gave his Council the benefit of his advice, and sound and prudent advice it was. The advice was this: that the administrative life of the council would cease on 7 June, and that after that date it would be open to any ratepayer to challenge the right of the Council of the county to collect or administer the rates. Now that opinion was confirmed by Mr McBreen, who was the County Solicitor. But the opinions of both these gentlemen were disregarded and now I would like to say this, that it must be highly gratifying to every person who is interested in local government in Ireland that county councils have such able and clear-headed officers as the defendant in this action and Mr McBreen, the solicitor to the Co. Council. No better advice could have been given by any two gentlemen.

Now what would have been the result if every Co. Council in Ireland pursued the course which the Co. Council of Cavan took in the present case? Why, nothing short of universal stoppage in the whole machinery of local government. There would be a condition something like that which would be produced like a general strike – a strike by every county officer, a strike by every rural council officer, lunatic asylum officers, and a strike by every road man. Why, there would be nothing except a condition of universal paralysis, produced by the death of the nerve-centres of local government – namely, the Co. Councils of the several administrative counties.

Now, the explanation of all this is to be found in a circular letter from the Local Government Board directing Co. Councils not to hold elections which were made imperative by statute. There is not a shred of legal authority for such a circular and it certainly came as a surprise to me that such a fatuous course should have been adopted by the Local Government Board. I have a good experience of the administration of the Local Government Board, both when at the Bar and since I came to preside in this Court, and I have never had anything but admiration for the thoroughness of its work, and the great ability and the great zeal displayed by its executive officers, but certainly a great blunder has been committed, but it turns out that small blame can be attached to the permanent officials of the department. The indiscreet intervention of the Attorney General at the beginning of this case accounts for everything. His counsel interrupted the proceedings for the purpose of informing the Court that some legislation was pending which would affect the machinery of elections. The only meaning of this was – the only meaning which I could ascribe to it – was that this Court was to hold up the administration of the law as it stood in the Statute Book and that the judgment of the Court was to be in some way moulded so as to suit the movements of politicians who, rightly or wrongly, think that the existing law should be altered. This Court knows nothing of politics or of future legislation.

Its duty is to administer the law as it is, and I hope that the day will never come when a judge takes guidance from a government officer who thinks that existing laws ought to be changed, Mr Healy, counsel for the defendants, resented the intrusion of the Attorney General, saying that since the days of the Stuart Kings, no such attempt had been made by the Crown to influence the Court. Well Mr Healy was absolutely right. I was really invited to exercise a kind of dispensing power under which I was to give some kind of dispensation to the Co. Council of Cavan, or its Returning Officer, from obedience to the law of the land. Why one would think that the Bill of Rights were regarded as a deader letter than Courts of Justice. There was absolutely no warrant for the interference of the Attorney General, and I have thought it necessary to say so much in order that the public may know that Courts of Justice still retain their absolute independence.

But now I must consider whether the plaintiff is entitled to an order for an interlocutory injunction compelling the defendant to proceed with the election. Having regard for the form of the action, I must look at it as a private suit between the plaintiffs and the defendant.

If it were brought in the name of the Attorney General at the relations of the plaintiffs, I should pay regard to the consequences to the public at large, but as it is, I must consider the plaintiffs in their purely private capacity. Mr Murphy urged this most forcibly and I yield entirely to his argument. Now interlocutory injunctions are only granted for the purpose of preventing irreparable loss pending the trial of the action, and I cannot see what irreparable or serious damage the plaintiff, O'Reilly, can suffer by not being declared the duly elected councillor for the Ballyconnell electoral division on 7 [should have been 4] June; and so far as I can see, I would be saving him from a position that might prove a very expensive one indeed if he insisted on continuing to fill it for any length of time. I do not consider it necessary to go into the question whether the plaintiff is disqualified for election as a county councillor by reason of holding a certain office or whether the proper procedure should not be by way of mandamus. I think that the answer to the application for an interlocutory injunction is to be found in the fact that interlocutory injunctions are only granted in the special cases that have been mentioned and, therefore, I am inclined to refuse the motion; but of course I must reserve the costs.

INDEX

A.

Act of Union 1801; p.25, p 59,
Agar-Robartes MP; p45
Arva;   Hiring Fair; p.60
Attack on RIC Barracks; p.10, De Valera fair day quote; p. 210.
Anglo-Celt; see Press
Anglo-Irish Truce; p 172 – 177,
Anglo-Irish Treaty; p 178-181,
Asquith Herbert. Premier; p 26, 115, 116, Third Home Rule Bill. Ch.3 p 41/42
In Dublin: p 67
Annesley Lady; p.22
AOH; p.20, 23, 68/69, 83,
Arigna; p 193/4, 195
Armour Rev. J B; p.51.
Arnold Josephine, Mrs. P.51, 57
Ashley Col. MP; p 126
Auxillary Police; p. 157-8, 159, 160,

B.

Bailieboro; p.78/79
Ballyconnell; Ch. 1, history of, Ch. 14 social history. Canal; p.16, 58, 224. Fair ; p16, 59
Joe Biggars /First Ulsters p.17/18, 222.
Electric Lights; p.51 Light Orchestra: p.24, p58. Masonic Hall; p.21Orange demonstration; p.85/86.Petty Sessions; p. 74/75, Sinn Féin Club; p. 70, 80, 87 , Sack of; p 193-198.
Ballinamore; p 195
Blacklion; p.27, 193.
Bawnboy Atrocity; p 169/170
Bands; Dance Bands all p.216/7
Baxter Philip (P.F.); p 69, 71, 94, 190
Baxter James or Baxter's; p 59/60, 70,
Baxter Joe; p 217
Belfast Balmoral Gathering/ Showgrounds; p.37
Chamber of Commerce; p 45/46
Boycott of goods; p 98-101, 162,
City Hall/First Parliament; p 169/170
Belturbet; p 70/71, 81,
Bennett W; p.20

Bennison J. J.; p.23, 24, 73
Black & Tans; p 160
Bloody Sunday; p 156-158, 227.
Boffin Ned; p 197.
Bonar Law Rt. Hon; p37-39, 47, 91,
Breiden Davy; p 222.
British Army; p 227.
Breffni O'Raghallaigh/'O'Rourke; p16
Brooke. Sir Basil; p 221, 223
Brooke John; p 224.
B. Specials/B Men; p 155, 219, 220
Bullock Thomas; p.51
Bullock S.F; p 51-2,

C.

Cairo Gang; p 156, 157,
Carson, Sir Edward; p.37, 45, 46, 47, 48, 54/55, 90/91, 108/109, 111, 120, 136, 137, 154, 162, 167,
Castlereagh Lord; p.25
Cavan East, by election; p 82-84.
Cavendish Bentinck, Lord Henry; p.110.
Childers Erskine; 178,
Churchill Winston; p.47, 170, 212
Church in Ireland, disestablished; p.25
Church of Ireland; p.29, 48/50, 64, Gazette; p.28, 31,37, 45, 111/115, Crozier, Bishop of Armagh; p.33, Bishop Darcy of Down; p.29/30, Gregg Most Rev. J A F, DD; p 121.
Bishop of Kilmore; p.33
Bishop of Ossary, reference to; p 34.
Synod[s]; p.29, 33,
Citizen Army the; p.67
Civil War The in Ballyconnell; p 191- 198.
Clancy Joe; p 24,
Clarke Mrs Tom; p 180.
Clements T.E.L. DL; p.139,
Clones; p. 161, 190,
Cockerhill Brig-Gen MP; p 117, 118,
Cock fighting; p. 218.
Coffey J C Dublin; p.40.
Collins M; p 116, 136, 156, 157, 167, 170, 178-181, 186-188, 189
Conall Cearnach; p.15/16
Cooper James MP; p 167, 189.

Cootehill Sinn Féin p 69, 77, 82/83, 184
Nominations; p 123,Boycotts; p 99,
Cosgrave W.T; p 68, 81, 197
Cosgrave W.T : p 68, 81,
County Cavan , WW1.Dead; p 61-63.
Craig Sir J; p 136, 154, 162, 164, 167, 170,
186-188,
Crawford Annie; p 95/96, 192/3, 194,
Crawford Robert; p 73, 191,
Crawford Sir William; p.30
Creameries Wrecked; p150-153,
Crom Castle/ Earl of Erne; p 46, 52.
Crozier Dr. Archbishop of Armagh.
Crozier John; p 27.
Crumley Patrick MP; p 27,
Cull Michael; p 193/4, 197.
Curry or Corry Master; p.22
Custom House, Dublin; p 167/8

D.

Dáil Éireann; p 84, 156, 162/3/4,
Dáil Courts; p125-136,
Reported Hearings; p 126 -130
Disrupted; p 133-135
Dalton Emmet; 189
Dalton "Brian Boru"; p.79
Darcy, Bishop of Down; p.29
Dardanelles/Gallipoli; p 65.
Davitt Michael; p23
Derrylin; p 27, 216, 219, 227,
De Valera Eamon; p 68/70, 77, 85, 136,
159, 162-4, 164, 167, 172-177, 220/1
Devlin Joe; p 20, 91, 164, 166
Dillon John (IPP); p 72, 79, 81
Dolan Catherine ; p 14.
Dolan Charles; p. 85,
Dolphin. F; p 24, 193,
Dolphin P; p 87/8/9, 197, 225.
Dolphin T.; p 87, 124, see Appendix 2., 195
Dolphins Hotel; p.56
Dougherty J.B; p 51
Drum John p.19-22, 70, 93, 95, 96, 124,
132, 193, 198.
Drum Ellie; p 73/74, 132,
Drum Emily; p 196
Drum Molly; p 74.
Drum Una; p 196
Drum, Co. Monaghan; p 138

Dublin Castle; p.25/26, 67,
The great lockout; p.59
Easter Rising; p 56
Dundalk Ambush; p. 172.

E.

Earl of Erne; p 46,
Easter Rising C.2 (ii), p.58, 67, 83, 155,
            Co. Cavan natives: p.60
Enniskillen Horse; Ch.3 (ii) p46/47
IRA Attack; 189, Ballyconnell Volunteers in
court; p.88/89,
Ennis A.W. p 222. Mill; (Laing's) p57, 221

F.

Fair Day; p 197
Fair Green; p 16, 56,
Falls C F; p.28, 189,
Farnham Lord; p.47
Farrelly Dr. Ned; p 216
Fastry; p. 73
Figgis Daryl; p.87.
Finlay William; p 124. See Appendix 2
Finnegan Bishop; p.78/79
Fitzgerald Desmond; p 85
Fitzmartin Private WW1; p. 57
Fitzpatrick Comm. Matt; p.190
Foster's Hardware Shop; p 194, 196.
Frangoch, Internment Camp; p 85.

G.

Gaelic Bar the; p.17, 20.
Gaffney Rev. B.; p 78/79, 81, 83,
Galligan P.P; p 60, 84, 85,123/4,165, 193
German Plot the; p 83, p 85,
Glasgow & Midlothian; p.54
Griffith Arthur. P 15. 22/23, Ch.5 67/84,
85, 115-117, 125, 136, 157, 165, 167,
173/174
Ballyconnell in: p/70/74
Bailieboro; p 78/79
Cootehill; p 77/78, 82,
Nominations; p 82, p.123.
Sunday Times article; p 118.
Grey Lord; 115,
Gormley Joe; p 213, 217
Gormley Tom; p 24.
Gladstone W.E; p.25/26, 51,
Land Acts; p.25/26, Home Rule Bills; p.25

Gráinne River p.15-16
Great War the; p57, 59, 61, Roll of
Honour, Ballyconnell area; p.62/63
Gwylynbrook Manor of; p.16

H.

Hamilton Duke of; p. 224
Hannay Rev. J.O; p.34
Henderson A. MP; p 110.
Henry Denis: p.51.
Home Rule Bill; p.22, 26, 33, 41, 45, 46,
47, 54, 59, 64, 68, Act. P 54, 56, 102, 111,
Question; p.27
House of Lords; p.25
Howth Gun running; p.53

I.

Impartial Reporter; see Press
Inniskillen Dragoons or Fuisiliers; p.47, p
62/63
IPP; p.23, 67/68, 73, 81, 82, 103,
Irish Self-Determination League; p.102
IRA; p 157, 160, 165, 167/8, 219/20.
IRB; p.17/18, 57, 67,
IRP Chiefs; p 135/6
Irish Meteorological Service; 212/3.
Irregulars; p 193/4, 195, 198

J.

Johnston R.H; p.47, 53, 81, 85,

K.

Kaisers Dream; p.65/66.
Kelly Michael Fr.; p 221/2
Kenworth Lt. Comm. MP; p 102.
King George V; p.169-172, 175/176, 180
King James II; p.16
Kirkpatrick L.S; p50
Kilmore Dioceses; p.16
Bishop Finnegan: p 78/9
Knockninny Fife & Drum Band; p.20

L.

Lawlor Gen. Tony; p. 189/190.
Lemass Sean; p 220, 223.
Lincoln Jail: p 102. 208.
Lisnaskea Guardians; p 161,
Lloyd George David; p.61, 68, 91, 103,
136, 153, 159, 161, 172
Peoples Budget; p.26

Caernarvon Speech; p 114/116, also
Appendix 1. 229/236.
Anglo-Irish Truce and Eamon de Valera; p
172-175., Anglo-Irish Treaty; 178-80.
Dream; 182-3.
Local Elections 1919; p 124/5, also see
Appendix 2
Locke Joseph; p. 213
Lough Rt.Hon.T; p.52

M.

Madden Lt. Col. DL JP; p 138
Maguire Rev B; p.27
**Markieviez Countess and Maude Gonne
Mahony Pierce;** p.79.
Malanaphy A. Ch.1 all, p 73, 195,
Malanaphy F p14, 19
Maloney G.V; p 83,
Mandela Nelson; p 181.
Martin Rev. R. D; p 140, 196,
Meehan F E MP; p 27.
**Military actions in west Cavan/south,
Fermanagh Ch. 6,** p 91-95, 96-97;
Milroy Seán; p 69, 77/78, 82, 102, 165,
197, Ch. 13 all p 199-208.
Monaghan Gaelic team; p.186
Mountain Road Band; p.20, 93,
MacEoin Gen Sean; p 60, 101, 189, 198
MacNeill Eoin; p.36, 78, 83,
McBride; p 85.
McCabe Francy; p 221.
McCabe Jas Main St; p.57.
McCabe James (Snugborough); **p 195**
McCaffrey Michael; p.53
McCorry P.E; p. 75.
McCullough Henry; p. 217.
McDonald Fr. Maynooth College,
reference to; p 106.
McElgunn Louis; p 179
McGee's; p 221
McGovern G. V.S; p 219
McGovern Tom 'Barney'; p 221/2.
McGrath Seán; p.195/6
McGuinness J; p 68,
McKenna T.P Co.C; p 83,
McKiernan Ned; p 213
McKiernan Pe; p 214.
McKinley LOL; p 28

McLaughlin Rev M; p.71.
McMonagle Dan; p.16
McMurrough Kavanagh; p.34
McNiece J F; p.50
McQuade Dr. Sam; p. 216
McQuade Dr. Ned
Mullery James S; p.74
Mulligan Master; p.22

N.

Ne Temere Decree; p.27/28, 33, 42.
Newtownbutler. Battle of; p.48
Ambush ; p 189, Volunteers in court; p 87.
Northcliffe Lord; p 175-176.

O.

O'Brien William; p.79
O'Connell Rev. P. PP VG: p. 69, 78/79, 81,
83, 184
O'Connell Street; p.36
O'Duffy Eoin; p. 129, 185
O'Flanagan Rev. Fr reference to; p.105
O'Grady Brian; p.17
O'Grady Bryan, Frank, Leo; p 24
O'Hanlon J.F.; p 82, 84,
O'Hanlon Willie; p.84
O'Kane P; p.16, 95
O'Kane JF; p 56
O'Kelly Seán T: p. 179
O'Mahoney Pierce; p. 34/35
O'Mahoney J; p. 85
O'Rahilly The; p. 56
O'Reilly Tom or Thomas; p. 17,18,19,
70/71, 124/5. Also appendix 2.
O'Reilly "The Leaguer" John;
p.69, 74, 128.
O'Reilly Monica; p. 90.
O'Reilly Eugene; p 223
Ovens W; p 194, 195
Owen Roe O'Neill; ref, to p. 81.

P.

Parliament Act; p 26/27, 40, 54, 176.
Parnell C.S; p.18/19, 23, 72,
Partition Scheme, Introduction ; p.103
Elections; p 161, Tyrone/Fermanagh result
and other results 167,
Bill 1920; p 136, 156,
Act: 164

Peace Conference 1920; p 140-149.
Speakers: Sir Nugent T.Everard; Mr. a
Fennell; Lord ffrench; Major O'Connor; Mr
Samuel Wray; Rev.Fr Kearney, Lord
McDonnell; Sir Stanley Harrington; John
Sweetman, Lord Shaftsbury; Sir Thomas
Esmonde; Rev. Fr. Cotter; Serjeant Hanna
KC; The O'Conor Don; Sir Horace
Plunkett; Capt. Stephen Gwynn; Mr I.
Varian; James Brady and Dr. Mcwalter.
Peace by Ordeal; p.136.
Peacock Rev; p.33
Pearse Padraig; p.36
Plunkett Count; p 68,79
Plunkett Sir Horace; p 52, 61, 119,
Press; Irish, British, American and
French daily/weekly papers and
periodicals quoted; United Ireland p17;
Christian Globe p31; The Irish Times p45;
News Letter p50; The Globe p55, 167;
Reuter's Agency p77; An English
newspaper p.79; Many English newspapers
p85; The Press Association p114; the Irish
Bulletin p114, 174; Sunday Times p118;
The Daily News p119, 120, 166; The New
Statesman p119; Manchester Guardian
p120, 151; Evening Standard p120; London
Times p120; the Daily Mail p 150;
Westminster Gazette p152; The London
Dispatch; ref to Nationalist Press p154;
London Daily herald p154; Evening News
p155; Truth p165; The Pall Mall p167; The
Philadelphia Public Ledger p170; The New
York Times p175; Liberté p 177; Excelsior
p179; Poblacht na hÉireann p184;
Local Press; The Anglo-Celt (Cavan) and
the Impartial Reporter (Enniskillen) are
acknowledged by numerous quoted reports
throughout the book
Press referred by; 'Peace by Ordeal' – the
Chicago Tribune, the Manchester Guardian,
the Daily Mail, the Irish Times.
Provisional Government; p. 186

R.

Red Branch Knights; p.15/16
Redmond John; p.26, 36, 41, 54/55, 61, 77,
RIC; p.19, 74, 159
Richardson R.M.; p 222.
Richardson John; p.194
Roe Estate; p 80/81
Roe S G; p.22
RUC; p.210, 213, 219
Rudden Barney; p.71
Ryan William; p. 196, 197

S.

Shaftsbury Earl of; p. 144/5. Also Ref's
Ch.9.
Shaw G B – letter; p.31/32
Shaw Lt. Gen. Fredrick; p 85/86,
Sheridan Capt. Seán; p 78, 189/190,
Sinn Féin: p.23, 160, 165,
Arbitration Courts; p 75-77.
Growth of: Ch 5, p 67/84, inc. East Cavan
by election and Arbitration Courts.
Ballyconnell; Founded; p 70, Volunteers
serving p. 87, Cavan town Club; p.74
Manifesto 1918; p 122., Local elections
1919; p 124/5. Also Appendix 2. P 237-252.
Slaters' Directory of Ireland; p. 16.
Smith Paddy TD; p 224
Smuts General Jan C; p 172, 175
Spanish flu the; p 80, 86.
Squad The; p.157.
Stack Austin; p 126. 174.
Star Cinema and Ballroom; p. 216
Star Plastics; p. 222
Sullivan Serjeant-at-law; p130/1.
Swanlinbar Chapel; p.23/24, UVF; p.53

T.

Tipperary County; p 85
Town Hall Cavan; Sinn Féin meetings; p.
69, 75
Trimble William Copeland; p.28, 32, 47,

U.

Ulster Day; p 46, 48, Covenant and
Declaration, signature. P.46, 48/51, 54
Various; p 64, 111,
Ulstershire; p 52, 179, 219.
Ulster/Irish Unionist Party (Council);
p.55, 61, 82, 87, 111, Belfast Easter Tuesday
1912; p. 37, Reference to; p. 185, 190,
Arms smuggling; p 53
United Irish League UIL; p.23, 68/69, 78

V.

Versailles Treaty of; p 91, 114.
Volunteers Irish; Ch 4 –p 56, 67, 85, 87 –
in court, National; p.56/57 Ulster; p 56, 87,
90,

W.

War of Independence; see ch. 6 p 85-101,
150,
Wattlebridge; p.87/88,
Weather forecast; p 212/3.
Westminster; p.22, 25, 27, 68, 82, 154,
General election 1918; p 84
Questions at p 47, 88/89, 126,
White Star Line/Titanic; p 41.
Wijtschate/Messines Ridge, Battle of
1917; p 64.
Winter Ormond Col.; p.156.
Wolseley Col; p.48
Woods Commander P; p 135,191,198.
World War 1 or the Great War ; Ch 4.
World War 2; p 210
Wyndham Act Land Purchase; p.23

Y.

Young Samuel, MP East Cavan.
Speech on third Home Rule Bill; ch 3 p
43-45, p.68, 78, 82.